The
New Rules
of the
Job Search
Game

The New Rules of the Job Search Game

WHY TODAY'S MANAGERS HIRE ... AND WHY THEY DON'T

Jackie Larson

AND

Cheri Comstock

BOB ADAMS, INC.
Holbrook, Massachusetts

Published by Bob Adams, Inc.
260 Center Street, Holbrook, MA 02343

ISBN: 1-55850-404-4

Printed in the United States of America.

J I H G F E D C

Library of Congress Cataloging-in-Publication Data
Larson, Jackie.
    The new rules of the job search game : why today's managers hire—and why
they don't / Jackie Larson and Cheri Comstock.
        p.   cm.
    Includes bibliographical references and index.
    ISBN 1-55850-404-4
    1. Job hunting. I. Comstock, Cheri. II. Title.
    HF5382.7.L365   1994
    650.14—dc20   94-36122
                                                                  CIP

This publication is designed to provide accurate and authoritative information with regard to the subject matter covered. It is sold with the understanding that the publisher is not engaged in rendering legal, accounting,
or other professional advice. If legal advice or other expert assistance is required, the services of a competent professional person should be sought.
    — From a *Declaration of Principles* jointly adopted by a Committee of the American Bar Association
and a Committee of Publishers and Associations

This book is available at quantity discounts for bulk purchases.
For information, call 1-800-872-5627.

The information about the companies Silicon Graphics, Inc., Callaway Golf, and Breed Technologies, Inc.,
was extracted from various information packets developed by those companies.

Visit our home page at http://www.adamsonline.com

To our husbands, Bill and Dave, who unselfishly shared us, our homes, our children, and our love over the past years;

to our children who, during their formative years, shared their mothers with telephones, resumes, and manuscripts;

and to our parents, who inspired and challenged us always to try the impossible, to never to give up, and who, through their "unconditional love," gave us the confidence and determination to "power on."

Table of Contents

Acknowledgments

We would like to thank Lee Nicholson who hired us against all odds, encouraged and motivated us to really "sell," and continues to be a mentor more than a decade later; Leilani Gayles who taught us to hire the "best of the best" and gave us the opportunity to develop a new business while maintaining the flexibility to be there for our children; Kathleen Flynn, our editing associate, whose effort helped make this project happen and whose creative attributes made the difference; Laura Graham, Suzanne Jennings, Mona Mitrani, Anne Williams, and Kenny Jahng who as our first employees worked tirelessly to make the vision a reality; and Dr. Stephen Covey and his assistant Patti Pallat, who inspired us "To be Proactive." We thank them for their encouragement, support, and the role models they became for our entire organization. We thank Wallace Kuralt for his "push" to write this book and his creative insight throughout the process. We would also like to extend our thanks to Dick Staron, our editor at Bob Adams, Inc., for keeping us striving for the best and having confidence in our ability.

Introduction

How This Book Will Help You

As corporate recruiters for a young, fast-growing company, we have seen how job seekers succeed—and how they fail. If you knew what we know, you would be much better able to locate and land a job worthy of your talents and ambitions. What this book will provide is a description of the complete process of hiring—from our side of the desk. It will give you the new rules and a map to follow in the changed job-seeking landscape of the '90s. After reading this book you will be on par with the few out there who have learned the secrets the hard way.

Perhaps you have gone to career counseling, sent out countless resumes, answered newspaper advertisements, and called every contact you know. Yet you find that interviews are rare and job offers even rarer. You feel that you are doing everything possible, but without much result.

It's neither your bad luck nor a lack of jobs. The job market has changed; the old rules don't apply any more. This book will take you inside the hiring process to explain these changes and lead you through the maze. You will learn how successful job hunters proceed and how you can adopt their methods. Your greatest challenge will be to adjust to the new market, to leave behind the comfortable and familiar job search of old, and to become competent in new ways that yield results.

Who We Are and What We Do

We have acted as an outside hiring organization for Silicon Graphics, Inc. since 1990. Silicon Graphics is a market leader in visual computing systems. The company has grown by nearly 50 percent annually since 1987, at a time when many of its larger competitors are downsizing. It is just the sort of company where many people would love to work.

As corporate recruiters we have witnessed great changes in the job market. We have also read through tall stacks of resumes and interviewed thousands of candidates for jobs ranging from sales representatives to regional general managers. In our four-plus years we have seen Silicon Graphics, Inc. add more than 2,000 employees. We have helped hire many people, but we have rejected many more.

These days we see many people with excellent credentials and experience who are looking for work. The market is flooded with talent. For every 1,000 resumes we read, we interview 80 people; out of that 80, about six get an offer. In this book, we will use real-life examples to describe common characteristics and strategies of people who made the final cut. We'll also give some examples of those who didn't make it.

This Book Is Different

There are many other job search strategy books on the market, but ours is unique for several reasons. It is written by people with direct and recent experience who are on the hiring side of the desk. As corporate recruiters, we are on the front lines daily. We also talk to ten other hiring managers a week. We know this business from the hiring side; we know what works and what doesn't.

Many books do give a lot of advice about tactics that are no longer very useful. We will explain what these are and why they don't work anymore, based on input from fast-growing, hiring companies in many different industries.

♦ We will explain how job hunters who are not the "best fit" usually get the job and how to become the sort of person that companies want to hire.

♦ We will describe how to find the promising companies in your field and the hiring managers within these companies. We will tell you how to use every conversation to bring you closer to your goal.

♦ Other job search books don't explain how to react to the new ways hiring is conducted. Few job search books, for instance, discuss what to do when you receive a phone call from someone at a company to which you've sent a resume. Few authors discuss the real purpose of this first phone call, although it has become a vital stage in the multi-step process of determining which job seekers will advance to the next stage of the interview process. In this book, we'll describe what we look for in such an interview. We'll also suggest ways to handle it, even if you aren't prepared.

♦ We will teach do's and don'ts that you never learned from job counselors. This information will reduce the time you waste on ineffective strategies. We will show you how to survive a phone screen and move to a face-to-face interview.

- We will also outline the changes in the job market and how you can turn them to your advantage.

It Sounds Great. It Isn't Easy.

Finding a good job is both important and difficult. It requires time, energy, and resolve. But you can do it. And we'll show you how.

We assume at this stage in your hunt you are getting fewer than three interviews a week for jobs paying what you want to earn and that you are looking for new and better strategies. Our goal in this book is to motivate you to change your old tactics—to try a bold and innovative approach. It is called the *Focus Method*. It isn't just hype, nor is it easy. But our approach works. We see it in action every day.

CHAPTER 1

That Was Then, This Is Now

Do you want to know...

- ...why companies are downsizing today?
- ...where the jobs are?
- ...what kinds of companies are hiring today?
- ...how many jobs are "hidden"—meaning never advertised?

Are you hearing conflicting information and want an insider's perspective on issues like...

- ...should you always send your resume?
- ...what if you're not an exact fit for the position?
- ...how do you decide which industry to target?

The 180 Degree Principle

It's quite heartrending to talk to so many people who think they are working effectively to find a job when they are doing nothing of the kind. The impetus for this book came from a compilation of some hiring statistics we've collected over the last four years.

- We have reviewed more than 20,000 resumes of job hunters making more than $40,000.
- For every thousand resumes we review, 80 get an interview and 6 receive an offer.
- Fifty percent are disqualified based on the initial phone "screen."
- Thousands of resumes are received each year and never seen by hiring managers.
- We have helped hire fewer than five people who sent in a blind resume in four years.
- Ninety percent of the jobs we hire for are unadvertised. The aver-

age number of resumes reviewed is 50 to 75. For an advertised job, the average number of resumes reviewed is 500 to 1,000.

To compete successfully in today's job market you must make a 180-degree turn in the way you're used to thinking and acting. The successful job hunter realizes that yesterday's self-focused mindset will not help you find a job today when hiring managers all want to know what *you* can do for *them*. The old rules were effective in the period in which they were formed, but times have changed. It's time to focus on small, fast-growing companies and the value you can add to them.

Sometimes we are reminded of a widower who would like to marry again. Thrust back into the dating scene after a 25-year hiatus, he's at a loss as to how to proceed. Where does one meet prospective spouses in the '90s? If only he were younger, smarter, and better-looking; perhaps it's no use. Friends and family contradict one another with helpful advice, confusing him further. Perhaps he should relax and stop trying; he might meet the woman of his dreams by chance. But even if he does, what then? How does he ask for a date? Will he make a fool of himself? *The old rules have changed; this much is clear to him, and he doesn't know the new ones, or how to learn them, except by painful trial and error.*

Looking for a job these days is equally frustrating and difficult for most people. The old ways, the ones that got you hired five or ten years ago, aren't working this time. Why and how these ways have changed, and what to do about it, is much less obvious.

For example, conventional wisdom asserts that large, well-established firms, such as Fortune 500 companies, are the places to find a job. As a result, some of these companies receive 250,000 resumes annually, according to a recent report on CBS News. Yet these companies are precisely the ones now laying off workers. In fact, a recent Dun and Bradstreet report predicts that most new jobs in America this year will open up at *small companies,* those with 1,000 employees or fewer. We're going to show you how to find those companies. We've found that job seekers spend too much time and money on old, ineffective tactics. One example of a venerated tactic with little result today is the unsolicited resume. As part of our research for this book, we have talked to managers at a variety of fast-growing companies. and we received similar answers everywhere. The great majority of such resumes end up in a file drawer or a database. Today, successful job hunters find out who's doing the hiring in a particular company and then make contact—in a persistent but charming manner—with that person. We'll explain how they do this in Chapter 7, "How To Generate the Hiring Manager's Interest."

The key to attracting the hiring manager's attention depends on your ability to demonstrate your knowledge of his or her company and industry. A totally new approach is required: *focus on only three companies at a time!*

Try concentrating your efforts so you gain the inside track to the best jobs. This will provide the highest payoff of results for your efforts. By focusing on a few companies, you can talk to competitors, suppliers, and customers and gain the help of assistants and your future peers. You'll learn how to focus on the company's needs—and turn 180 degrees away from the old tactics of a "me, me, me" approach.

In today's market the number of applicants for each position is so high that companies use absolutely every opportunity to weed them out. At each stage in the process they are working to narrow the field of candidates. The hiring process resembles a funnel. Lots of people start at the top, but only a few make it through. Without a clear understanding of what goes on inside that funnel, it's difficult to improve your chances. Being taken out of the running, however, is not necessarily final—*if* you know what to do about it. In this book we'll explain ways to put yourself back in contention after you've been "screened out." You'll learn how to turn a "no" into a "yes" at each point in the hiring practice.

As at many other companies, our ideal job candidate is always someone who has held the exact job somewhere else. And like many other companies, three times out of four we don't hire such a person. Why? Because someone else, not the "perfect fit," convinces us that he or she is in fact the best candidate. Those successful job hunters demonstrate superior communication skills and persistence with charm.

Communication is crucial in the hiring process. We see only about one person in ten who can communicate effectively. Far too many people have confused "communication" with aggressive, relentless verbosity. They are forgetting that communication is a two-way process, and that asking questions and listening closely to the answers are vital parts of this process.

You may encounter unexpected difficulties moving on to the next stage of the funnel after an interview. Let's imagine you have just completed an interview. It seemed to go well, as far as you can tell. What can you do now to improve your chances of receiving a favorable decision? There are some great ways to strengthen your case, although most people don't know what they are—and it's not sending a thank-you letter.

Many excellent, productive workers have either been laid off or have good reason to fear that they will be soon. Having always worked hard in their careers, they're hoping they'll be lucky and that something will turn up. However, based on current labor statistics and our own experience, we can tell you that nothing is likely to turn up—unless job hunters change their thinking and tactics. The job market is bad, and it is getting worse.

Why? World economics. Large American companies are reducing the number of levels of management. For example, before a company reduces its workforce, it may have ten levels between the factory worker and the president. After downsizing, the same company has four levels between the hourly workers and the CEO. They must eliminate job divisions and departments in order to remain competitive in an increasingly global market, one without boundaries. In addition, many jobs, no longer only the unskilled ones, are going overseas where labor costs are lower.

During the first month of 1994, corporate America announced layoffs of more than 100,000 people, with more to come. Cutbacks in military spending will also make things worse, as thousands of defense-related industries lose their best customer. It is estimated that these industries *alone* will cut 2.6 million jobs in the next five years.[1]

The Good News about Job Hunting Today

Despite the dire news—much of it true—that you've heard about the American economy in recent years, there are bright spots amid the gloom. We will briefly discuss the reasons behind the changes in the job market and explain how this has altered hiring practices at most firms. Then we will outline some of the fallacies still being taught by many job search experts and explain why the old methods are not likely to work anymore. Finally, we give a composite portrait of today's successful job hunter.

> *One must never lose time in vainly regretting the past nor in complaining about the changes which cause us discomfort, for change is the very essence of life.*
> — ANATOLE FRANCE

In many ways, what we are seeing today is a second Industrial Revolution. The first one, which started in the United States about 150 years ago and changed the nation from an agricultural to an industrial economy, wasn't easy or painless either. Yet our early industrialization led to greater productivity and opportunity, higher standards of living, and our rise to the status of a world power.

In the same way, the changes that are occurring now are, in the long run, positive. The moves in our large corporations, the cuts in military and defense spending, can all make the United States more competitive in the increasingly global economy. Consider the example of Ford Motor Company, which has adapted to a new market with radical changes. Ford studied its competitor Honda, and learned from its example. Ford's old hierarchical reporting structure, rigid supplier-vendor and union relationships, outdated design technology—all were broken down in the quest to improve.

One important trend is the growing influence of small companies. Firms

1 *Fortune*, March 8, 1993, "The New Unemployed," p. 41.

unwilling or slow to change are being replaced piecemeal by successful smaller businesses. *These "upstarts" have invented new and better methods of doing business. Job prospects in these companies could not be brighter.*

The American Dream isn't dead. It's just more elusive. The Bureau of Labor Statistics predicts a 20-percent growth in employment between 1990 and 2005. This means some 24.6 million new jobs. The biggest growth will be in high-skill, high-wage occupations, particularly those involving computers or health care.

Additionally, Dun and Bradstreet reported that small companies, *with fewer than a thousand employees, accounted for almost 90 percent of new jobs in 1993.*

Largest Growth Industries [2]

Construction	32% increase in hiring
Transportation	31%
Utilities	31%
Manufacturing	27%
Service	26%
Retail	22%

According to an American Express study, companies employing between a hundred to a thousand people, representing a mere 4 percent of all companies nationwide, are expected to create 33 percent of the new jobs over the next two years, perhaps 2 million in all. Even smaller companies are expected to add 4 million jobs, but they represent more than 90 percent of U.S. business firms.[3] For this reason, finding a job by random resume-blitzing is rather like winning at darts while blindfolded.

Surprise! Six Changes in Hiring Practices and the Job Market

The employment picture has changed significantly, and so have hiring practices. These changes have made a big impact on the way hiring managers go about their daily routine. Some of these changes seem quite logical; others are counterintuitive. We think they will all surprise you. Keep them in mind as you start to develop your personal job search strategy.

Surprise #1
We don't hire the "best fit"!

Often, we do not hire the best fit for the particular position. Here is a job description of the ideal candidate for one specific position.

As many as 75 percent of the people we helped hire did not have all the

---

2 Dun and Bradstreet Corporation, 1993.
3 American Express Study, May 10, 1993, "Mid-Sized Companies Will Generate Two Million Jobs in Next Two Years, According to an American Express Outlook."

required qualifications. Most of these "unfit" candidates had two qualities: superior communication skills and the ability to wed persistence with charm. In Chapters 6 and 7 we'll tell you what works and what doesn't in today's competitive marketplace, using the examples of these "unfit" candidates.

Surprise #2
Switching Industries Isn't a Cure-All

An ideal candidate is an exact match from a competitor, even though, as we said, in many cases that person is not hired. This *does not* mean, however, that we are likely to go completely out of the field and hire someone from an unrelated industry.

What this means for the job hunter is that if you think that simply switching fields from a shrinking to a high-growth industry is going to solve all your problems, you may be wrong.

A Human Resources manager whose only experience is in an insurance firm will find it almost impossible to land a job with a computer company. There are too many unemployed human resource managers who do have the technology experience. On the other hand, this doesn't mean that you're stuck in the same field all your life. It does mean that you need to look carefully at what you've already done, and think creatively about where there is an industry and job relationship you can leverage.

For example, consider the laid-off marketing manager for an envelope company. What does he know, and where could it be helpful? Well, he knows the names, numbers, and communications needs of many businesses who use lots of envelopes, along with their mail volume and other related information.

Silicon Graphics, the world's premiere vendor of high-performance 3D graphics workstations and supercomputer-class RISC multi-CPU servers, is significantly expanding its presence throughout the Midwest. We are currently looking for *experienced* Sales Representatives and Systems Engineers.

SALES REPRESENTATIVES

We have several openings for Sales Representatives who have the experience and maturity to sell our extremely high-performance 3D graphics workstations and our supercomputer-class RISC multiprocessor computer servers to Fortune 500 corporations. You must have at least 5 years of experience selling high-end graphics and/or CPU technologies and must be a top performer, a self-starter and a self-motivator. You must have prior experience managing a sales team consisting of yourself, a pre-sales Systems Engineer, and a post-sales Systems Support Engineer, and have prior experience selling $250,000+ technologies into markets such as CAD/CAM/CAE, pharmaceutical, CFD, visual simulation, medical, video, and universities. A background in computer science and/or engineering is preferred, and a strong working knowledge of client/server computing, symmetric multiprocessing (SMP), 3D graphics, UNIX, C and Fortran is required.

All this would be of great use to a fax machine manufacturer. Here are some other examples of how job skills can be leveraged:

- ◆ Elementary teacher to educational toys Sales Representative
- ◆ Hotel Manager or Resort Activities Coordinator to Manager of an upscale retirement community
- ◆ Ex-military officer in charge of managing transport vehicles to manager of a rental car fleet or courier company
- ◆ V.P. of Marketing for a bank to V.P. of Marketing for a mutual fund company

We call thinking this way *leveraging your skill set*. Many skills can be leveraged, as Chapter 3 explains. See Appendix C for some examples of successful industry transfers.

Surprise #3
The Hidden Job Market is Better Hidden Than Ever

Many jobs are not advertised because the job hunters who have stayed in contact with hiring managers over a period of months are in line when a job opens up. That is the real secret of small, high-growth companies. *If a fast-growth company does not have a job for you today, chances are one will open up in the next 12 months.* Often we never get to our file of unsolicited resumes, because we have three people who used the telephone effectively to find us and keep us in the loop.

So if you're using the venerable job-search techniques of the past—sending lots of resumes out, answering dozens of newspaper ads, and hoping that your search firms are working for you—you probably want to change your strategy to find a job worthy of your talents and ambitions.

Most organizations try to fill their jobs before the position is ever posted. At fast-growth companies, a large percentage of positions go to job hunters who were referred by a current employee. By the end of this book, you will have all the tools necessary to find and land those hidden jobs.

Surprise #4
We Don't Like Resume Hunts

Many of the current books about job hunting, and some of the largest outplacement firms, suggest a technique that we'll call "Keep the resume hidden." This game involves trying to get an interview without sending your resume because you believe the prospective employer is just trying to get rid of you politely when he or she says, "Send me your resume and then we'll talk." Although this might be true in some cases, it is certainly not true in all, and it's a remarkably effective way to demolish whatever chance of getting hired you once had. The following voice mail I received from a director with several managerial positions to fill demonstrates this.

> "...Can you call Jeff Snipes for me? He keeps calling, and he doesn't send a resume, and that really annoys me. I have not returned his call because I don't want to get locked into a conversation without having a chance to preview the resume. I think it is contrived when people do that and I find it annoying."

What a wonderful first impression to make on a hiring manager. Please, fax your resume. We really want to see it. First, we want to evaluate your written communication skills; a good resume usually indicates a person who can think and convey ideas clearly.

Second, we are too busy to spend more than two minutes on the phone with someone without seeing a resume. In a company that is growing at 30 to 40 percent a year, everyone already has more work than he or she can handle.

Surprise #5
The Age of the Phone Interview Has Arrived

Fifty percent of our prospective candidates are disqualified after the first phone call that we make to them. Once upon a time, job hunters sent out resumes, and then the company followed up with a brief phone call to the job hunter to schedule one or more face-to-face interviews, to be flown in at company expense if necessary. Or they were in college and signed up for an on-campus interview. It seldom works that way anymore, first, because so many companies aren't hiring, and second, because those that are hiring don't have the time to interview so many possibly unqualified applicants. Moreover, the average cost of flying a candidate to company headquarters is $1,600.[4] A phone call is less expensive, in terms of both money and time.

Smaller, high-growth companies typically do not have employees who have time to spend days and weeks doing on-campus interviews. Following is a list of some typical companies who conduct on-campus interviews. They are generally big and not growing in their employee numbers significantly.

Typical Companies Conducting On-Campus College Interviews			
Company	Location	1993 Employee*	1991 Employee
BF Goodrich	Akron, OH	12,450	11,892
Bankers Trust Co.	NY, NY	10,371	12,114
Chemical Bank Retail Banking Group Corp.	NY, NY	39,687	29,139

4 *USA Today*, Wednesday, June 16, 1993, p. 5B.

Company	Location	1993 Employee*	1991 Employee
Compaq	Houston, TX	9,500	9,700
Deloitte & Touche	Wllton, CT	15,300	20,246
Kimberly Clark Corp.	Dallas, TX	41,286	37,000
NCR Corp. Micro Ele. Div.	Dayton, OH	1,300	1,440
Proctor & Gamble Co.	Cincinnati, OH	106,000	79,000
Scott Paper Co.	Philadelphia, PA	26,700	29,400
Texaco	White Plains, NY	38,000	37,067

If they are adding employees, the competition for the available positions is intense.

Our process, therefore, has been structured to weed out the uncommitted. The phone interview catches many people off guard. When we call and find out that the would-be employee knows nothing about our company, including why he wants to work there, his chances diminish.

In our phone interview we also like to use situation analysis, asking how one would react to a certain hypothetical set of circumstances. We do it to see what kind of thinker the applicant is. Can he take any available information and come up with a suitable response? Can she think on her feet?

One of four people does the initial phone interview: a Human Resources person, someone who works for the hiring manager, the hiring manager himself, or an executive search firm. We believe there is little available knowledge on this crucial part of the journey. In Chapter 8 we will tell you about the most common blunders we notice on the phone interview and how to sharpen these skills.

Surprise #6
The Guerrilla Interview Plan

Most people are more prepared for the face-to-face interview. But here, too, there have been changes. For example, you will often be interviewed by two or more people at the same time. This helps build a consensus among decision makers and allows more analysis of the candidate's response.

Sometimes we have the candidate talk to one person right after another all day. It sounds like a secret-police interrogation technique, but be happy if this happens to you. No firm would expend that much effort and time on someone unless they were very interested. You might wonder what companies are looking for when they do this. One important thing is consistency of answers. Does the candidate seem solid, or is he changing his responses according to what he thinks the interviewer wants? Does she exhibit the kind of energy and drive needed to excel in this fast-paced environment? After a day of interviews you—and the company—will both know the answer to these questions.

Strategies the Experts Teach that No Longer Work

We assume you are reading this book so you can change your job search into something that results in a good job offer or offers. To continue on the path of the "tried and true" will only bring the same results you've had so far in your search process. To bring about different results, you will need to use different strategies and techniques.

Then	Now
1. An unemployed person was seen as incompetent, lazy, or some sort of problem employee.	1. There are many extremely capable and talented individuals who, through no fault of their own, either do not have a job or are about to lose one.
2. The "numbers game" worked. The more resumes and cover letters the job hunter sent out, the greater the likelihood of an interview.	2. Job hunters who focus on three great companies at a time and persistently pursue them have the most interviews in the shortest time.
3. In the interview process the job hunters were encouraged to talk most of the time about their best qualities.	3. Gaining the hiring manager's attention is achieved by a thorough understanding of the business environment and the challenges facing the organization. Good probing questions and listening skills are highly desirable.
4. Resumes and cover letters offset-printed on high-quality paper were important in creating a good first impression.	4. Job hunters who customize resumes for each particular company, job opening, and hiring manager have a much greater probability of a second look or a call back. Mail campaigns don't work.
5. Most business communications took place through the mail.	5. Most business communications take place through the telephone.
6. The place to find the best prospective employers after networking, search firms, and ads failed to work was in the reference section of your local library.	6. Most of what's in the reference section is outdated and too well known to be a good source of leads. Most successful job hunters today spend their library time using tools like InfoTrak and Nexus and reviewing current periodicals to identify the most current information on hot companies.
7. A hiring manager's task was to find the best candidate for the job.	7. A hiring manager's task is to make his division the best, most profitable part of the company. Smart job hunters learn how to show they can add to his success.
8. Employment agencies and executive recruiters were great sources of job opportunities.	8. Most success stories we see involve jobs found through the job hunter's own efforts.
9. Normally, one person made the decision to hire—and whom to hire.	9. Many companies involve several individuals and departments in the decision to add additional employees, and in who will be selected.

Then	Now
10. You left a message with a secretary to get a manager to call you back.	10. Voice mail messages are the norm. A compliment and a clear, concise message left on voice mail is the best way to get your point across. It may take a number of messages to get your call returned, and you will probably need the help of an administrator to schedule a call.
11. The administrator or secretary was seen as a roadblock in getting to the hiring manager.	11. The assistant to the hiring manager may be the most helpful and knowledgeable about how to approach the hiring manager.

There is no one easy way to get a good job in today's market. To some degree you must adjust your strategy to the company you're targeting. As a general rule, the smaller the company, the less formal the hiring process. As companies get larger, more outside influences are involved, and an applicant must work harder to keep his name in front of all the decision makers.

Nonetheless, there are some traits that are important no matter where you want to work. In researching this book, we talked to executives and hiring managers in dozens of high-growth companies. We found among them a remarkable degree of unanimity on the description of successful job candidates.

Nine Traits of Successful Job Seekers

1. *They have recognized the changes in the job market*, both in how companies go about hiring and what companies expect from a candidate. The successful don't waste time on relatively ineffective tactics like formal resumes, search firms, newspaper advertisements, resume-blitzing, surface networking, and cover letters.

2. *They don't rely much on friends, headhunters, or people who promise to call them back.* They know that finding a good job is essentially their own responsibility.

3. *They have a positive attitude.* They know their own strengths and can describe them clearly and succinctly. Even in the worst of times, this allows them to present themselves enthusiastically.

4. Related to this positive attitude is *strong motivation*. Such people are not content simply to take the first job that comes along; they want a good one. As a result, they spend time planning their job-search strategy and establish specific goals—a certain number of interviews per week, for example.

5. *They focus their efforts.* First, successful job hunters locate fields that are relevant to their previous experience. Next, they identify the top companies in these fields. Then they sort out these compa-

nies and contact them, *concentrating on just three at a time*. This is a totally new approach. We call it the *Focus Method*.

What does this mean, concentrating on a company? For one thing, it means talking to everyone possible associated with the company. Sales representatives, secretaries, customers, and even competitors can yield valuable clues about a company: where the opportunities are, who's responsible for hiring, and the challenges facing the organization.

6. However, *they also can recognize a dead end when they see one*. If a company isn't hiring, a hundred calls won't help. Successful candidates do enough research on a company to know before they start that it's worth the effort.

7. *They take advantage of all available technology* to bring themselves to a company's attention: telephones, voice mail, faxes, E-Mail and a personal computer to tailor their resume to each situation. They spend at least six hours a day using these tools, especially on the telephone. On the research side, they use tools like InfoTrak and Nexus and CompuServ.

8. They are *persistent but charming*. Such candidates may call the hiring manager seven times, but they will eventually make the hiring manager *want* to talk to them.

9. Successful job candidates also *demonstrate that they can communicate well*. How? For one thing they listen carefully, and try to understand what they hear. They don't talk more than half of the time, and they ask good questions. They do not easily become defensive or rattled. And they try to learn from their failures, rather than becoming too easily discouraged or stubbornly persisting with the same ineffective tactics.

From this portrait of the typical successful job hunter, it's obvious that finding work is also a job; one that requires skill, daring, hard work, and imagination. It is also clear that finding a job is a highly rational process, not one that relies on luck or connections. Successful job hunters develop a specific plan of action to guide them as they progress in their job search. The completion of these successful methods and strategies is summarized as the Focus Method.

What makes men great is their ability to decide
what is important, and then focus their attention
on it.   — ANONYMOUS

The Focus Method: A Revolutionary Seven-Step Strategy to Find the Best Hiring Companies

We want to outline the process of finding the great and growing companies to target. After looking at the steps, you may be tempted to go back to the old ways of want ad shopping and sending resumes. Don't! Don't be intimidated by this method's apparent complexity. In reality, it's a seven-step process that requires substantially less time to find a great job than the old method did.

The most important thing to remember is—we didn't invent this method; we compiled it. The Focus Method is a summary of the different ways that those who have obtained great jobs went about their search.

We're advocating the tried, tested and many-times-validated method that managers in high-growth companies and successful job hunters tell us works. Throughout the rest of the book we'll explain and demystify each step. For the moment, however, read through the seven steps to give yourself a map of where you're going and how to get there.

Seven Steps of the Focus Method

The key rules for a successful job hunt are to be looking where the other job hunters don't, to focus on the small, fast-growing, hiring company, and to work a few (three or four) at a time. Focus on the information that people who buy stock look at; don't look where all the other job hunters look. (Your objective is to spend time on jobs where your competition is generally not focusing.)

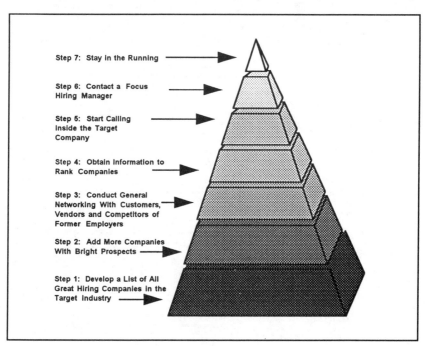

Step 7: Stay In the Running

Step 6: Contact a Focus Hiring Manager

Step 5: Start Calling Inside the Target Company

Step 4: Obtain Information to Rank Companies

Step 3: Conduct General Networking With Customers, Vendors and Competitors of Former Employers

Step 2: Add More Companies With Bright Prospects

Step 1: Develop a List of All Great Hiring Companies in the Target Industry

THE FOCUS METHOD

1. Develop a list of all great hiring companies.
    a. Decide which broad industry to target based on your prior background, interest, and experience.
    b. Go to the library and find these five issues of magazines:

        ♦ Business Week's "100 Best Small Companies."
        ♦ Fortune's "100 Fastest-Growing Companies."
        ♦ Forbes's "200 Best Small Companies."
        ♦ Inc.'s "100 Fastest-Growing Public Companies."
        ♦ Inc.'s "500 List of Most Rapidly Growing Private Companies."

        If you are interested in an international job, the larger companies have international offices; you can check *International Business's* "100 Fastest-Growing International Companies."
    c. Review each of these issues and write down the names of any companies in your targeted industry along with any information about them.
    d. Find the companies' corporate headquarters and phone numbers if not listed in the magazines. (You might have to call information [(area code) 555-1212] to find some of the numbers.) The *Directory of Corporate Affiliates* and *Ward's Business Listing of Private/Public Companies* lists many of these headquarters, and you can ask your librarian for help if it's not listed there.
    e. Call the headquarters and see whether there is a location in your preferred geographic area. If there is ask them to mail an investor relations package, or an annual report at the minimum. If the company isn't publicly traded, ask for a public relations (PR) packet or a recruitment/employment package.

2. Add to your list more companies with bright prospects, defined as companies whose "stock is a recommended purchase" by the experts. These are usually companies who...

    ♦ ...are hiring many new employees (greater than 20 percent per year).
    ♦ ...are consistently increasing sales/revenue and profits (greater than 20 percent per year).
    ♦ ...have a new, innovative product that is the best or a close second in its market niche.

    a. Ask any librarian for local business periodicals, review the Business section in the local newspapers, and add any possibilities to your list.
    b. If you're not choosy about location, review last year's issues of the *Investors Business Daily*, of the *Wall Street Journal Transcript* and add any company in your focused industry whose prospects look bright.
    c. Get annual reports sent for some of the small company, aggressive-growth and industry-specific or select-industry mutual funds. Look for your industry segment in the annual report and add those companies to your list.
    d. Call the financial newsletters or some of those listed in *Hulbert's Guide to Financial Newsletters*. Ask to be sent a sample, and add their recommended stock buys in your industry to your list.
    e. Call any stock brokers in your area and ask for their recommended "Buy Stocks" in your industry.

3. Conduct your general networking.
   a. Add any customers, suppliers, vendors, or competitors of the companies you've worked for who might be doing well. If you don't know, add them to your list and call their headquarters for an investor or public relations package.
   b. Call the Chambers of Commerce and Economic Development Groups in the towns of your interest. Ask for the industrial recruiter who is responsible for talking to new companies, and request her help. Does she know of any fast-growing companies in the area?
   c. Determine whether your target industry has an annual trade show. If so, this is your best source of contacts. Make plans to attend. Ask for a copy of the attending companies and try to match any with others you find through different sources. These are great opportunities to review the products. Talk with the competitors and collect business cards; introduce yourself only to ask questions and learn more. You are still only researching and evaluating. Successful job hunters do not spent their time chasing down jobs where their competition is intense, or where the company is not great and growing.
   d. Call your alumni office, because many have listings of all alumni and their employers and phone numbers. Call any in your industry for advice.

4. Obtain enough information (number of employees, sales, and profits for the last three years) for each company to rank them A, B or C.
   a. Many job hunters start with the companies in their geographic areas. They call them and ask for a packet, and if they can't get one, they go back to the library and ask for help in finding the information on the company. (The library will have any published articles and annual reports; but it takes a lot longer to compile than making one phone call and having all the information sent directly.) You need enough information to determine whether each company can be ranked as an A. Is it as big as you'd like? Are its sales revenues and net income increasing? Does it have a unique product? Is it in a location you would like?
   b. Complete a list of:
      ♦ A's—companies you want to pursue further
      ♦ B's—companies you might want to pursue further later after or if your A's are exhausted
      ♦ C's—companies to drop or eliminate
   c. Work on your A's in alphabetical groups of three or four at a time unless they rank themselves for you in another way, such as location or fit with your background. Call Standard & Poors at 800-642-2858 and pay $9.95 each for a company profile, or go to the library and find any articles written in the last three years, copy them, and bring them home to read. Have a file on each company.

5. Start using the telephone.
   a. Call the receptionist or secretary and ask for the name of the person to whom you would report
   b. Talk to that person's secretary
   c. Talk to a peer
   d. Talk to a customer and
   e. Talk to a sales representative
   f. Talk to a dealer or distributor and see whether you can evaluate the product personally
      If it appears that any of your first four A-target companies will probably not be hiring someone like you in the next year, put it on the bottom of the list and look at the next one on your list. Don't forget to keep in periodic contact with peers in the company in case hiring needs change.

6. Contact a hiring manager at a focus company.
   a. Put together a customized resume for a specific job you might be qualified for at each of your first three A's, with a similar cover letter. Fax it to the person you would work directly for—the hiring manager.
   b. Call the hiring manager and let her know you are following up on your fax. Leave a voice mail message once a week for three weeks, and resend your fax each week.
   c. If you can't get her in person and she doesn't return your call after three well-spaced messages, ask her assistant or secretary for help. Try to schedule a time on her calendar for a telephone conversation. Most hiring managers are just busy; it's not that they are not interested.
   d. Proceed with a phone conversation. Ask for a next step. Uncover any concerns the hiring manager might have. If there isn't a possibility of a position now, ask whether she thinks there might be one in the next year.
   e. If you can't turn around a concern, ask for her advice on other people you can talk to—people in her company or a competitor's company, or perhaps customers.

7. How to stay in the running.
   a. Whether or not there is a next step, leave a voice mail message the next day thanking her for her insight, advice, etc. Offer another compliment and express your interest, excitement, and enthusiasm in moving forward (if you didn't get a definite rejection).
   b. Keep checking back until you receive a definite yes or no. Ask how often you should check (they might be interviewing many candidates). If you're not being scheduled for a second interview, your chances at this point are extremely small.
   c. Fax a copy of a recent article you found in the library (a "just-thinking-of-you" fax), or send a book or small, less than $10 gift on a subject in which the hiring manager is personally interested.
   d. STAY IN TOUCH. Call and check about once a quarter. If you haven't had any success after a year, drop them from your list.

CHAPTER 2

It's Choice...Not Chance

Are you...

♦ ...starting to get distraught about your job search, because networking, newspaper ads, and search firms aren't yielding many face-to-face interviews?

♦ ...looking for a more effective way to look for your next job?

♦ ...starting to wonder whether all the great jobs are gone forever?

Is it...

♦ ...a mystery why and how some people are lucky enough to land a great job?

♦ ...depressing to work more than three or four hours a day on your job search?

♦ ...difficult to overcome feelings of anger, apathy or defeat?

> *Destiny is not a matter of chance, it is a matter of choice. It is not a thing to be waited for, it is a thing to be achieved.*
> — WILLIAM JENNINGS BRYAN

Once you master the techniques outlined in this book and understand the principles behind them, the result will be an increase in both your financial security and your peace of mind. You will know that you can find a good job, through your own efforts, any time you want. Does it sound impossible? It's not.

Remember the traits of the successful job hunter in Chapter 1? Now that you've seen the changes in the job market (Trait 1), this chapter will show you how to implement Traits 2–4: taking responsibility, developing a positive attitude, and finding strong motivation to achieve.

Every successful job hunter we've worked with regards job hunting as a "mission." The real secret to any job, whether it's job hunting itself, doing a payroll, or writing a symphony, is having a mission. This involves, in part, "beginning with the end in mind" as Dr. Stephen Covey describes it in his best-selling book *The 7 Habits of Highly Effective People.*

It's obvious that the mission here is to get a job—right? No. Your mission for this aspect of life really depends on where you want to be at the end of one year, at the end of four years. Do you just want to get a job, any job that will pay the rent? If you want more than that, then what? To make a lot of money? To improve the lives of others? To find an outlet for your creativity?

The Magic Solution to Finding a Job

Everyone wants to find the great job with the great company by the fastest and easiest route possible. Many job hunters think sending out nice resumes, contacting search firms or headhunters, responding to newspaper ads, and calling and checking with all their business contacts, friends, and relatives should produce this job. But statistics from the nation's largest outplacement firm, Drake, Beam, Morin, Inc., released in *USA Today*, March 17, 1994, indicate the following success rate *for 1993*:

Managers

Search Firms	9%
Mailings	2%
Ads	14%
Target Networking	61%
Other	9%
Consulting	5%

Senior Executives (150K+)

Search Firms	10%
Mailings	2%
Ads	4%
Target Networking	74%
Other	2%
Consulting	10%

The first three choices are low-risk, low-success solutions. The people in our database have about a 5-percent success rate using these methods.

So what is the magic solution? Successful job hunters we see have a deep, driving desire to learn and get ahead. They are determined to be in the group of 2.1 million that *is* going to be hired this year. They are willing to take some ego risks and try new, different ways of going after what they want.

They picture themselves where they want to be in one year and four years. Whatever "okay" offer that comes along is not good enough.

Externalization
Most job hunters we talk to who have been searching unsuccessfully for more than six months have excellent reasons for their lack of success, invariably related to causes beyond their control. Following is a list of the most common answers we hear:

+ I don't have enough contacts (or as many as John has).
+ I perceive calling people on the telephone as being beneath my dignity.
+ I'm too old/too young.
+ I don't have enough experience.
+ I'm overqualified.
+ I'm in a dying industry, and I can't get out without going back to school.
+ I'm waiting for the economy to pick back up, because no one's hiring many people.
+ No one returns my calls, and I'm just getting rejection letters.

As James Allen once said, "Men are anxious to improve their circumstances, but are unwilling to improve themselves; they therefore remain bound." It is much easier on our self-esteem if we can blame our failure at anything on causes beyond our control, such as timing or luck.

We see this variety of wishful thinking in many job hunters we talk to. They don't want to accept the responsibility for finding—or failing to find—a good job. Psychologists call this tendency to place responsibility outside one's control *externalization*. The following case study illustrates it in action.

College Graduate Case Study: Paul

Paul graduated with honors in May of 1994 with a degree in Political Science. He had hoped to get an internship before he graduated, but the school hadn't been able to line anything up.

During the spring months Paul was involved in finishing his coursework, but he did contact the career placement center. He was disappointed in the options available through the center—the counselors didn't seem to have much time to help him find open jobs.

His job search did not begin in earnest until after graduation. A month after graduation, Paul had talked to seven individuals, had one face-to-face interview (arranged by a family friend), and had sent his resume in response to ads.

Paul's parents and family were assisting him. They identified a list of names from their beach club association of member executives and their companies. Paul had started contacting each one of these individuals and was spending about 15 to 20 hours on the job search per week. He talked to his brother, a human resource professional, and he was helping him to develop a plan. After his brother gave him some feedback about his job search and outlined an action plan, Paul was supposed to get back to him with periodic updates. He is waiting to return his calls, however, until he has some real progress to show.

Successful job hunters we've worked with who find a great job in today's tight market go out and find it themselves. Unless you are so obviously and brilliantly talented that companies are calling *you* and begging you to work for them (in which case you don't need our book), you must recognize that the job you get is mostly your own responsibility. Whether you find a good one—or find one at all—depends almost entirely on how much time, effort, and persistence you are willing to put into mastering the necessary skills and using them. The successful job hunter keeps knocking on different doors in different ways.

There are plenty of opportunities out there, and we're going to help you find them.

Most of Us Fear Change

When we talk to job hunters about risk and new strategies, many become angry. There is a part of every job hunter that would rather be unemployed, take a job at half the "ideal" salary, and sell off their possessions, than acquire the strategies of job hunting that we see work over and over again. The job hunters who are able to overcome this fearful part of themselves are the ones who triumph and land the good jobs with the great companies. Our job is to make sure you're one of them! Just remember, we all wish life's rewards would come easily and without sacrifice. But it is only when we see job hunting as a journey for change and self-actualization that we can begin on the road to our dreams.

People who are always able to find managers who want to interview them, and who land the best jobs, often have the following unconventional ideas about their search process.

- ◆ There are lots of people getting great jobs and I'm going to figure out what they did.
- ◆ I'm not going to make excuses for anything. Excuses never have anything to do with finding a solution. I will not use the word "but" in any conversation; for instance, I will never say, "I want to find a job but...no one's hiring people like me."

♦ I am going to learn new ways of job searching and improve myself. I'm going to *make* it happen.

To get the most out of this book, read it actively. Try one of the methods described here that's new to you. Start with a small, manageable goal and attain it. Reward yourself and then try something that's a bigger stretch. Evaluate your progress daily and weekly. Which new strategies are working best? Which do you need to modify? Reread this book often. Practice the new techniques we'll describe by yourself and with a friend.

How to Overcome Feelings of Anger, Apathy, and Defeat

You gain strength, courage, and confidence by every experience in which you really stop to look fear in the face. You are able to say to yourself, "I lived through this horror. I can take the next thing that comes along." You must do the thing you think you cannot do.
— ELEANOR ROOSEVELT

At some point in the job-search process, most job hunters hit a wall and see no end in sight. They experience self-doubt and a decline in confidence. Because they have been doing everything they think they should be, they begin to wonder whether there is something really wrong with them.

We believe that self-confidence is linked to motivation. If you believe you can succeed, you are much more motivated to try things that will work. If your self-confidence is low, which for many people it is at this point, you'll do even less.

We have sent along many technically qualified candidates to hiring managers, who later tell us things like:

♦ "Joe has a chip on his shoulder...he comes across kind of down and out," or

♦ "Sue is technically qualified...but she just came across too strongly...like she's desperate and will take the first job that comes along."

Try as you might, a feeling of depression and desperation, unfortunately, is hard to hide from other people. You cannot indulge these unproductive emotions. The hiring managers we talk to want to see a demonstration of energy and controlled enthusiasm.

We choose our attitude and our reaction to every situation. There are millions of new unemployed college graduates. There are millions of capable, experienced and laid-off professionals. The ones who choose to see this experience as part of their growth and self-actualization will come across much better and more positively.

Job hunters who get discouraged usually do so because they are doing all the things the experts still teach, but finding many of these techniques don't work anymore. If you keep trying without results, you'll soon give up.

For example, think about a puppy. If you lay a wire that causes a mild electrical shock to your pet each time it tries to leave your yard, pretty soon it will stop trying to cross the line. After a while, you can even remove the wire and the pet still won't leave the yard because it has built up a database of memories of being shocked.

You can't let your lack of results in the past stop you now. The "wire" of old tactics is gone and the world is open to you.

Failure can lead to whole new opportunities. Many of the people we've helped hire were in "positions of failure" as some might describe it. They were laid off, forced to leave an organization trying to regain its footing in the fiercely competitive global economy. Now they are in an organization with high growth, high profits, and maximum opportunity for advancement—and enjoying it. These winners looked at their job search as a tremendous opportunity to be in a much better place than they were in the past. With this positive attitude, they were able to conduct their search much more effectively, even when the external situation looked bleak.

Fear of change and discouragement when methods don't work are the two biggest roadblocks to a successful job search. We are constantly helping to hire people who, though they do not meet all the requirements listed for a given position, have won the job they want through their own efforts. *Successful job hunters, like the one we're about to describe, use skills most job hunters possess but don't use.*

Underemployed Case Study: Michael

A business major, Michael graduated three years ago from Clark University. His goal was to sell computers directly for a computer manufacturer. He was unable to get such a job, so he went to work for a retail PC dealership. After a time, the company was looking worse and worse financially, and Michael knew that its days were numbered. He decided to pursue his original goal of working for a computer manufacturer, even though everything he read suggested that computer manufacturing employment growth was down and retail employment growth was up. He spent two weeks reading business and computer industry periodicals, looking for companies in every part of the computer hardware business that were small, growing and profitable.

He made a "hit list" of 50 companies and decided to target two at a time. He kept his resume on his PC so he could tailor it easily to each company and position. He called and talked to everyone he could at his targeted companies: the receptionist, two different people in Human Resources, people in investor relations. He averaged about eight people per company.

He sent out his resume but had no callbacks. He found out the hiring manager's name at each company and followed up with a phone call every time. He did not give up until he got through, even though this took sometimes as many as eight calls. He spent most of his time on the phone asking questions about the company. These questions included,

- What are your most important goals?
- What do you think about the company's future?
- Are you hiring now and for what kinds of positions?
- What does your company look for in the people they hire?

These questions opened up excellent opportunities to demonstrate his ability to listen as well as articulate his value added. His lack of qualifications appeared to be a barrier. Along the way, he was told that he needed:

- at least five years of sales experience
- an engineering degree
- Workstation/UNIX experience, not personal computer and MS-DOS experience.

But Michael refused to give up. He systematically and doggedly pursued these companies, asking his contacts questions like:

"What's the worst thing that can happen if you give me an interview? I promise I won't waste your time," and
"You can put me up against any of my competitors for this job and I won't disappoint you. Paper does not do me justice!"

If he managed to get an interview, Michael always asked his interviewer for ideas and "hot buttons" for his interview with the next person. He would never take no for an answer. Instead, he always tried to find out why the answer had been no, because he wanted to completely understand the interviewer's objections and overcome them. Throughout the process, Michael read everything he could about UNIX and workstations. He took a night class on the subject at his local college.

Michael was confident in his abilities, set on his mission, and convinced he could be a valuable asset to the right firm. After two months of pursuing his top-choice company, Michael began his job as that company's new rep.

Most job hunters have intelligence and skills to offer a prospective employer, but they don't put these items to work for them because they are afraid of rejection. It's easier to hear nothing from sending a blind resume, or to call twice, not have your calls returned, and give up than it is to pick up the telephone and hear "No" directly in your ear. Many job hunters spend an inordinate amount of time shuffling through "potential" company lists, making out numerous resumes and cover letters, and passing all kinds of prospective employers in their car every day. It's easier than facing rejection.

In this book we will show you how job hunters who have less experience, the wrong degree, etc., for any given position can succeed if they know what they want, are committed to that mission, have articulated a plan and spend their time on job-hunting activities with the greatest likelihood of success.

How Successful Job Hunters "Make Things Happen"

While all of us may be uncomfortable about putting our egos on the line, successful people don't let that discomfort stop them from making the effort.

We have learned from our associations with executives that the one skill that is most valuable in determining a person's success is the ability to "power on," to make things happen. Successful job hunters are able to rally themselves each day and motivate themselves to forge on in the face of adversity—with a smile. Why with a smile? Because it seems that the ability to seize the initiative belongs to those who take each obstacle as a personal challenge. They realize they will encounter resistance and discouragement, but they decide that fear of it won't stop them. Successful job searchers challenge themselves because they know that the highest rewards go to those who are able to find a job through their own efforts.

What If You're Not Really Qualified for a Position?

Notice Michael's weakness. His dream job "required" experience in selling to scientific engineering customers, and he didn't have this. He needed to know an entire new operating system and he needed to have five or more years of experience. These are realistic disqualifiers. Everyone Michael talked to stated these requirements for this kind of job. But Michael stayed ahead of the others by...

1. ...*identifying his weakness*. Many job hunters are afraid to find out what the problem is. They let a "Dear John letter" pacify them into thinking that it's something beyond their control.

2. ...*setting out to fill the gap*. Michael pursued his self-training on UNIX and workstations with a vengeance. He never stopped asking for advice and information from anyone who could increase his expertise.

Spend some time identifying your strengths and weaknesses, not for the purpose of finding some real internal problem but because you might not know something that your competitors in the job market know about. Working on weakness is part of overcoming fear. Michael and hundreds of other success stories swallow their pride. They ask for advice and favors, and sometimes they get rejected. But, they all see it as part of the process of getting from point A to point B. The following chart details some of the skills employees look for.

EMPLOYEE CHARACTERISTICS SMALL COMPANIES LOOK FOR

- High energy
- Quick thinking
- Makes things happen
- Effective use of limited resources
- Experience in a high-growth, dynamic, or changing group
- Creative solutions to unique problems
- Situation assessment and decisiveness
- Can arouse enthusiasm in other employees
- Tenacity / working issues to completion
- Knowledge of industry / specific company challenges
- Able to think outside company / industry experience
- Works well without defined parameters
- Not rules-oriented / thinking beyond policy and procedure
- Understands and anticipates needs of internal and external customers
- Looks for new ways to accomplish goals instead of always relying on past experience

---

Success is simply a matter of luck. Ask any failure.
— EARL WILSON

Identifying Your Mission

You need objectives. You need focus and direction. Most of all, you need the sense of accomplishment that comes from achieving what you set out to do. It's important to make plans, even if you decide to change them, so that at least for the moment you know where you're going and you can have a sense of progress.

What is your mission? Many people don't think in these terms. They are just trying to avoid failure, protect their self-esteem, and get back to the point where they were before they lost their jobs. But in order to develop a dynamic action plan, you must first develop a mission that gives you a destination to work toward. Finding a job is like organizing a vacation. Do you drive down the nearest highway until you find a place you like or do you focus on a destination and then figure out the best way to get there?

A specific description of what you want to do, followed by achievable goals and detailed action plans, is crucial to any job search strategy. Michael had a driving, burning mission to work directly for a computer manufacturer. Against the odds, he attained his dream. That dream and many other job hunters' dreams begin with a mission. Case after case in our files exemplifies the importance of this determination.

> *If your determination is fixed, I do not counsel you to despair. Great works are performed not by strength, but perseverance.*
> — SAMUEL JOHNSON

In order to be specific, you have to know what you want. In writing your mission statement, you have to come to grips with who you are and where you want to go. For some it's easy—you want a job just like the one you had, but with a company that's growing, not laying people off.

What to Do if You Can't Define a Concrete Mission

Don't despair. Deciding exactly what you want to go after is one of the hardest parts of job hunting. But the benefit—being able to articulate to a hiring manager exactly what you want—is astronomical. *Remember, no manager has the time or inclination to be your career counselor.* Job search action starts with this first small step.

A mission statement is a guideline, not an oath sealed in blood. There's no reason you can't change your mission if you find out later it's not the one you want. It's better, though, to have a target and aim at it, even if you adjust it later, than to fire wildly into darkness. Not everyone knows exactly where they are going when they start the journey. They define it more as they talk to people along the way. The best way is to sit down with a piece of paper and ask:

- What have I done that I've been really proud of?
- What makes me feel productive?
- What gives me the most fulfillment?

Make a list of what you're good at. Think about and define who you really are; a positive, concise self-image is vital in your job search. An important early step in your search is to find a friend or relative who can coach you. This person can't develop your mission for you, but he or she can help you better identify your strengths and weaknesses and help you decide what you really want. It's not easy to ask for help, but your coach can assist you all along the job search, so it's important to enlist his or her help at the beginning. The best person to coach you is a good friend and colleague from work. He will be able to give you honest feedback from a professional point of view.

After you make your list of strengths and weaknesses list, give it to your coach and see whether it rings true to him. Sometimes we have a better idea of who we think we "should" be then who we actually are. Your coach should know you well enough to help you with this step. Role-play with your partner to gain valuable feedback on your interviewing skills and personnel mannerisms. Appendix B at the back of this book offers some further resources to help your career development plan.

A good way to decide on a vacation destination is to talk with people who have already been there. Similarly, a great way to decide where you want to go in your career is to talk to people in the job you think you want. Most people are more than happy to talk about themselves, their careers, and what they've learned. If you feel uncomfortable about approaching someone else, read the sections in Chapter 3 entitled "What Most Job Hunters Never Learn about Networking" and "How Not to Be Perceived As a Pest."

How to Develop an Action Plan

Many job hunters tell us that they are doing everything they can to find a job. Sometimes they ask for our advice and help. When we dig into exactly what they've been doing for the last six months, we find many have no written plan and no real record of what they've done—who they've talked to, and what the follow-up has been. We'll get a list of a hundred different contact names and companies. Seldom do we see any follow-up plan.

It's just like any high achievement; many people may seek the goal, but few are willing to take the hard steps to get there. Nothing comes as easily as others think. *The process of writing an action plan separates those job hunters who make things happen from those who wait for us to find their resumes in our stacks of unopened mail.*

Many job hunters resist a written plan because it imposes deadlines, commitments, and personal responsibility for making things happen. But we don't see many people obtaining a job with a great company that do it another way. The following case study demonstrates the importance of following a plan.

Laid-Off Case Study: Ron

Ron was the service manager for a publishing firm when his company went through a downsizing and he was let go. He took advantage of the outplacement service he was offered, but didn't expect *the firm to get him a job. He spent the first week focusing his mind on the job ahead. He made sure he could relate clearly, objectively, and without bitterness his past experience and the reason for the layoff. In addition, he explored his career options and targeted his search. Because he had free access to the outplacement service, he sent out a mass mailing of 1,000 resumes, but received only 15 responses. Instead of using the mail service, **he decided to use the phone to get his next position.***

Ron found his best opportunities by networking, meaning he began with the name of an acquaintance, called, asked for advice and asked for names of other people he might call for advice. He realized "networking" really meant calling a lot of people he didn't know but who were referred or found through other people; some he even got by calling the receptionist and asking for the name of the V.P. of Marketing. He started by contacting 50 friends, business acquaintances, and former employers and asking for advice in his job search. They gave him any leads they could and told him which companies were hiring. By the time he finished his job search, he had contacted more than 400 people.

After drawing up an aggressive action plan, he set definite goals to add two new names per day to his contact list and to spend at least five hours on the phone daily. Before he called any references, he made sure to find out any information he could about each company. He looked up information on their competition, market share, product line, and business structure. After an initial phone screen, he studied each company even more extensively. Ron always tried to find what he could do for the company, not what they could do for him.

He developed a ratings system to track his job search progress and to help motivate him to keep up the pace. He documented each call and its result. Ron spent 40 to 50 hours per week (not including commuting time) looking for the right job. He contacted a few search firms, but they were of minimal help.

Ron arranged informational meetings with the vice presidents of some of the fastest-growing subsidiaries of his former firm's parent company. At the time, no one had any openings, but Ron used these meetings to find out which companies were doing well and might be prospects in the future. Four months after his initial contact, one of the subsidiaries had an opening for a national service manager. The vice president called Ron for a formal interview and offered him the job. After nine months, Ron is the now the one on the hiring side of the desk.

As Ron and others like him tell us, a successful job search is getting from point A to point B by taking all the small steps in between. Each item on the sample successful plan is a small step, but success comes to those who do each one. They begin with the end in sight. In other words, they have their mission, but they realize it will not be accomplished in a few giant steps, but lots of well thought-out smaller ones.

Why Document Your Progress?

An effective action plan is a documented review of results. The daily planner and contact management report are crucial to the ability of the job hunter to stay organized and follow up. Planning carefully lets you predict where you are going and how you are spending your time. An analysis of results allows you to evaluate progress, making sure productivity is maximized.

Additionally, the number of people you keep in contact with could be in the hundreds, particularly when you include all the networking contacts from newspaper editors to economic development advisers, to competitors, customers, and suppliers for each of your hot list of targeted companies. Each contact should be nurtured: A small token of appreciation for their time is always well taken.

Contact management information like the form at the end of this chapter is invaluable for follow-up. Keep it in a loose-leaf notebook, alphabetical by company or geography, as this information will be invaluable for follow up. If you are supposed to call someone in a month, note it in your day manager and on the contact management information.

Again, your phone, fax, and PC should be humming—working on this project as if you had a key strategic task to complete with the highest levels of productivity and efficiency.

What Is Your Work Ethic?

If you typically spent 45 hours on the job, you should carry the same daily plan in to your job search activities. Most of this time will be spent on sleuthing activities, general information gathering on the telephone. Don't be distracted in your quest—stay focused on your plan. Ron committed 40 to 50 hours a week to his job search and he rewarded himself as he achieved goals. Remember, finding a job is a job in itself. Your energy, drive, work ethic, and determination will show and impress your future employer.

The pages that follow give other examples of some basic systems for keeping all your information organized and easy to access. You can adapt these to your needs; the idea is to use tools that will maximize your productivity.

Sample Success Action Plan

GOAL 1: Develop planning and organization systems and a contact management process.

1. Develop company profile information.

2. Develop contact report
3. Devise monthly and weekly goal setting. (See following pages.)
4. Develop monthly and daily action plans. (See following pages.)
5. Read a time-management book—invest in a daily planner.

GOAL 2: Find 15 companies growing/hiring. Target time frame for completion: 2 weeks.

1. Read about and identify 50 or more companies that may be possible employers from the published lists of fast-growth companies in the targeted industry.
2. Who are the fastest-growing competitors, suppliers, and customers of the company you last worked for? Find the fastest-growing companies within the sphere of your previous position.
3. Call the companies' public relations department and/or investor relations department; go to the library and find as much information you as can.
4. Prioritize the list (**A** for urgent activities, **B** for secondary activities, **C** for activities with dubious payoff).

GOAL 3: Target three hot companies to begin contacting. Find five new contacts or names per day.

1. Call companies in order to gather more information.
2. Compose a pre-call introduction letter for each company, department, manager, or known opportunity.
3. Cold call to identify hiring managers in targeted companies (see Chapter 3).
4. Send 15 introductory letters per week.
5. Make a yes/no decision on keeping the hot companies on your list every week.

GOAL 4: Obtain eight phone conversations per day.

1. Make 25 phone calls a day.
2. Spend four hours a day on the telephone.

GOAL 5: Obtain two face-to-face interviews per week and obtain one 2nd-level interview every two weeks.

SAMPLE CONTACT REPORT

Company:	XYZ Systems	**Address:**	245 Celia Ln.
Contact:	Joe Smith		
Phone:	919-555-xxxx Ext. 643		
Title:	Product Manager	**City:**	Fairfield
Sec:	Susan Jones	**State:**	NC
Dear:	Joe	**Zip Code:**	27793

Call:	7-7-94	**Re:**	Info. interview
Meeting:	7-10-94	**Re:**	Info. interview
To do:	Send Forbes article	**Re:**	XYZ growth

Last Results: Contacted 7-1-94
Referred by: Jim Serandon (Company Q, Inc.)

Mkt.:	Color Printers, Monitors	**Public:**	No
#/Field Offices:	3	**Av. Sales:**	$30 mil
# of Emp.	75 (60 last yr.)		

Strengths: Niche product, excellent technology, fast growth
Weaknesses: Cust. svc. decline over last yr.

Asst. 1:	Jerry Wright	**Asst. 2:**	Pam Shields
Title:	Mktg. Rep.	**Title:**	Mktg. Rep.
Phone:	Ext. 645	**Phone:**	Ext. 640
Last Reached:	6-10-94	**Last Reached:**	6-25-94

Notes:
Only available 12-3 M-F

SAMPLE CONTACT REPORT

Company:	Superstar, Inc.	**Address:**	344 Merelake Rd.
Contact:	Jackie Samson		
Phone:	919-555-xxxx Ext.: 643		
Title:	VP Customer Support	**City:**	Overland
Sec:	Jamie West	**State:**	NC
Dear:	Jackie	**Zip Code:**	26627

Call:	3/31/94	**Re:**	Info. interview
Meeting:		**Re:**	Info. interview
To do:	Send Forbes article	**Re:**	Superstar growth

Last Results:	Sent cover letter
Referred by:	Jim Serandon (Company Q, Inc.)

Mkt.:	Niche pharmaceutical manufacturer	**Public:**	No
#/Field Offices:	3	**Av. Sales:**	'93—190 mil
			'92—90 mil

# of Emp.:	75 (60 last year)

Strengths:	Niche prod., exc. technology, fast growth
Weaknesses:	Fast growth may lead to cust. svc. decline

Asst. 1:	Tom Avery	**Asst. 2:**	Anne Williams
Title:	Mktg Rep	**Title:**	Cust Serv Mgr
Phone:	Ext. 645	**Home:**	Ext. 644
Last Reach:	11/1/94		

Notes:
Best to reach after 8:30 a.m.
Likes analytical approach to problem solving
Under pressure from CEO because of delivery problems
Needs to hire someone—position not announced yet

Sample Daily Action Plans
Day 1

6:00	Exercise
	"
7:00	Breakfast, read *Wall Street Journal*
	Review today's PLAN
8:00	Fax customized letter and resumes to target managers
	"
9:00	Follow up on telephone with letters sent via fax to 8 managers
	"
10:00	"
11:00	"
	Meet with career partner—practice interviewing skills or conduct practice phone interview
12:00	"
	"
1:00	"
	Travel
2:00	Informational interview with peer at target company
	"
3:00	Travel
	Call 6 referrals from informational meetings
4:00	"
	Cold call for 15 additional contracts at target customers
5:00	"
	Dinner
6:00	"
7:00	Take class on new library research technologies

Sample Daily Action Plans
Day 2

6:00	Exercise
	"
7:00	Breakfast, read *Wall Street Journal*
	Review today's PLAN and any articles or information on companies to contact
8:00	"
	Cold calling for new names in target companies
9:00	"
	"
10:00	Attempt to contact managers or leave voice mail for manager to return call
	"
11:00	"
	Travel
12:00	Lunch meeting with business news editor—Terri Jones
	"
1:00	"
	Travel
2:00	Break—walk
	Call new contacts at target company including manufacturing, operations, production control, and quality managers
3:00	"
	"
4:00	Library—research new companies identified and review current issues of *Fortune, Forbes,* and *Business Week*
	"
5:00	"
	Dinner
6:00	"
	"
7:00	
8:00	Read motivational book

Progress Report for Week 1			
Activity	*Goal*	*Actual Number*	*Actual Time*
Phone Calls: Information Gathering	30	22	17 hours
Phone Calls: Hiring Managers	5	2	2 hours
Introduction Letters and Resume Faxes	20	15	9 hours
Telephone Interviews/Screenings	5	1	4 hours
Face-to-Face Interviews with Hiring Manager	3		
2nd-Level Face-to-Face Interviews			
Face-to-Face Informational Interviews	4	4	6 hours

....

CHAPTER 3

The Mystery Unravels: Where Are the Jobs?

Do you want to know...

♦ ...where the jobs are?

♦ ...what kinds of companies are hiring today and how to find them?

♦ ...how many jobs are "hidden"?

Have you...

♦ ...called more than 50 network contacts?

♦ ...answered every ad you could?

♦ ...sent a resume and cover letter to more than a hundred companies without result?

Do you...

♦ ...avoid networking and phone calling because you're afraid you won't make a good impression?

♦ ...need to know how to tell the great companies from the mediocre ones?

> *There is very little difference in people, but that little difference makes a big difference. The little difference is attitude. The big difference is whether or not it is positive or negative.*
> — CLEMENT STONE

The purpose of this chapter is to teach you the new secrets of the hidden job market: effective techniques for finding the engines of job growth in the '90s—the small, dynamic, growing companies. Remember traits five through seven of successful job hunters in Chapter 1?

 # Five: They focus their efforts. First, they locate fields that are relevant to their previous experience. Next, they identify the top companies in these fields. Then they sort out these companies and contact them, concentrating on just three at a time.

What does it mean to concentrate on a company? For one thing it means talking to everyone possible. Sales representatives, secretaries, customers, and even competitors can yield valuable clues about a company—where the opportunities are and who's responsible for hiring.

 # Six: They also can recognize a dead end when they see one. If a company isn't hiring, a hundred calls won't help. Successful candidates do enough research on a company to know before they start that it's worth the effort.

 # Seven: They take advantage of all available technology to bring themselves to a company's attention: telephones, voice mail, faxes, and a personal computer to tailor their resume to each situation. In researching companies they use electronic databases like Infotrak and NEXIS/LEXIS. They spend at least six hours a day using these tools.

New Search Strategies: How to Find a Job where the Competition Is Less

Some job hunters think that research means accumulating company names and addresses. Many of the other job-hunting experts list in their manuals or books pages and pages of reference sources that range from Standard and Poor's various bound volumes to Trade Association manuals. We've talked to thousands of unsuccessful job hunters who have spent weeks pouring through these reference manuals, accumulating company names and addresses and following up by mailing a resume.

There are several problems with this approach. The information is usually dated, and most of the information is on larger companies—usually those with over a thousand employees—that are not hiring. A study done by American Express in 1993[1] highlights the explosive growth happening in companies employing between a hundred and a thousand people. The study sees no job growth at the giant outfits. One reason is that the established mid-sized firms are having better luck getting loans from banks today. The rebound in construction has affected the explosive growth in many smaller companies. According to this study, mid-sized companies will be hiring in the following areas listed in descending order (see Fig. 3.1): wholesale and retail trade, construction, manufacturing, and services.

Most people have never heard of many of these new companies; they were 1980s start-ups and represent only 4% of companies nationwide.[2] It's

---

1 "Mid-Sized Companies Will Generate Two Million New Jobs In Next Two Years, According to American Express Outlook," *American Express Travel-Related Services Company, Inc. News Release*, May 10, 1993.
2 *ibid*

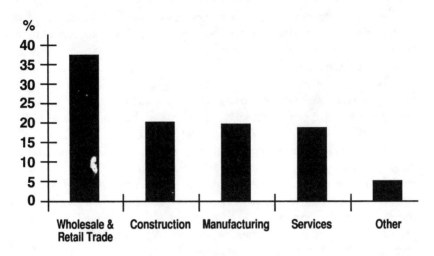

Figure 3.1
Where mid-sized companies will be hiring, based on a 1993 American Express study.

easy to see why it is so tough to find a great job with a growing, hiring company. In order to be successful, you must figure out how and where to find these new job engines. These companies are in effect "hiding." It is almost impossible to find any of them in the traditional sources cited by the experts in the past.

If the information is over a year or two old, chances are that either the company has doubled in size again and everyone else in the job-hunting market place has found them, or the business has since taken a nose-dive. Very few companies today operate in a static environment. One of the tricks we've heard from successful job hunters is to find new and current information about possible prospective employers. But great research means much more than that. Successful job hunters tell us that true researching involves finding specific information that gives a *strong indication* of whether a company is hiring for the job they desire. Following is a case study from our database of job hunters. Read it and judge whether Joe's research techniques are likely to land him the job of his choice.

Laid-Off Case Study: Joe

> *Joe had worked as a credit manager for an automotive supply wholesaler for fifteen years when he found out that he would be laid off in a month.*
> *First he called all his friends and business acquaintances to ask for contacts. He then called the 50 or so names he was given. He got*

through to around 30 percent of these people, but no one he talked to had any positions open. Many secretaries directed him to Human Resources or said they would forward the message; many managers never returned his calls even though he called twice. When he reached someone's voice mail, he never left a message, considering this a waste of time. Several people he called did ask for his resume and told him to try back in few months. Joe always made a note in his planner and called back after exactly one month.

Next, he looked up the largest automotive firms and sent out resumes and cover letters to more than 50 companies. At first there was no response to his letters, but Joe knew it would take time.

In the meantime, he called a search firm that his brother had used successfully five years earlier. The interviewer at the search firm seemed interested and said he might have something in the next two weeks.

So far he hadn't had any face-to-face interviews, so he considered calling his former company's customers, vendors, and largest competitor to see whether any of them were hiring.

At this writing Joe has been conducting his job hunt for over nine months and he still has had very few interviews for jobs he would like to have. What's wrong?

Six years ago, when Fortune 500 companies were creating new jobs, these methods would probably have worked. But as we noted earlier, the larger, well-established companies are no longer hiring in significant numbers. They are restructuring—downsizing—in order to keep pace in a globally competitive market. This isn't expected to change anytime in the 1990s; it is a symptom of fundamental changes in the world economy, not just a temporary slowdown.

It's Not News, but Fortune 500 Companies are Flooded with Resumes.

These companies receive 50,000 to 250,000 resumes a year, many unsolicited. What happens to all those resumes? Usually nothing at all; they are filed and forgotten. There are simply too many with which to cope. As Joe discovered, sending unsolicited resumes to the Fortune 500 companies yields little or no progress in finding a job. Indeed, almost any company today with any name recognition at all receives more resumes than it can even file.

A new technology using computer scanners and computer databases automatically inputs the resume without any human evaluation. Stacks and stacks are simply opened by clerks and optically scanned into a computer database. One of the more popular of these is called Resumix, an applicant-tracking and resume-scanning system. Resumix generates a skill summary after the initial scan. When a position comes open, a requisition listing the particular skill set that will be needed is entered, and Resumix searches the data bank of resumes, pulling out only those that match the requisition's skill set. Therefore, it is very important to list skills on your resume that you know will be in demand. This system is used to identify an exact match to a position, and a less-than-perfect fit yields no action on your resume.

The chances are slim that any one resume will ever be retrieved. So again, savvy job hunters never send an unsolicited resume and expect anyone to read it. Many people tell us this is old news. So why are thousands and thousands of blind resumes being received every month? It's a mystery to us.

You should also bear in mind that any job hunter fortunate enough to land a new job with a large, well-known company could soon face the unemployment line once again. Downsizing and layoffs have become an accepted way of doing business for most large companies. Wouldn't it be great to be part of a company on its way *up* instead?

Some job hunters target the well-known names, which also generally means the big ones, on the erroneous assumption that these firms offer greater job security. Not so. There is more job security in a small company with some great products than a large one struggling to maintain its market share. And small companies offer other great benefits over large ones. Opportunity for stock options is one such benefit; if the company does well, the job hunter can look forward to considerable financial rewards, although most people moving from a large to a small company should expect a 20% decrease in base pay, which may offset that benefit slightly.[3] Remember, too, that at a small company you'll be a bigger cog in a smaller wheel, with more input into the decision-making process. You can develop more experience across different functional areas. The one benefit we hear most is "no red tape." You can actually get things done and obtain decisions in a timely fashion.

The solution is knowing how to locate and approach the fast-growing companies that are hiring. It is easy to find such companies once you learn where and how to look. Successful job hunters know that the secret is to find the company before everyone else does and to get in on the ground floor.

The first and simplest rule: Think small. Small businesses represent the real power of new job creation. *Nine out of ten new jobs created this year will be in small companies that...*

- ...have carved out a niche market
- ...add value in ways their competitors don't
- ...are globally competitive
- ...rarely use search firms and expensive ads
- ...don't have the resources to recruit on campus[4]

3 "Targeting Small Companies: It's Definitely Who You Know." *Networks, The Quarterly Publication of Exec-U-Net*, Vol. III No. 4, 1993, p.3.
4 "Out of College: What's Next?" *Fortune*, 7/12/93; p. 58.

If a company is small but is also growing and hiring, chances are it doesn't have the time or the people to recruit actively. Moreover, hiring search firms is expensive. Almost without exception, people we've talked to in fast-growth companies who are in charge of hiring would prefer a well-prepared job hunter to contact them. It saves time and money, and it also saves the need to run ads, go through hundreds of resumes, and follow up with people. The small fast-growth companies want you to hit the ground running. Your knowledge of their organization, market, and challenges is what hiring managers are looking for in the people they hire. The key is being well prepared—as you will be when you finish this book.

Even though they are the best place in town to get a job, these smaller companies receive far fewer resumes than the larger Fortune 500s and even fewer follow-up phone calls from prospective job hunters. *Therefore, the competition for any particular job is less.*

Simply finding small companies is not enough, however. Although a lot of small and medium-sized companies are hiring, less than 10 percent of them are doing 70 percent of the hiring.[5] *Therefore, you must find the right companies. This is where the research comes in.*

We have found that successful job hunters have discovered an entirely new way to conduct research. They do not rely on the large reference manuals listing dozens of established large companies. The fast-growing "upstarts" are not found in the traditional financial analysis books like Dun & Bradstreet's listings. Books or articles about *"the best places to work"* are also misleading. While these may, indeed, be great companies to work for, they are not necessarily good places to find jobs. As we've explained, even profitable companies are downsizing these days. Almost without exception, most job hunters spend their first six months targeting the larger, well-known companies, even though most know these companies are not hiring in any significant numbers. If you are a college graduate and depending on college recruiting to land you a job, you may want to find out how many students from your school or even nationally a given company plans to hire. The numbers are sometimes staggeringly competitive—500 interviews for 5 slots. Many new college graduates assume that on-campus recruiting will yield them a job, when school after school tells us less than a third of the graduates are finding this true.

For a Job Hunter, the "Looking" Process is a Never-Ending Search in Places Most People would Never Think to Check.

The places where stock buyers look, for example, are invaluable. Think about it. If you want to make money in the stock market, you're typically looking for a company that has captured or created a distinct niche in the market

---

5 "Targeting Small Companies: It's Definitely Who You Know." *Networks, The Quarterly Publication of Exec-U-Net,* Vol. III No. 4, 1993, p.3.

and therefore has something better to offer than the "big boys." You would hope to find a company growing by 50 percent a year or more. These booming little companies get money one of three ways:

- Venture capital or an initial public offering of their stock
- An offering of more of their stock
- A business loan

Such upstarts typically need more money or capital than they can borrow from a bank, and thus, are eager to spread the word of their success to potential investors, in order to obtain more money to finance their rapid expansion. *Such businesses are a job hunter's dream.* The way they go about acquiring that money opens them up not only to potential new investors but also to a savvy job hunter like you. One approach is simply to visit all your local office parks and executive suites. The directory in the lobby lists all the young upstarts. Go in to the offices and act lost, browse the company literature, ask about what the business does, and then go to the next one. Some startups in these office parks or executive suites may be one- or two-man operations but they may be "booming businesses" looking for someone just like you. You'd be surprised how many great global companies started in a founder's garage or basement.

The Research Process

In the section that follows we will describe the steps involved in doing research, in the general order in which you should do them. An important aspect of this kind of job search to keep in mind, however, is its circular quality. Although we advise starting with printed (or computerized) sources and proceeding to human sources after you've learned enough to ask intelligent questions, this does not mean that your reading stops at that point. Ideally people's suggestions should lead you back to do more reading, as well as leading you to other people.

Where to Look to Find the Growing, Hiring Companies

We recommend at least two weeks initially to conduct a personal and professional inventory—to take stock of what you know, what you can do, and where this knowledge and these skills could be valuable to a possible employer. Define your mission.

Don't overlook the obvious. If you have been laid off, or are simply trying to upgrade your job, you already know or have access to a good deal of information about your competitors, your vendors and your customers. All of these are places you or a coworker knows about; they are in an industry with which you already have experience. Savvy job hunters always cover these easy sources first. They are easy because if a company is growing and hiring, it would love to hire someone from a competitor, vendor, or supplier—someone who won't have a large learning curve. When you are looking for companies to research, put these on the top of your list. We'll discuss later in this chapter how to evaluate them.

Start with periodicals. Your reading program should start with the most general sources of information and gradually narrow and deepen. Large business and investment magazines such as *Inc., Fortune, Forbes,* and *Business Week* are the best places to begin. All of these magazines occasionally have issues identifying, listing and ranking great, small, fast growing companies. *Fortune* has an issue ranking the top 200 small companies; *Inc.* has its annual "*Inc.* 500" listing. Articles on companies to watch that are doing well in a specific area are regular features; indeed, every issue of all four magazines contains several clues to a job hunter leading to potential employers. Most large public libraries and business school sections of college libraries will keep back issues of these publications covering several years. They are as follows:

FIRST PLACES TO LOOK FOR GROWING COMPANIES

 Business Week's "100 Best Small Companies"

 Fortune's "100 Fastest-Growing Companies"

 Forbes's "200 Best Small Companies"

 Inc.'s "100 Fastest-Growing Public Companies"

 Inc.'s "500 Most Rapidly Growing Private Companies"

 For international jobs, International Business' "100 Fastest-Growing International Companies" is the place to look. The larger of the fast-growth companies will have international offices and will be on a prior list.

Here is an example of one of these companies. In 1993, ControlAir Inc., a high-growth manufacturing company in Amherst, N.H., was number 199 on the *Inc.* 500. It was the first time ControlAir Inc. appeared on the Inc. 500 list, and the company received no apparent increase in resumes or other inquiries from individuals interested in employment. A small progressive company, ControlAir Inc. is establishing itself in a mature industry with aggressive global market development and a successful new product introduction strategy. A privately held company, it grew 1,269% over three years.

Or take another example. Each issue of *Fortune* has a "Hot Products" column. Those hot products are sometimes owned by a hot company. If the industry is in your background, add it to your list. *Forbes* has a monthly column called "Companies to Watch"; these too are usually good prospects. Almost every current business periodical you could pick up will have good leads. Michael, the job hunter profile in Chapter 2, has a brother-in-law who is a stockbroker. When Michael was job hunting, he would have his brother-in-law mail all his business periodicals every month; and he would go through them page by page. A write-up in *Fortune* initiated his interest in the company where he found his dream job.

Here is a sample of the table of contents from one issue of *Forbes* (November 8, 1993). Much of this information would be of interest to a job hunter.

Company Profiles 220
The Honor Roll 228
The 200 Best Small Companies in America 230
The Best (and Worst) Paid Chief Executives 250
Who Runs the 200 Best 252
Rankings 266
How to Reach the 200 Best 276
How to Invest in Foreign Up and Comers 286
Foreign Company Profiles 288
The Best Small Companies Outside the U.S. 294

Newspapers are another helpful, general source. The library will have newspaper indices of local and national newspapers, as well as the articles themselves on microfilm. If you are confining your search to the area where you currently live, the local newspaper's business section for the past two years will offer useful information about new companies that have moved into town, products they offer, and how they are doing. For those whose search is not restricted geographically, we suggest the *Wall Street Journal* as the most comprehensive source of business news. If you don't read this paper already, start.

Libraries are increasingly computerized, which can speed your search. For example, the full-text version of the last few years of the national newspapers are now on CD-ROM, which permits quick searching using key words, ending eyestrain in the microfilm room. InfoTrak allows you to search many newspapers and periodicals by subject. It's a sort of vast, computerized version of the old *Reader's Guide to Periodical Literature*. Other databases are devoted exclusively to business and financial subjects. The Directory of Corporate Affiliates identifies small privately and publicly held companies. Whenever you find information you think you can use, jot it down, along with the name of the article's author. That name may come in handy later.

A word about university libraries. Policies differ. Some will allow anyone in the community to come in and use their facilities freely; others place restrictions, and a few won't let you in the door without a student ID. Find out. University libraries can be a valuable source of information impossible or expensive to obtain elsewhere. If you have to take a class at your local university to get library privileges, a course in these new information technologies, like InfoTrak, might be just the thing.

Search the indices in the *Reader's Guide* for company names you already know, and look also under more general topics that might lead to more company names. Go back no further than two years; you don't want out-of-date information. Keep notes of all the companies in your field that are doing well; on file cards, in a notebook, or in your computer, if you have a laptop or portable.

Mutual Funds

Another likely place to find aggressively growing small companies is in the mutual fund industry. There are so many funds now that they group themselves by what kinds of industries they invest in. As you probably know, mutual funds are currently the investment vehicle of choice, because the current interest rate is too low for investors to make any money buying certificates of deposit (C.D.'s) or keeping savings accounts. Individuals can own stock shares of many different companies by investing in a single mutual fund. Each individual fund (and there are thousands) consolidates the stocks of hundreds of different possible great companies. A mutual fund is managed by a company (such as Fidelity or Vanguard or Templeton), or rather, by fund managers hired by the company, people whose expertise is in buying stocks likely to go up or increase in value.

In the investor trade these people are called "stock pickers." Their sole function is to find companies whose earnings or profitability—or both—are expected to increase. Typically, large earnings and profitability are followed by large increases in employee hiring. If fund managers can find companies other stock pickers haven't yet found, they will do even better. Stock pickers for mutual funds, who often have hundreds of people scouting the country (and sometimes the world) for companies they think are going to be great in the future, usually talk extensively with a company's executive officers before investing in that company. How do they obtain access to these "top dogs"? Simple. The "top dogs" need more money to grow and expand, and that means they want their company's stock to go up. If a mutual fund manager has five billion dollars (many have much more than this to invest), you can bet he or she is going to see and hear a lot of privileged information you probably won't get from reading the newspaper.

To make a long story short, you can get access to thousands of these possible future "stars" simply by calling the mutual fund company (usually an 800 number) and asking for a prospectus and annual report. As you can see from the following, the fund's stocks are conveniently segmented by industry. Your best move is to pick the ones in your target industry which you've never heard of and add them to your list.

Most mutual funds today differentiate themselves on the basis of what types of company stocks and/or bonds they invest in. Search the "Aggressive Growth" and "Small Company" categories for companies in your field. Investor magazines often list and rate these funds. You should also find "select" funds that focus on your industry of interest, such as Fidelity Select Retail or GT Global Telecommunications. The prospectus or annual report of each of these funds lists the great growth companies they hold.

Many firms also have small company funds. Speak to the fund representative and ask for their recommendation of funds with *small* high-growth companies.

Following is a partial prospectus from Fidelity's Select Broadcast and Media Portfolios as an example. Look for companies you haven't heard of before—they are the small companies to target in this industry.

Advertising
Advertising Agencies
Foote, Cone & Belding
    Communications, Inc.
Interpublic Group of Companies, Inc.
Omnicom Group, Inc.

Broadcasting
Cable TV Operators
BET Holdings, Inc. Class A
Cablevision Systems Corp.
Century Communications Corp.
Comcast Corp. Class A
Falcon Cable Systems Co.
Gaylord Entertainment Co. Class A
Jones Intercable, Inc.
Jones Intercable, Inc. Class A
Liberty Media Corp. Class A
QVC Network, Inc.
TCA Cable TV, Inc.
Tele-Communication, Inc. Class A

Turner Broadcasting System, Inc. Class B
Viacom Inc.
Radio Broadcasting
Infinity Broadcasting Corp. Class A
International Cablecasting Technologies, Inc.

Television Broadcasting
CBS, Inc.
Capital Cities/ABC, Inc.
Grupo Televisa SA De CV ADR
Heritage Media Crop. Class A
Home Shopping Network, Inc.
Multimedia, Inc.
Silver King Communications, Inc.

Cellular
Cellular and Communication Services
Contel Cellular, Inc. Class A
McCaw Cellular Communications, Inc. Class A
Mobile Telecommunications Technologies, Inc.
ProNet, Inc.

Fidelity Investments, one of the largest mutual fund companies, is one excellent source of hot leads for fast-growing companies. Their telephone number is 1-800-544-8888. Call to ask for a prospectus and annual report that includes the companies the fund holds.

There are also thousands of investor newsletters on the market. Almost every brokerage firm has a monthly investor newsletter, and every one will have articles about companies whose stock is likely to go up. (A company's stock usually goes up if its revenues and/or profitability are predicted to grow rapidly.)

There are hundreds of investor newsletters for sale. Every one will list recommendations for companies their experts feel will do well. There is generally a description of the kind of business the company is involved in and why the expert believes the stock or company's value should increase.

On page 48 we have listed possible funds from which to search for small, growing companies. To use this information, call the investment company and ask for the prospectus and annual report on the fund you're interested in. (If you don't have the fund's phone number, call Information: 1-800-555-1212.) For example, if you call Information for Jones & Babson's toll-free number, you will find that it is 1-800-422-2766. Call Jones & Babson and ask for the prospectus and annual report on Babson Enterprise Fund 2. This prospectus and/or annual report will include a list of all the fast-growth companies Jones and Babson identified as "high growth" in their Babson Enterprise Fund 2.

A brief explanation of the information contained in fund listings might be helpful to the noninvestor:

The first column lists annual average return over the last 12 months. Babson Enterprise had a return of 20.8%. If you had sent them $1,000 two months ago, you would now have $1,208. The fund may hold several hundred stocks of different companies. Some may have increased in value by 100%, some may have lost 20%. These gains and losses are based on the expectations of all the investors in the world concerning how the particular company will do in the future. As a general rule of thumb, the higher the return, the better the stock picker who manages the fund. So target the funds whose stocks have done the best.

Weighted average P/E, or price/earnings ratio, is the price of the stock divided by the earnings or profits per outstanding share of stock issued of the companies. For example,

$$\frac{\text{Stock Price}}{\text{Earnings/Share}} \quad \frac{25.1}{0.76} = 33$$

The higher the P/E, the more investors know about the stock and have purchased it in hopes that it will go up significantly. The higher the P/E, the higher the hopes and the more speculative or risky the investment. High P/E's are what a job hunter like you looks for. Of course, a low P/E may just mean others haven't "found" the company yet.

Median market cap, or capitalization, is the average size of the company the fund holds. Less than 1 means less than 1 billion in sales, which is something else a job hunter looks for. Less than .5 means less than $500 million in sales revenues.

Fund/ Company	Total annual average 6/83–6/93	Return last 12 months	Weighted average P/E	Median market cap ($bil)
Babson Enterprise Fund 2/ Jones & Babson	—	20.8	21.2	0.1
AIM Aggressive Growth(c)AIM	—	49.6	NA	NA
American Capital Emerging Growth-A/American Cap.	11.1	41.7	31.8	1.3
Evergreen Limited Market/ Lieber	16.0	15.8	19.0	0.1
Fidelity Low-Priced Stock/ Fidelity Investments	—	23.6	15.2	0.1
Fidelity OTC Portfolio/ Fidelity Investments	—	17.6	19.8	0.4
Founders Discovery Fund/ Founders	—	26.7	26.0	0.2
Gabelli Small Cap Growth/ Gabelli	—	18.9	21.0	0.2
Hancock Special Equities-A/ Hancock	—	54.1	35.5	0.6
Hartwell Emerging Growth/ Hartwell	10.1	32.5	40.3	0.6
Invesco Emerging Growth/ Invesco	—	40.6	30.3	0.3
James Venture Fund/Janus	—	18.9	20.1	0.7
Kaufmann Fund/Kaufmann	—	33.3	27.5	0.2
MFS Emerging Growth/MFS	10.0	38.1	32.3	0.6
Mutual of Omaha Growth/ Mutual of Omaha	12.3	24.8	32.1	0.3
Oberweis Emerging Growth/ Oberweis	—	32.5	24.6	0.1
Oppenheimer Discovery/ Oppenheimer	—	34.0	27.0	0.3

How aggressive growth, small-company investors evaluate a company will give the job hunter the "inside scoop." They look for companies whose revenues (total sales) are going to increase by more than 30% per year.

Investors evaluate a great deal of information in order to get a realistic projected growth rate—information such as future products in the pipeline, management expertise and decision-making capabilities, what the competition is like, and many other similar factors. Let them do some of the work for you.

Newsletters

Many newsletters will send a free trial copy for potential investors (you) to evaluate. Some smart job hunters find the company of their dreams that no one else knows about in these newsletters. To help you determine which newsletters are the better predictors, we'll list the top ones based on relative risk and past performance according to *The Hulbert Guide to Financial Newsletters*. (By Mark Hulbert; Dearborn Financial Publishing, 1993.)

1. The Chartist (Average) Actual Cash Account

2. Value Line Investment Survey ($55/10 issues); 1-800-634-3583[6]

3. Zweig Forecast; 516-785-1300

4. The Value Line OTC Special Situations Service

5. Individual Investor Special Situation Report; 212-943-8773

6. Louis Navellier's MPT Review; 702-831-1396

7. Medical Technology Stock Letter; 510-843-1857

8. The Growth Stock Outlook

9. BI Research (studies small and relatively unknown companies only), P.O. Box 133, Redding, CT, 06875 ($80/yr.)

Okay, you have read back issues of newspapers and magazines and investor newsletters covering the past two years or so. You have a list of thriving companies in your general field of expertise. What's next?

How to Contact People and Obtain Information

Sometimes you'll want to contact real people as part of the general search you've been conducting already; at other times you will be looking for more specialized information. A job hunter should be involved in as many "outside" activities as possible, including the PTA, the School Board, the Town Council, local planning board meetings, church, hospitals, trade associations, women in management, and so on. Proactive job hunters volunteer their time consulting and doing whatever else they can to meet people and find out who they know and where they're employed.

6 Out of their 1,700-stock universe, Value Line picks 100 that have the best potential.

Journalists

A creative source of information about expanding small and medium-sized companies is your local newspaper's business editor and writers. Newspaper people, although busy, view their readers as their customers and are therefore likely to be helpful. Remember, the whole job of business editors and writers is to cover companies and their news. They will know which small companies are planning to move or have recently moved into your area, which are growing, and which are marketing great new products.

While you are doing your homework in the local library and reviewing old business sections, remember to jot down who wrote the articles in which you found new target companies to add to your list. These are the people to contact for information.

Newspaper people are not always easy to catch, of course; when they are available depends on when they go to press and when their deadlines are. If you consistently call just before press, you'll never even get a call back. Find out when they are just over press time and you'll get much more cooperation. Often it's at really strange times. Also, since business writers have to do most of their research during, right before, or right after business hours, you may need to meet them at some odd hour to fit their schedule.

Receptionist:	The News and Observer...
Job Hunter:	Hi, is Joe Writer in?
Receptionist:	No, he's not, could I take a message?
Job Hunter:	Yes, that would be great, could you ask him to call me? It's regarding the article he wrote on Company X last month.

Note—A newspaper editor or writer may be under a particular publishing deadline and so have no time to call you back. Try to time your phone call so there are no imminent deadlines pending. You should be able to find this out from the receptionist.

If the reporter or business editor doesn't call you back after two messages (unlikely), the third call should go something like this:

Receptionist	The News and Observer...
Job Hunter:	Hi, I was wondering if you could help me?
Receptionist:	I'll try, what is it?
Job Hunter:	I've been playing telephone tag with Joe Writer. Could you advise me as to the best time to reach him? I'm going to be in and out the next few days.
Receptionist:	Well, I really don't know his schedule.
Job Hunter:	Oh, yes, I'm sorry, you couldn't keep track of all those writ-

ers. Is there someone up in the Business department who might?

Receptionist: Well, his manager Bob Jones might have his schedule.

Job Hunter: Great, thank you!

Or, you get a call back from Joe Writer:

Joe Writer: Hi, this Joe Writer, I was returning your call regarding Company X.

Job Hunter: Thank you so much for returning my call. I want to first say, I really enjoyed the article; you have a nice concise style.

Joe Writer: Well, thank you.

Job Hunter: I wanted to ask your advice. I am in the process of leaving Company Z (say this even if you're unemployed) or I am a recent graduate of UNC and I thought you would probably have some insight for me regarding Company X. Do you think they're doing well? Who did you speak with when you wrote your article?

Joe Writer: Well, I interviewed Sam Johnson, the CEO, and I got the impression that they are doing well.

Job Hunter: What did you think about the company? Would it be a place you'd like to work if you were me?

Joe Writer: Well, they are just introducing a new product. There are probably 500 employees, and the CEO seemed like a good guy. What is your background?

Job Hunter: I'm looking for a position in the advertising or promotions area.

Joe Writer: I'm not sure if they'd be a good place or not.

Job Hunter: Do you think I should talk to some more people there? Is there anyone else you met or do you have any other names who work there so I can at least make some contacts? (Newspaper people will appreciate your tenacity and they will empathize. They often have to try to talk to people who don't necessarily want to talk to them.)

Joe Writer: Let me look in my file...Oh yeah, Susan Water is the V.P. of Sales and Marketing. You could call her.

Job Hunter: You have been so helpful! Have you seen any other growing, small dynamic companies in the area that maybe I should contact?...Are there any other reporters there who cover business news?

Joe Writer: Well, there's x, y & z...

Even if you don't get any good information this time, send a handwritten thank-you for the reporter's help and time. Plan to check back with her in a month or two months. Ask the next time whether she's heard of any new companies moving to the area. Job hunters who keep their "feelers" out constantly and spend a lot of their time talking to people and reading current financial or business news always seem to find these great, fast-growing companies. One successful job hunter told us she found out about the company she targeted from her neighbor, who was a cable installer for the local power company. Whenever a new company was moving into the area, he always knew as soon as they broke ground because he had them on his installation schedule.

People who take time to be genuinely interested in other people they meet seem to find the best jobs the fastest. If you haven't been in the habit of asking people all about themselves, now is a good time to start. It's amazing how well people respond to simple questions like, "How did you get started here? What do you like best about this company? How do you see the prospects for this industry?" Learn to listen and express appreciation. Even after you've landed a great job, continue to collect names and occupations, because you never know when you'll be looking again.

Venture Capital Firms

Another possible source of information is the *venture capital firms* in the area where you want to work. Venture capital firms provide capital money for start-up companies in exchange for equity or partial ownership or stock in these new businesses. Venture capital firms get money from wealthy individuals who don't have time to track down these potentially lucrative start-ups. They pool the individual investors' monies together and then help finance their start-up or expansion in exchange for part ownership of the company. The part-owner relationship, of course, ensures that the connection between the start-up and the venture capital firms will persist long after the initial capital investment. For this reason, venture capitalists are often looking for talent to help manage these new, fast-growing firms, and they help place many senior level managers within these firms.

Here's a sample role play that works well:

Job Hunter:	"Hi, this is Donna Lutz. May I speak with one of the partners, please?"
Receptionist:	May I ask what it's in regard to?
Job Hunter:	Well yes, and maybe you could help me, too. I was interested in talking to one of them regarding a new business start-up. Are they currently investing in new start-ups or are they only accumulating a pool of capital at the current time? (You sound like you are a potential client.)
Receptionist:	Well, I'm not really sure, perhaps you should talk to Joe Wells.

Job Hunter:	Is he one of the partners? (Most venture capital firms are pretty small—less than 50 people.)
Receptionist:	Yes, he is.
Job Hunter:	Thank you so much for your help, and what did you say your name was? (You'll probably need her help tracking Joe Wells down in the future.)

When you speak to Joe, this is how the dialogue might go:

Joe:	Hi, this is Joe Wells.
Job Hunter:	Hi, this is Steve Job Hunter. Thank you for taking my call, Joe. I just wanted to ask for your advice. A friend told me you know just about everything about every start-up business in this area. (Pay a compliment.)
Joe:	I know many of them.
Job Hunter:	I'm in the process of leaving Company X (or I'm a recent graduate of University X). My background is in Y (give the briefest possible description). If you were me, are there any of these companies that you would make contact with? What kinds of successes have you had recently in identifying successful start-ups? Would giving you my resume help?
Joe:	Why don't you fax me a resume and we'll talk after that?
Job Hunter:	Terrific, you have been so helpful. I'll drop it off with your secretary tomorrow. (You might get the opportunity to at least introduce yourself in person, but if you say I'll bring it to *you*, the person will see this as a possible infringement of their time and they will tell you to just put it in the mail.)

Remember, most people are helpful if they are approached benevolently, and…

- ◆ they are asked for their help directly.
- ◆ they see a demonstrated interest in understanding their business by the person asking.
- ◆ they are made to feel important, as they are helping those less fortunate, especially if the less fortunate person is sincere in expressing gratitude and appreciation.
- ◆ they are complimented and asked again for their advice.

If you get a rebuff—if someone says "I can't help you" or "I don't have time to help you" or "you should be speaking to Human Resources"—*give them a second compliment and ask them again for their help.* We see this approach work nine times out of ten. But if the person is in the middle of a project don't push speaking right now. Ask him for a few minutes at a specific time. For example, the venture capitalist may say, "I only talk to my customers about the startups in the area." Respond with, "I can appreciate that—it's just that I've heard you know more about promising startups than anyone in the area—I'd appreciate just a couple of minutes of your time." The venture capitalist usually responds with, "O.K., what industry are you looking at specifically?"

Many people find it difficult to put themselves purposely and actively beneath someone else. Everyone is striving to make herself look and sound important. This attitude keeps the job hunter from finding a job. People help the humble and less fortunate, not the ego mongers. You are less fortunate, since they have a job or information that you may need. The very few who ask for our help get it. Greg, one job hunter, asked for help, and we probably spent a year talking to him a couple times a month trying to find a position for him. Many other job hunters call and are working so hard to make themselves look good and sound important that they turn us off from attempting to help them.

Economic Development Advisors

Another good source of information, especially if you're looking for a job in a specific county, is the county or state Economic Development Advisors. Although they are known by different names in different places, their purpose is always the same—to bring new business into the area in order to increase the tax base and add to the region's prosperity. You can find this organization with the help of your local or regional Chamber of Commerce. Its members are invaluable friends to make. They know about every new business in the area and any old ones that are in the process of building, thinking about building, or moving in.

How does the job hunter find out the names of the people in this group he or she should talk to? The first place to look is in the local phone book. Call the Town or City Manager and ask who is in charge of working with companies who are interested in building in the town or city. Then call the County and State Offices and ask the same question. Who knows, they may assume you're someone calling about possibly building a BMW plant. You'll get the names easily; just remember to speak with confidence.

Of course, your local Chamber of Commerce publishes an updated list of most companies located in most towns and cities. Any one of those companies that is interested in growing and hiring probably will belong to the local Chamber of Commerce. Such lists are usually mailed to anyone who calls and typically include the names of the companies, their basic business, a contact name, and a phone number.

Here's a sample role play with Jan Smart who works for the Council on Economic Growth.

Secretary: Council on Economic Growth, may I help you?

Job Hunter:	Is Jan in? This is Steve Job Hunter.
Secretary:	Yes, may I ask what it is in regard to?
Job Hunter:	Yes, I'm with Company X and I wanted to ask her advice on some personal issues (or) Yes, I'm at the University of North Carolina and I wanted to ask her advice on a personal issue.
Secretary:	I'll put you through.
Jan Smart:	Jan Smart.
Job Hunter:	Hi, Jan, this is Steve Job Hunter. I'm in the process of leaving NTI and I wanted to ask for some advice from you. Is that okay?
Jan Smart:	I'm pretty tied up today. (Expect a rebuff.)
Job Hunter:	I've heard you are the expert on new companies in the area—I'd appreciate just a few minutes of your time.
Jan Smart:	Sure, go ahead.
Job Hunter:	First of all, tell me, how are things going in attracting new businesses? It sure seems like you're doing a great job! I remember seeing an article in the newspaper a while ago about Company Z purchasing land on Weston Parkway. That was a real coup. (Other possible questions: How long have you been here? How many new business have you worked on?)
Jan Smart:	Thank you very much. Well let's see, we brought in four new businesses in the last year, and we have good prospects for at least three new ones right now.
Job Hunter:	That's terrific, it must be really challenging competing against all the other areas wanting new companies. How have you guys done so well? (Remember, sincere compliments and questions work miracles at opening people up.)
Jan Smart:	*Continues talking about the reasons for their success.*
Job Hunter:	Jan (people love the sound of their own name, use it a couple times in conversations), you obviously have a lot of contacts. I was wondering, if you were me—recently graduated from UNC in business (or in the process of leaving an accounting position at Company NTI), which of those companies would you call about a possible position?
Jan Smart:	Well, I would call Company J, since they are also in the technology field.
Job Hunter:	That's a good idea. (Always acknowledge their ideas as being good.) What else could you tell me about Company J?
Jan Smart:	*Continues dialogue.*
Job Hunter:	Do you know the names of any people who work there as a starting point for me?
Jan Smart:	Well, Stan Jacobs is the President, and Julie Target is in charge of the logistics of the move.

> *Job Hunter:* That's terrific, is there anyone else you can think of?
>
> *Jan Smart:* No, not really, that's it.
>
> *Job Hunter:* Jan, you've been such a help to me in my job search. Are there any other places you think I should call or people you know who might be interested in my background? I'm a real "can do anything" type of person.

We assume you have already located a listing from the Council on Economic Growth of all companies in your area and have researched the small "unknown" ones.

There is also a local Entrepreneurial Development Organization in most regions. This organization supports the growth of new companies by providing information on how to obtain private financing or small-business loans. Such a group can be a good source of information about promising new companies in a particular geographic area.

If your industry hosts trade shows in your area, consider attending. Trade shows represent a great opportunity to meet representatives of the hot companies. They also offer a chance to see new products demonstrated and to evaluate the image of a given company or industry. You can collect dozens of business cards. Talk to customers of targeted companies and receive real feedback on products and services.

What Most Job Hunters Never Learn about Networking

So far we have been talking about general sources of information. *Sometimes, though, the crucial information to help narrow your choice is available only from people inside an industry or company organization. This is where networking becomes crucial.* Presumably, you're reading this book because networking has not led to many interviews or job offers. Like many people, you may think networking involves calling everyone on your Christmas card mailing list and asking each whether he or she knows anyone who is hiring—calling 50 to 200 people.

How to Ask for Advice

If you had talked to and helped hire as many people as we have, however, you would find that the successful networkers use an entirely different system from the one described in the previous paragraph. First, when they call a friend or acquaintance they typically ask for advice only, saying things like: "I am in the process of leaving company X or graduating from the University of X, and I was wondering if I could ask for your advice. Could you take a look at my resume and advise me on where and how I should focus my job search efforts?" People are generally more helpful when approached this way. Most people who have a job are glad they do and love to advise the "less fortunate."

So put your ego away and ask for help directly. If it helps you get a job (and it will), who cares?

How Not to Be Perceived As a Pest

Many job hunters continue to ask their acquaintances for help the wrong way. Many call or ask someone they meet at a social event and say, "I'm going to be laid off soon, or I'm graduating from UNC, and I was wondering whether your company is hiring or has any job openings?" This acquaintance really doesn't know you or your business capabilities, and his defenses immediately go up. He thinks, "Oh no, another unqualified pest wanting me to find her a job," or "If I send her to Joe Smith, the hiring manager over in Accounting, and she's a 'dud,' it'll make me look bad, so I'll just keep my information to myself." We hear this scenario repeated every day. A positive, practiced approach will work networking miracles.

Two other differences we have observed in successful networkers: They typically network with anywhere from 400 to 800 people, and they keep track of every contact for repeated bi-monthly follow-ups. Seems impossible? It's not, as successful job hunters report. When you are hesitating to pick up the phone and your stomach is churning, just remember that there are thousands of job hunters cemented behind their desks, typing useless cover letters, stuck in place by fear of picking up the phone. We all like to protect our egos, but let's not do so by avoiding the methods that really work. We would all prefer to have a new job come after sending out letters and resumes or calling headhunters or answering blind ads. And those methods worked— five years ago, but not today.

A successful networker may *start* with the 25 people on his Christmas mailing list, but when he calls back to the office where he faxed a resume, the recipient usually has some advice like: "Well, company X and company Y are doing well, from what I hear." The job hunter next asks whether he knows anyone who works there to use as a name to "get his foot in the door." Then the successful job hunter keeps probing:

"Well, what about any of your customers or vendors or competitors—are any of them doing well? Are there people in your company who know a lot of people in other companies whom I could possibly call and ask for advice?"

The first part of networking simply involves gathering information about companies, casting as wide a net as you possibly can. The second part involves making the companies aware of you. Actually, the distinction is not clear-cut; both these processes are ongoing and circular, *since a crucial part of making yourself an attractive prospect in the company's eyes is your knowledge of that company.* You might look at the following steps as *starting to look for work*, rather than simply *gathering information*—but we don't advise creating this artificial, meaningless distinction. Research is the root and branch of job hunting. It involves not only library research but the whole process of networking—talking to prospective employers about what their most pressing problems are, or their most significant challenges. Such discussions can occasionally lead a hiring manager actually to create a job specifically for you and your talents. This is why you want to *find and talk to hiring managers.*

When you are the first to talk to a manager about her challenges, you are there before the crowds that respond to a posted job or an advertised position in the newspaper. *Would you rather compete against two or three or 1,000 people?* On the other hand, this isn't what either you or the hiring manager came into the discussion expecting. If someone asks to see your resume while you are in the process of learning about their company, or others they know of, great. If someone doesn't, you have still gathered knowledge that will be helpful as you continue your quest.

After you have gathered information about as many companies as you can, *you will want to narrow and refine your search.* Let's assume you have a list of anywhere from 25 to 125 companies that pertain to your field of expertise and seem to be prospering. You don't want to send resumes to all of these places; you couldn't keep track of them.

First you need to weed them out. You don't know how well they're doing. Sort out the likely prospects, the ones that are expanding fairly rapidly, from the less likely ones. The easiest way to do this is to call the corporate headquarters (we'll explain how in Chapter 4), find out whether there are any office locations in your area, and ask to be sent information. Many companies will send out a recruitment package to prospective employees or keep some press clippings and general product/service information on hand, no matter how small a company they are. Ask whether they are publicly traded or whether they plan to be—most companies have someone handling Investor or Public Relations, even if that's not anyone's official title. The people at corporate headquarters are very knowledgeable about the company and will be happy to send out information. If the company doesn't have anyone responsible for public or investor relations, you may want to inquire whether it is hiring, since it is probably very small indeed.

Pulling It All Together: How to Pick the Best Companies

Once you've gone this far in gathering information about your list of companies, you need to impose some order on the chaos of data and create a list that ranks them according to several important characteristics. For example, give each company a score from one to ten on the following traits.

> ♦ *Growth in total employment.* Employment growth should be over 20% a year to be a hot prospect. The annual report will give the total number of employees; just compare the last several years. Ex-

ample: 1991—200 employees. 1992—250 employees. 1993—300 employees.

♦ *Rate of sales or revenue growth and potential profitability.* (Many won't have profits yet—these are sometimes the best start-ups.) Good: over 30 percent. Bad: less than 20 percent. Example: 1991—Sales, $100 Mil., Net Income, $5 mil. 1992—Sales, $130 Mil., Net Income, $13 Mil. 1993—Sales, $175 Mil., Net Income, $33 Mil. Look for a trend upward in both areas.

♦ *Your "fit" within their industry.* Bad: going from aircraft engine manufacturing to retail. Good: going from aircraft engine manufacturing to truck manufacturing. (See Appendix C for more examples.)

♦ *Long-term market prospects.* Good: the company appears to have found a different and better way of doing something. Patented products can be imitated, and the company may spend time in court defending its patents. See how fast they introduce new products in comparison to the competition. Is their competitive advantage a lower price? If so, steer clear; it's only a matter of time and technology before someone else is cheaper. The best small companies that grow into big companies are number one or a strong number two in their market niche. The product or service needs to be different enough so that it isn't competing on price.

♦ *Diversity of products and company markets.* Is the company dependent on one product or focused on a single industry? Good: multiple product lines targeted at unique markets. Bad: one targeted industry or segment of customers, such as the defense industry. One-product companies or those that rely on a few large customers are a high risk.

♦ *Indebtedness.* Is the company self-financed or is it leveraging future profits to carry a large debt? Companies that grow with discipline and self-financing are a better prospect for longevity. The lower the debt percentage, the less risk associated with going to work with the company.

♦ *Global market share.* Is the company expanding overseas now, or is it planning to in the future? Not all products/services can be exported, but aggressive companies always look for new markets. Good: 20 percent of sales overseas or more than 20-percent growth in foreign sales. Bad: regional product with no geographic diversification.

♦ *Quality of Management.* Are the company's managers known for their vision and innovation? Do they grasp the market of the future? Are they committed to change to stay competitive?

♦ *Company culture.* Is the company known for treating its employees well, or does it have a reputation for disregarding the individual employee in quest of corporate profits?

The sources of information on which this scale based should all share one crucial trait: The news they offer should be fresh. We can't overstate the importance of having recent information, whether you are buying stock or searching for a job.

Restrict Your Focus to Your Expertise

Like others, these small, growing companies are likely to hire a person who comes from an identical or similar industry, or else a recent college graduate who demonstrates a lot of knowledge of the industry, either from having taken relevant courses in college, from educating himself in a subject, or both.

Sue has chosen to look for a job in an expanding field. What do you think of her prospects?

Laid-Off Case Study: Sue

Sue, formerly a Human Resources representative in the food service industry, has been out of work for six months. Because of the downturn in food service, she decided to focus on another industry. Reading the help wanted advertisements to see what sorts of firms were hiring, she decided that the fast-growing bio-tech field was a good one to target.

Every week she read the help wanted ads in her local newspaper, as well as those from six other newspapers in the library. She sent her resume and cover letter to at least three companies a week. Usually there was no response, which Sue expected, but a few did call back.

She had prepared a two-minute account of her work history and made sure to cover that at the beginning of each conversation. After each phone call she always went to the library to read the Dun and Bradstreet and Value Line reports on the company in case they called back for a face-to-face interview.

After the phone interview, she wrote a thank-you note and then waited no longer than a week for a call-back. Sue then called the company. When they didn't return her call, she assumed they were no longer interested, and started over with another company.

She never gave up, and began sending out about five resumes per week. After reading a book about careers in health service industries, she began sending out resumes to pharmaceutical companies.

Sue still has not found a job in biotechnology or health care. She's doing some consulting for a few pharmaceutical companies. If she does this long enough, she might get enough experience to be hired in the industry. But this can be a lengthy, austere route to the job she wants.

At this point you should easily be able to spot four major flaws in Sue's strategy. First, she was trying to break into a field in which she had no experience. Second, she was not doing enough research to overcome this handicap. Third, she was spending far too much time on unproductive tactics such as reading and replying to classified advertisements. Fourth, almost no one returns a single phone call placed by someone he doesn't know. She gives up too early.

How to Be Creative and Unique

Successful job hunters often find either a new star in a shrinking industry or else a closely related industry. For example, the automotive and related-components industry is very broad. One might consider moving from GM to a smaller company, Breed Technology, Inc., that manufactures airbag sensors, the hot new product for the auto industry. Think creatively and read extensively. Appendix C contains some further ideas to help you point your thinking in the right direction. Again, all the aforementioned business periodicals contain columns on "Companies to Watch" and other similar great clues to hot prospects for the job hunter.

Given the choice, companies want to hire someone from a competitor, vendor, customer, or closely related industry—or someone who has somehow taught herself the industry. Rising-star companies almost never want to hire someone who knows nothing about their company, business, market, or industry. Why should they, when there are others who have displayed an understanding of their needs knocking on the door?

But perhaps you are a recent graduate, without significant experience or extensive training in the area in which you want to work. College students and recent graduates have a hard time leveraging a nonexistent professional background, which is why students who co-op or do internships often have an easier time obtaining the great jobs. Some college students get in by doing volunteer work in their chosen area of interest in order to obtain a background. But there are other new college graduates, like the one we're about to describe, who do not have many of the requirements for a particular job and who still, through commitment to a mission, persevere and land the job of their dreams. *They know how important their research is to filling in the knowledge gaps,* and they go the extra mile to set themselves apart from the thousands of other graduates who haven't made the 180-degree turn.

New College Graduate/Underemployed Case Study: Donna

Donna, a 1991 graduate of Miami University in Ohio, majored in business and worked her way through school. Knowing she had an aptitude for sales, she decided to target the pharmaceutical industry. First she got on the Pharmaceutical Manufacturers Association's mailing list. Then she looked up the fastest-growing and most profitable companies and focused her efforts on the "least well known" three. She called each company's Investor Relations Department. Donna asked, as a prospective investor, to have information sent on the company, product, and prospectus, along with annual and quarterly reports. She then called Human Resources and was politely told by each company that they only hire new graduates who have nursing or pharmacy degrees and that they really prefer those who have sold for another pharmaceutical company.

Donna couldn't get a job in the pharmaceutical industry. She went ahead and took a low-paying sales job, but she spent every spare minute researching the fastest-growing pharmaceutical companies' products and competition. She talked to the pharmaceutical industry's local sales staff and took the local sales reps of each company to lunch. Eventually Donna went on some calls with the sales reps on her days off. She learned the challenges of selling pharmaceuticals by directly observing the sales reps and the customers.

She asked her new associates whether all the pharmaceutical sales reps in their company had the background described by the human resources manager. The answer was "of course not," so she continued on in her research and networking efforts. She talked to several local doctors and hospitals about the industry and what they wanted from their pharmaceutical sales reps.

Donna got the names of the pharmaceutical hiring managers in the geographic locations she preferred, then relentlessly and positively pursued them. (We'll tell you how to do this without being a pest.) The whole research/networking process took a year, but Donna was hired by an expanding pharmaceutical company and is now one of her company's most successful salespeople. She still does not have a pharmacy or nursing degree!

What did Donna do right? First, she was committed to a clear mission based on her desires and aptitude. Next, she focused her search on fast-growing but hidden companies. She used every tool to gain the information she needed—but she didn't take the data at face value. Instead, she deepened her research to get the inside scoop on her target companies and their requirements. One of the most important steps Donna took was to focus on a small number of companies. Why was this so necessary?

How to Make Research Pay Off

What do we mean by focus? It is the process of understanding what is actually taking place at a given company. Is the company hiring? Who is hiring? What divisions or locations are expanding? Who are the hiring managers and the people who work for them? Focus is finding out about the products, the competition, prospects for the future. It's talking to many people within the company to learn this inside information. This may mean talking to more than 50 people associated with one company!

Focus does not mean you limit your opportunities. Flexibility is also important. If a hot tip on a great job in a great company is presented to you, it should be added to your "hot list."

At this point you should have a list of prospects considerably longer than three. *Why, then, focus on only three at a time?* It is the 180 Degree Principle. The 180 Degree principle means that instead of focusing on why you're such a great job seeker, or why you left your last job, you put your energy into learning more about the company you approach. Again, what are the challenges the organization encounters? What must go right in order for the organization, department, or company to be successful in its mission or goals? Focus on your potential future employer and become the kind of person companies want to hire today. Why limit the number of companies?

1. By focusing on a few, you can take the time to make sure the company is really growing and hiring before you spend a lot of time pursuing it.

2. Companies prefer to hire someone who can demonstrate an understanding of their business and who can effectively articulate how he or she could make a contribution. It is difficult to do this with more than three companies at any one time; you can't keep all the facts straight. Every day we call people back and ask them why they are interested in coming to work with us. The rare one out of ten who can credibly answer is the person who almost always gets the job offer.

3. The insider knowledge enables you to make contact with confidence! You can tailor your resume and your cover letter focused on the *employer's needs*—not your requirements. Review our examples of effectively focused cover letters on pages 146-147.

4. If you receive a call back or are able to reach by telephone a hiring manager to whom you have sent a letter and resume, it is crucial to be prepared for the phone screen. This is where most of the job hunters we talk to are weeded out. *Nothing impresses a hiring manager less than to call someone who has sent a resume, ask him why he sent it, and hear an answer like, "I saw the job posted,"* or *"I heard through friends that your company was hiring."* Doing your research ahead of time, and having the facts at hand is the only good way to ensure that you won't find yourself saying things like this. Instead, say, "I've admired your company for several years. Your ability to be the best at what you do and your zeal

for excellence in product innovation, customer satisfaction, and attracting the best and brightest makes me want to be part of your team."

Almost without exception, every job hunter we have brought on board has displayed an intimate knowledge—achieved by hard work—of the company, its product, and its competitors. There are exceptions, but not many.

Summary: Who Are the Companies and where Are the Jobs?

One of the most important facets of a successful job search is knowing how to find the companies and managers that are hiring. In conducting your research, remember the following:

1. Focus your efforts on the small and medium-sized companies, where nine out of ten new jobs are created.
2. Use nontraditional resources, such as investor information, in your research.
3. Find a new star in your industry or a closely related field.
4. Rank the companies you contact and focus on three companies at a time.
5. Network with up to 800 people, keep track of each one of them, and follow up with them every two months.
6. Ask your contacts for help directly, be humble, and remember that people love to give advice.

The successful job hunter realizes that this process is not linear. Such an in-depth, focused research strategy requires flexibility and strong analytical skills—but it works!

CHAPTER 4

The New Way to Find Out about a Great Company: Case Study Profiles of Silicon Graphics Inc., Breed Technologies, Inc., and Callaway Golf

Many unsuccessful job hunters we talk to fail because their research is inadequate. They either know almost nothing about the company or they have done only a brief review of some objective facts found in the annual report or in Dun & Bradstreet reports.

By now you understand that this is a sure-fire guarantee against moving on to the next step. After all, for every job opening, there will be a few people who have spent days researching the company. For hiring managers the research issue becomes a convenient screening mechanism. Fast-growth companies want to hire someone who has taken the time to understand the business, not a desperate job seeker who responds to an ad before he knows whether the company is a place he'd like to work.

Fast-growth companies hire enthusiastic, hard-working people who know the company and its products, are impressed by what they've seen and heard, and have a mission in life to work for the best!

Following is an account of the path taken by one job hunter to research three of his "A" companies, along with the results of that research. The job hunter is now prepared enough to begin some conversations with employees at each company. Successful job hunters we talk to almost always have this kind of background information prior to sending a resume. Each of the three companies he looked at is in a different industry—computers, automotive, and leisure—yet the sources of information are generally the same: the places where people investing in stock look.

How to Begin the Research Process on an "A" Company

1. The job hunter visits his local university or public library to find corporate headquarters, or he can call 1-800-555-1212 to see whether the company has a toll-free number. The librarian refers him to the Security Exchange Commission's database, which records all financial documents filed by every public company. While at the library, he also looks in *Standard and Poor's Corporate Records* and *Ward's Business Index* for added information. Not as much information is available on privately held companies, but there will be some record of the headquarters location at least for most private companies. He then calls the investor relations department at corporate headquarters to ask for an annual report and any other information sent to potential investors of their stock. Next he asks to be switched to Human Resources or the people who handle hiring and ask whether they have a recruitment package or any information they send to possible new hires. It is important to document the entire process—who you talked to and when you should expect to receive the information. If you don't receive the information within the anticipated time frame, call again.

2. While the job hunter is waiting for this information, he goes to the library and asks the librarian to help him find everything written about the company in the last year from the *Wall Street Journal*, *Forbes*, *Fortune*, *Business Week*, and specific computer industry publications. There are *short cuts* to this information if the job hunter has more money than time. A profile from *Fortune* costs around $30 and can be faxed or sent by overnight courier for those in a rush. If you are a current customer at a brokerage or mutual fund company, you may get reports at nominal fees. Any job hunter can contact Standard & Poors for an eight-to-nine page investment report for around $10. The phone number is 800-642-2858.

3. Next he calls the local headquarters and asks whether there is an office anywhere near him. Most companies sell *something*, whether it is a product or a service. He finds out the name of the sales representative, dealer, or person who handles his area of the country. Depending on how comfortable he feels, he can approach them one of two ways: through the front door or through the back door.

How to Use the Front-Door Method to Find Information

The job hunter tells the sales representative that he's heard great things about the company/product/service, and he's exploring other companies in his field. Then he asks whether the representative would help him by explaining why he went to work there and why that was a good or bad decision.

How to Use the Back Door Method to Find Information

The job hunter calls as a potential customer and contacts the sales rep, dealer, or whoever is in charge of marketing the service and tells them he's interested in their product. (In most cases you *could* be a potential customer.) He asks them why he should consider their product or service rather than another company's.

By doing these three things, the job hunter finds out a wealth of great information that will help him to decide whether the company is truly a great company to work for.

He now can be honestly enthusiastic about wanting to work for the company and can clearly enunciate the reasons why.

What to Look For to Determine if a Company is Hiring

There are four financial highlights to consider:

A. Growth in Employment

B. Growth in Sales Revenue & Profitability

C. Debt

D. Future Predicted Growth

Sample Research Information on a Target "A" Company

Silicon Graphics, Inc.

Sales at Silicon Graphics, Inc. (prior to the MIPS acquisition) had grown from $152 million in 1988 to more than $1 billion in 1993. That's an average increase in revenues of 50 percent per year. Profits or income has doubled over the period from 43¢ a share to $1.30 a share or from $7 million in 1989 to more than $95 million in 1993.[1] The Value Line Investment Survey, which is in most libraries, ranks 1,700 companies from one to five (one being the best) on timeliness or relative price/performance over the next twelve months. Silicon Graphics's ranking is currently a one.[2]

The best companies with the brightest, most secure futures have less than one-third of their total capitalization or stockholders' equity financed by debt. According to SGI's 1993 Annual Report, long-term debt as a percentage of stockholder's equity is just 4 percent. SGI has plenty of money to weather any future downturns extremely well. Based on past history and future projections, 1994 is another high-growth year.

The latest Annual Report also contains information on four new products. The Challenge server provides customers with a powerful new cost-effective distributed solution; it is in place in automotive, aerospace, pharmaceutical, and educational accounts for file and database management applications and for digital media network management. Another new product, the Onyx, is aimed at the high-end graphics workstation market. The Indy combines the graphics workstation with full digital media capabilities including a built-in camcorder, for less than $5,000. The company's new growth will be based on these products in virtual reality, digital film, and video production. Because annual reports can sometimes be almost a

1   SGI 1993 Financial Highlights.
2   from *Value Line*, April 30, 1993.

year old, and because business changes quickly, be sure to ask for a copy of the most recent quarterly report.

From these sources you also will find out that the company is twelve years old, has little long-term debt, became a Fortune 500 company in 1992, and that it has a global market share. Silicon Graphics has 52 offices in the United States, and 44 overseas. It also has three manufacturing sites: one in the United States, one in Japan, and one in Switzerland.

Silicon Graphics is the undisputed technical leader in its market. It is the leading innovator in more than a dozen major market segments, and the breadth of its product line is unmatched in the industry. Its products are the benchmark in an industry where competitors have been driven to commodity prices and resultant profits.

While only the White House could definitively say why Silicon Graphics was chosen as the site for President Clinton's 1993 high-technology initiative announcement, a number of aspects of the company were probably appealing to the White House. First, Silicon Graphics' leading-edge technology provided an optimal backdrop for the important event. Second, Silicon Graphics' fast growth and success illustrate what an entrepreneurial company—founded with federal funding—can achieve by contributing to new jobs, offering new technologies and playing an important role in the economy. Third, the company's unique culture was built on an open and nonhierarchical management structure, diverse workforce, constantly changing environment and an emphasis on empowering and respecting individuals.[3]

For example, the company credo "The Spirit of SGI" is a strong reflection of the ethics and values of SGI. It is well known by all employees and exemplifies the ideal employee.

The Spirit of SGI:

We who...
are open and receptive,
hear and understand.
Talk straight and honest,
are heard and understood

We who...
seek solutions rather than blame,
fuel and sustain our growth.
Empower others and delegate,
find our scope increased

We who...
are full of enthusiasm and fun,
watch it spill over and catch on.
Respect, trust, and support, are
lifted above our squabbles.

We who...
set objectives and propagate
them, find our objectives met.
Encourage creativity, see results

Following are some other summary press releases the job hunter will find in the library:

A New Partner for the Illogical Mind
by Lois F. Lunin

During a symposium held on January 27, 1993, Edward R. McCracken, president and chief executive officer of Silicon Graphics, Inc. (SGI) announced that the era of the traditional supercomputer has ended, and a new age in supercomputing is just beginning. At the symposium, McCracken introduced a new computer line that SGI claims incorporates the power of up to 18 Cray Y-MP class supercomputers into a single RISC-based system.

from *Information Today*, v10n3, pp. 13-14. March 1993.

Industrial Light & Magic Sets Special Effects Partnership

Movie maker George Lucas's closely held Industrial Light & Magic and computer maker Silicon Graphics Inc. have agreed to pool resources in the lucrative field of visual effects and film production.

3 *The Presidential Visit: Reinventing American Business in the 21st Century.* Silicon Graphics, Inc. February 22, 1993.

Silicon Graphics supplies computers used by special effects companies to manipulate images. Industrial Light & Magic has won awards for using computers to create fantastic creatures in movies such as "Terminator 2" and "The Abyss."

from *The Wall Street Journal*; 4/8/93; p. B2

Largest Private-Sector Employers

In Santa Clara County, California—ranked by number of full-time equivalent employees.

Name (rank 1993)	Percent change from previous year
Intel Corp (14)	+8.6%
Pacific Bell (13)	–5.1%
FMC Corp (12)	–14.6%
Varian Associates Inc. (15)	–9.6%
Lucky (19)	+11.5%
Advanced Micro Devices Inc. (16)	–14.1%
Safeway Inc. (11)	–32.7%
Selectron Corp	unavailable
Silicon Graphics Inc.	+19%
ESI Inc.	+4.4%
Applied Materials Inc.	+8.3%
Macy's	–20%

COVER STORY

"Dinosaur had 'to move with an attitude'"
by Tim Friend
USA TODAY

Jurassic Park isn't just about science—it is science.

And because of boundaries broken in robotics and computer graphics, and attention paid to scientific accuracy, the dinosaurs in the new Steven Spielberg movie are as close as anyone will get in this lifetime to bringing them back from extinction.

- Silicon Graphics computers—the world's fastest for 3-D graphics—were used to "replicate" dinosaurs, including herds of brachiosaurs, stampeding gallimimuses and full-body and most running shots.
- More than 200 new software programs were created for the fluid movement, color, texture and attitude.
- $1.7 million worth of Silicon Graphics and Apple Macintosh computers were used to create real-time images for movie set control room monitors and CD-ROM screens in the park's touring jeeps.
- Full-size live-action dinos were created for the T-rex, triceratops, adult velociraptors, velociraptor hatching, brachiosaurus head and neck, and the venom spitting dilophosaur—the one with the "killer lugie," says Winston.

Silicon Graphics, Inc.
"Nintendo Agreement is Set to Create 3-D Game System"
from *The Wall Street Journal*
Tuesday August 24, 1993

Silicon Graphics Inc. and the U.S. unit of Japan's Nintendo Co. have teamed up to produce a powerful new video game system.

Under the agreement, which was expected, Nintendo will use specialized Silicon Graphics computer chips designed to perform the calculations required to produce three-dimensional images.

The product, which will be developed specifically for Nintendo, will be unveiled in arcades next year and will be available for home use by late 1996, the companies said. The target U.S. price for the home system is under $250.

Under terms of the agreement, Nintendo will pay royalties to Silicon Graphics, Mountain View, Calif., for use of the licensed, three-dimensional technology. Software will be supplied by Nintendo and its licenses.

"Silicon Graphics' Next Stop: The Living Room"
from *The Wall Street Transcript Magazine Weekly*
June 14, 1993

If 1993 ended tomorrow, it would still go down as a blockbuster year at Silicon Graphics Inc. In late January, the company surprised other computer makers with new machines that rival the power of Cray Research Inc.'s supercomputers. That helped push its stock to an all-time high of 33. In February, the company leaped into the media spotlight when President Bill Clinton and Vice President Al Gore used a visit to its Mountain View (Calif.) headquarters to kick off their national technology initiative. And the company's 3-D graphics workstations, which have been creating movie special effects since *The Abyss* in 1987, played a key role in creating Steven Spielberg's upcoming *Jurassic Park*. SGI machines will even appear in scenes of the modern-day dinosaur tale.

But none of this may be as important as what Silicon Graphics still has on its calendar. Before the year is out, Chairman James H. Clark and Chief Executive Edward R. McCracken expect to position SGI squarely in the middle of what could prove to be a huge new market. As computers, communications, consumer electronics, and digital media converge, cable-TV operators and phone companies are planning information superhighways to carry digitized movies, interactive games, video phone calls, and on-line shopping. These "digital media" services will require powerful computers called servers to store reams of digitized data as well as technology to reproduce graphic images on TV screens.

SGI computers are used to model drugs at Genentech, design cars at Ford, and develop aircraft at Boeing. Such customers will be SGI's mainstay for years. But because of its advanced graphics and history in Hollywood, SGI is becoming a serious player in the emerging world of digital media. "I keep getting drawn into the consumer area," says McCracken.

DIGITAL DEALS
Silicon Graphics has signed up partners...

Product	Partner
DIGITAL FILM SYSTEM	Eastman Kodak Co.
MOVIE SPECIAL EFFECTS	Lucasfilm Ltd.
INTERACTIVE GAMES	Magic Edge Inc.

...but bigger ones are on the way	
DIGITAL CABLE-TV SERVERS	Time Warner, TCI

This company has cleared some very high hurdles, notes an industry veteran, "I think you have to give a lot of credit to McCracken, who really managed the company through some very significant challenges in the last several months. That included a very significant acquisition, a major change in the product line, and the introduction of a significant number of new products. SGI has come through that all very cleanly.

"Going forward, I see here a strong market position, very strong technology, a competitive advantage, in terms of time and scale. Very deep on the management side for a smaller company, and excellent visibility on the technical road map, as well. I think SGI is doing all the right things."

...

SGI negotiated the MIPS acquisition skillfully, agrees an investment advisor. "Silicon Graphics did one of the most amazing mergers and came out with flying colors. Silicon Graphics acquired a company called MIPS...."

...

"That has allowed SGI to acquire the core technology that's in its computers, that is, the microprocessor. It has allowed SGI to ensure its viability and survivability in the market."

The MIPS buy makes good long-term sense to one Wall Streeter, "The company has clearly established a very strong franchise in its marketplace. SGI made an acquisition last year that was somewhat controversial, but which has turned out very well. And, I think he has built a real team so that the company can continue to grow...."

...

The cultural development of SGI was highlighted by another: "Silicon Graphics leveraged a leadership capability in 3D graphics into a profitable, high-growth opportunity within the technical workstation market, within the technical computing market. So, as consumers have become more oriented toward a visual approach, if you will, SGI's visualization capabilities have been increasingly valued. And, as SGI has been able to deliver that capability at ever-lower price points; the company has been able to address broader and broader and more price-processing capability to move up into the really high-performance technical computing market, taking on competitors such as Convex for example. I think this company, from a technology and product point of view, is doing quite well, but I think the culture that the CEO and his team have fostered at the company has instilled great enthusiasm here. I think that the enthusiasm and sense of direction are truly strategic advantages."

Breed Technologies

Breed Technologies, Inc.—Excerpts from the 1993 Annual Report

Breed Technologies, Inc. is a worldwide leader in the design, development and manufacture of automotive airbag crash sensors and airbag systems. It is the only U.S. company that offers a complete line of electronic, electro-mechanical and mechanical airbag products. More than 23 million Breed sensors have been installed in passenger vehicles. For the 1994 model year, Breed's sensor products will be used in seven of the top ten selling U.S. vehicles.

Breed Technologies' airbag systems are gaining increasing market acceptance. Our airbag inflators and module products incorporate proprietary design and manufacturing technology that offer quality, safety and reliability. By 1995, Breed's electrical and mechanical airbag designs will be used by vehicle manufacturers on four continents.

Breed Technologies has operations in eight locations and employs approximately 1800 people in the United States, Mexico, England and Italy. Its executive offices are located in Lakeland, FL, with manufacturing facilities in Florida, Texas and Mexico; engineering and sales offices are located in the United States, England and Italy.

In 1993, Breed's first year as a public company (New York Stock Exchange: BDT), sales and earnings increased dramatically as the use of airbag systems in cars and light trucks proliferated.

Revenues (in $ millions)		
1991—78.1	1992—88.6	1993—153.5
Net Earnings (in $ millions)		
1991—22.3	1992—3.5	1993—16.8
Net Earnings Per Share (in dollars)		
1991—.09	1992—.13	1993—.59

Operations

To prepare for the potential of increased sensor unit sales in fiscal 1994, this past year saw the substantial expansion of capacity in our Mexican sensor and wire harness plants. It also marked growth in our Lakeland, FL, propellant, inflator, and module manufacturing plant. Outside the United States, Breed Italia, S.r.l. in Turin, Italy, began operations with the opening of a sales office in support of Fiat Auto. Staff levels expanded at the Breed European Operations Center in Coventry, England, as we increased local applications-engineering services and sales and marketing activity for our European customers. We continue to expand our local resources in support of existing and anticipated business with customers in Europe.

Business Expansion

Fiscal 1993 provided a number of firsts for Breed Technologies. We began supplying Jaguar driver and passenger all-mechanical airbag (AMS) systems for all the SJ-S and SJ-6 models in worldwide markets.

In the third quarter, Breed made its first shipments of our all-mechanical facebag systems to Fiat. These airbag systems are being offered as an option for several vehicles in the Tip 2/3 family (mid-sized vehicles) and have met with favorable market acceptance.

Fiscal 1993 was a positive year for our electro-mechanical sensors (EMS). Total product sales increased almost 60% over last year. We added Nissan to our customer list, supplying all of the airbag sensors used in their U.S.-produced vehicles. We also provided all sensors for Mazda's expanded U.S. airbag production, marking a 525% increase in Breed's Mazda business for the year.

Our largest sensor customers in fiscal 1993 were Ford and Delco Electronics (General Motors). Ford unit volumes increased 26% over fiscal 1992, while Delco-GM volumes increased 83%. In June 1993, the Company signed a new supply agreement with Delco-GM for the continuation of its sole-source position with Delco-GM for electro-mechanical, ball-in-tube sensors through the 1995 model year.

Product Development

In particular, we are pleased with the progress on the development of our next generation inflators, and we look for increasing customer activity with these products. The results of our electronic sensor development efforts in 1993 also have been favorable.

We are also pleased to report progress with our SRS-40 retrofit airbag system, which comprises a European or Asian style AMS facebag specifically designed for new or used vehicles manufactured without airbags.

The Future
Breed Technologies has accomplished a great deal in a short period of time. We have transformed ourselves from a small research-oriented engineering company to a mass-production automotive supplier.

Breed, Yesterday And Today
Although the Company was founded less than seven years ago (under the name Breed Automotive Corporation), its roots in airbag technology go back more than two decades. Allen Breed, Chairman and Chief Executive Officer of Breed Technologies, founded the Company's predecessor, Breed Corporation, in 1961. Breed Corporation's primary business was safety and arming mechanisms for military ordinance. As early as 1968 Breed engineers applied this experience and technology toward the development of automotive crash sensors for airbag systems. Development continued for the next two decades until Breed sensor designs were selected by several auto makers. In the mid 1980s, Breed's airbag sensor manufacturing began. In late 1986, the Company was established as a spin-off from Breed Corporation's defense business and was renamed Breed Technologies, Inc. in 1992.

Sensors
In recent years, Breed has been the largest airbag crash sensor manufacturer in the world, and business should continue to grow along with the increase in airbag installations.

Securities and Exchange Commission
Washington, D.C. 20549
Annual Report Pursuant to Section 13 or 15 (d) of the Securities Exchange Act of 1934
Breed Technologies

Item 1. Business
Breed Technologies, Inc. (the "Company" or "Breed") is a worldwide leader in the design, development, manufacture, and sale of crash sensors used in automotive airbag systems. The Company estimates that, in the 1993 model year, magnetically-biased electromechanical "ball-in-tube" sensors ("EMS sensors") supplied by the Company and its licensees were used in approximately 59% of all airbag-equipped cars produced in the United States. Products based on the Company's technology also are installed in cars produced and sold in Japan and Europe. In addition to crash sensors, the Company sells complete all-mechanical airbag systems ("AMS systems") that contain all necessary airbag components in a self-contained unit installed in the steering wheel. Building upon its expertise in the supply of critical components of airbag systems to major automobile manufacturers and its experience in high volume production of sensing devices, the Company is expanding its product line to include a range of driver-side and passenger-side electrically initiated airbag inflators. The Company also plans to sell electronic sensors and complete electrically initiated airbag systems.

Fiscal year ended June 30, 1993		
Customers	**Amount (in thousands)**	**Percentage of Sales**
Ford	$64,073	41.7%
Delco-GM	48,968	31.9
Mazda	18,051	11.8
Nissan	12,285	8.0
Jaguar	8,983	5.8
Other	1,166	0.8
Total net sales	$153,526	100.0%

Results for 1993 Compared with 1992

Gross margins for the year were 32.3 percent compared to 29.4 percent for 1992, reflecting the increased efficiencies achieved by a higher utilization of production capacity for both sensors and airbag systems, lower purchased material costs of raw materials and parts, and savings relates to the in-sourcing of a number of parts and processes. Manufacturing and material cost performance also was improved with the assistance of our suppliers to better coordinate material flows and product changes.

Nature of Business and Summary of Significant Accounting Policies
Nature of Business and Major Customers

Sales by the Company to Ford for fiscal 1993, 1992 and 1991 accounted for 42%, 62% and 59%, respectively, of the Company's annual net sales for such years. Sales by the Company to Delco-GM for fiscal 1993, 1992 and 1991 accounted for 32%, 31% and 37%, respectively, of the Company's annual net sales for such years.[4]

Equity Research Report from Olde Discount Stockbrokers
Breed Technologies

Initial Buy

We recommend that aggressive investors take initial positions for the following reasons:

♦ Breed Technologies' net revenues for the second quarter ended December 31, 1993, increased 82.1% over the comparable period last year to $69.5 million. Net income increased to $10.3 million, or $0.34 per share, compared with $3.6 million, or $0.13 per share.

♦ The National Highway Safety Administration requires that all U.S. passenger cars and light trucks have driver-side and passenger-side airbags by 1998. All trucks, buses and multi-purpose passenger vehicles are required to have airbags by 1999. Independent sources estimate that the airbag industry will grow at a 37% average annual rate through 1999.

♦ 1994 U.S. automotive sales are expected to show strong growth over 1993, reaching 15 million by year-end. With a 59% U.S. market share, this should benefit its revenue growth, as approximately two to three sensors are placed in each auto manufactured.

♦ Breed has a 59% U.S. market share with its electromechanical sensors. Although the company is facing increasing competition from TRW, Morton International and OEA International, it should be able to maintain its competitive edge with its 21 patents covering a broad range of its products and $12 million in planned R & D expenditures for fiscal 1994.

We believe that with Breed's definitive market share in the airbag industry, and strong customer relations and product development, the company will be a strong competitor going forward. We recommend that aggressive investors take initial positions. Our 18 to 24 month price target is $45.

Breed Technologies, "When Allen met Johnnie," Forbes 400, Oct. 18, 1993.

The bright son of a Chicago doctor, Breed earned an engineering degree at Northwestern University in 1959, did a brief stint at RCA and joined the Gruen Watch Co. in 1955. At Gruen he learned that the same machines used to produce a wristwatch's tiny gears could be used to produce safety and arming mechanisms for military munitions.

4   1993 Breed Technology Annual Report

In 1957 Breed left Gruen and formed his first company. The Waltham Watch Co. was moving its watchmaking operations to Switzerland. Breed and a partner bought some of Waltham's leftover equipment and began making safety and arming devices for the military. The company, REDM, was a success. In 1960 the 33-year-old Breed took the company public. But a year later Breed had a falling-out with the board; he resigned, left the company with around $300,000 and started a new company, Breed Corp. Says senior executive Ted Thuen, who has worked with Breed for 25 years: "Allen had this never-say-die attitude. He just regrouped and started something new"…

But while Allen Breed is a gifted engineer and inventor, he isn't much at running businesses. "Administrative duties," he readily admits, "aren't my strong point."

After a promising start making trigger mechanisms for things like antitank weapons, Breed Corp. was all but bankrupt by 1969, and Allen Breed's life began a frightening downward spiral. The problem: Breed had patented a ball and tube fuse that measures velocity and time changes. The Pentagon wanted title to Breed's fuse patent, but Breed wouldn't give it up and demanded higher royalties. Then the government canceled Breed's contract. Breed lost most of his net worth—cash, stocks, some Manhattan real estate—when Breed Corp. collapsed. His marriage soon failed, too.

But he didn't lose his do-or-die spirit. Says his lawyer of many years, Geoffrey Stewart of Hale & Dorr: "Allen just turned around and said, 'Let's find something new to make.' "

That something new was the firing device to inflate collision airbags in cars.

In the late 1960s, Breed had heard some fellow defense contractors discussing the new automobile airbag technology. His ears pricked up when he heard that auto manufacturers needed a cheap trigger device—a sensor—that would explode the bags at the right time. The trigger had to be able to tell the difference between a parking-lot fender-bender and a head-on, high-speed crash.

Breed thought he had just the right product, his patented ball-and-tube sensor used to fire rockets. The sensor was strong enough not to explode if the shell was dropped on solid concrete, but sensitive enough to deploy under pressure from the firing pin in a rocket launcher. Breed figured he could make a lot of money if he could adapt his sensor to trigger cars' airbags…

Fortunately, auto makers were looking at airbags again. But in 1984, just as he was preparing to go after more airbag sensor orders from the car makers, Breed suffered a heart attack. Leaving the automotive side of the company in younger brother David's hands, he went off to the Pritikin Longevity Center in Downingtown, PA. It was there that he met Johnnie Tanner, a tough-as-nails woman who would turn his life—business and personal—around. Says longtime employee Ted Thuen:

"Allen is a brilliant, brilliant engineer, but he's also the kind of guy who would go through a wall when there's a door nearby. Johnnie Breed is there to show Allen the door"…

In the early 1980's, when Ronald Reagan privatized many areas of government contracting, Johnnie Tanner was granted her own charter. Her own company, Ground Transportation Services, was born.

Today, Ground Transportation has nine offices in eight cities, specializing in buying transportation tickets for servicemen and women. The company processes close to 1.5 million tickets; Johnnie says revenues are $20 million and that her travel businesses earn her around $800,000 a year.

But starting her own business was hard on Johnnie's health and her marriage. In 1985 she checked herself into the Pritikin Longevity Center, where one of her fellow patients, a shy fellow wearing a baby-blue polyester leisure suit and thick eyeglasses, was Allen Breed…

They both believed in their ability to overcome obstacles. "Once he started to talk," Johnnie remembers, "I thought, 'This has got to be the most optimistic person I've ever met' "…

Once his health improved, Allen Breed wanted to get back to making airbag sensors. But Breed Corp. needed working capital. Allen asked Johnnie to invest in and help him run the company. Soon after, he asked her to marry him. By July 1987, 22 months after their chance meeting at Pritikin, Johnnie had agreed to all three proposals.

Allen Breed gave Johnnie free rein to examine the company and suggest any changes she though necessary. Her quick, analytical mind quickly convinced her that while Breed Corp. had potentially valuable patents, as a business organization it was a mess...

She wanted the company to look more like TRW or Motorola, which had separate automotive and defense divisions.

To make Breed Corp. look more like a company Detroit could do business with, Johnnie decided to separate the automotive business from the defense business by creating a new company, Breed Automotive, which would specialize in producing the airbag sensors. (The defense side of the business was sold in 1989.)

After restructuring the company, Johnnie found she was stepping on the sensitive toes of Breed Automotive's president, David Breed. David and Johnnie clashed often and unpleasantly. "David Breed had set up a plan for the way the company should work, and it wasn't wrong," says Allen Breed's lawyer Stewart. "Johnnie came in and started setting the company straight. David grew very resentful. He couldn't believe that this Southern woman, who had never finished college, was telling him, with his umpteen degrees, how things should be run"...

Once she had spun off the new company, Breed Automotive, out of the old Breed Corp., Johnnie went courting favor with Detroit's car makers by asking them to suggest people to help run the new Breed Automotive...

With Vince Russo in charge of Breed Automotive's day-to-day operations, the company won big contracts for its airbag sensors from General Motors' Delco division and Ford. Today the company accounts for about 60% of the U.S. crash sensor market. Sales zoomed from $7.7 million in 1988, over $150 million last year, when Breed earned $16.8 million...

Now operating from a 488-acre headquarters complex in Lakeland, Fla., and with three production plants in Mexico, the Breeds say they're ready for their next challenges. And challenges there will be. For example, some auto people and highway and safety experts think Breed's electromechanical sensor might be eclipsed by an all-electronic sensor. Johnnie Breed says she and her husband have a new, all-electronic sensor ready for production.

Callaway Golf

"Hot Clubs and Hot Stocks:

Big Bertha has Callaway sizzling. But are golf stocks overheated?"
from *Business Week*
February 21, 1994

...Douglas Johnson, who manages the Seattle-based $220 million SAFECO Equity Fund Inc., has been a Callaway convert for a while now. In Orlando, he got to swing the new irons on a course Callaway rented. Says Johnson, "I'm going to buy a set, and I haven't bought a set of clubs in four years. They're the best in the market."

He feels the same about Callaway's shares. Johnson added the stock to his fund's portfolio just after Callaway went public at 20 a share in February 1992. It soon split 2 for 1. Today, buoyed by an eye-popping 114% jump in 1993 earnings, to $41.2 million on a 93% increase in revenues to $254.6 million, it's trading at 67%.

...

...true believers such as Johnson have fueled the popularity of golf-related new issues. Callaway tops the leader board in size and price.

...

In addition, a more robust economy should help. Sales of golf equipment, which fell in 1991, have been recovering slowly, with 1993 estimates at $1.4 billion, according to the PGA. "The golfing public has put off their purchase of iron sets for a lot of reasons," says Allan Beyer, senior vice-president at market researcher Audits & Surveys."

Callaway Is Seeking Lead Role In Golfing
by Larry Dorman
from *The New York Times*, February 12, 1994

When Ely Callaway, the owner of Callaway Golf, took his company public in 1992, he hit the business equivalent of a 600-yard drive. Fueled by soaring sales of the revolutionary golf club that Mr. Callaway invented, the stock has more than tripled since then, jumping by almost 6 percent just this week.

...

Last week at the PGA Merchandise Show, a trade show sponsored by the Professional Golfers Association of America in Orlando, Fla., Callaway Golf introduced Big Bertha irons, based on the same technology that have made its Big Bertha drivers and woods the top sellers in the country.

"We already are the No. 1 producer of metal woods, and we see this as our opportunity to become the major producer of irons in golf," Mr. Callaway, who is the chief executive officer, said, "In 40 years, no major manufacturer has dominated the market in both woods and irons. We want to be the first company to do that."

...

An Impressive Record

That might seem fanciful, but a look at Mr. Callaway's record suggests that it might be a mistake to bet against him. When he bought the company in 1983, after careers in textiles and wine making, it was a smaller maker of hickory-shaft putters and wedges marketed by mail order. There were five employees, including Mr. Callaway, in a 1,500 square foot plant in Carlsbad, Calif. Annual sales were $500,000.

Five years later, sales were $4.8 million. Five years after that, in 1993, the company had sales of $254.6 million, 1,200 workers and had expanded its plant to 250,000 square feet. Net income for 1993 more than doubled, to $42.9 million, from 1992 after having tripled each year since 1990.

...

Steve DeLuca, director of research at Cruttenden & Company in Irvine, Calif., said, "But we think they can sustainably grow the business at above market rate, meaning above 20-plus percent."

...

Women professionals especially love the club. The Big Bertha is the No. 1 driver on the Ladies Professional Golfers Association Tour. According to figures compiled by Darrell Survey, a company that tracks that equipment used by tournament professionals, Big Bertha was the club of choice of 36 percent of the L.P.G.A. players in the first 11 months of 1993.

It was an even bigger hit on the Senior PGA Tour, where 58 percent of the over-50-year old set used the driver among the players on the regular PGA Tour, where Taylor Made drivers, also made in Carlsbad, had 26.39 percent of the market, compared with Callaway's 17.53 percent.

"America's 100 Fastest-Growing Companies"

by Andrew E. Serwer

from *Fortune*, August 9, 1993

New businesses can be created out of the most unlikely products. "If I can make it by improving a 300-year-old piece of Scottish athletic equipment, anyone can," says Ely Callaway. Many thousands of golfers swear that Callaway Golf has brought their game to another level with the Big Bertha driver, the company's flagship product. Bertha's head is almost 25% bigger but not heavier than an ordinary driver's, so even a duffer is better able to launch the ball like power hitter Long John Daly. Bertha has helped make the dollar sales of Callaway clubs the highest in the U.S.

This is the third round of business success for the septuagenarian Ely Callaway. He worked his way up in the textile business and made it to No. 2 at Burlington Industries, but was passed over for CEO and left in 1973. He then migrated to California and founded Callaway Vineyard & Winery, which he sold to Hiram Walker in 1981 for about $14 million. While puttering around on the golf course, Callaway came across a club he liked so much that he bought the maker. Callaway slapped on his surname and built the company to its present size from almost nothing over ten years. Clubmakers had long dreamed of building a bigger head; Callaway took advantage of a new stainless steel casting technology to do it and introduced Big Bertha two years ago.

It's simple, says this super salesman in his engaging Georgia twang. "Being successful means creating products with significantly greater satisfaction to customers. Everyone wants a better product. *Companies should give it to 'em!*"

	Sales Annual Growth Rate 3–5 years	E.P.S./Annual Growth Rate, 100 Rank
Callaway Golf	120%	243% 1

Callaway Golf Drives Hard With Innovative Product Line

by John A. Jones, February 9, 1993

from *Investor's Business Daily*

Since Callaway Golf Co. made its first stock issue a year ago this company has proved again the virtue of building a better mouse trap. In this case Chairman Ely Callaway built a better golf club—and didn't wait for the world to beat a path to his door.

Based in Carlsbad, Calif., Callaway Golf has grown from four employees in the early '80s to some 600 now, designing and producing a full line of high-quality golf clubs at premium prices.

Management's Letter to Shareholders

from 1993 Annual Report

1993 has been another very good year for Callaway Golf. Some of the highlights are:

- Sales increased to $254.6 million—up 93% from $132.1 million in 1992. We believe we are now the largest golf club manufacturer in the U.S. in terms of sales dollars.
- We signed an exclusive licensing agreement with Nordstrom, one of the world's leading specialty fashion retailers. Nordstrom will design, finance, produce and sell the apparel under a joint Nordstrom-Callaway Golf label.

- We completed construction and began operations in our new 75,000 square foot manufacturing and warehousing plant and have leased an additional 33,000 square feet of manufacturing and warehousing space as a part of our planned expansion.
- During 1993, the Company established the Callaway Golf Company Foundation, a charitable foundation for the funding of activities which are beneficial to our community, as well as to our employees. During 1993 the company contributed $1.0 million and Ely Callaway personally donated 20,000 shares of his Callaway Golf stock to the Callaway Golf Company Foundation.
- Big Bertha Drivers were the Number One driver used by the professionals on 3 of the 4 U.S. tours for all of 1993—the Senior PGA, the LPGA and the Nike tour. Big Bertha Drivers were in the Number Two position of driver counts for the entire 1993 season on the regular PGA tour. See page 6 for further details on our tour activities.
- Through our research and development efforts of 1993, we were able to announce in January 1994 two significant new products.

The Product

For the first five years of the Company's existence it concentrated mainly on the production and sale of golf clubs designed primarily for the golfer's short game. Wedges and putters using the patented Callaway Steel Core Hickory Stick shafts accounted for 90% of the Company's sales from 1982 through 1987. The company introduced a full set of Hickory Stick irons in 1985 followed by its Bobby Jones Hickory Stick woods and irons in 1986. While these products were highly acclaimed for their beauty, function, and feel, total annual sales did not exceed $3 million.

Recognizing that truly great innovation in golf club performance required improved clubhead design, the Company began its development of the S2H2 concept.

Thus in 1988, we saw the beginning of a radical change in the Company's direction and in its potential. The Company entered the 1990s with a remarkable new family of products recognized around the world as superior golf clubs made with the S2H2 concept. These are fundamentally unlike any other golf clubs in appearance, feel and function. They have non-existent or very short light-weight hoses, and the shafts are "bore through."

Personal Investing

from *Fortune*

An interview with Todger Anderson, manager of Westcore Midco Growth Fund.

Portfolio Talk
"Mid-cap Stocks: Still Room for Growth"

Callaway Golf is another consumer stock we like. The company makes golf clubs. Normally I avoid athletic equipment because the market tends to be faddish, but Callaway is here to stay. It developed a stainless-steel driver called Big Bertha that has a bigger sweet spot than usual, so the average golfer can hit better drives. Even more exciting is Callaway's new Big Bertha seven-wood that you use in place of your long irons. The company's founder and CEO, Ely Callaway, is a superb manager. The stock trades at 17 times this year's estimated earnings. We think earnings can grow at a 20% rate for each of the next three or four years.

CHAPTER 5

Narrow Your List to the "A" Companies: A Case Study

Case Profile of Vince Jacobson

Vince was employed as a marketing manager for a large pharmaceutical company whose profits and sales revenues had steadily increased throughout the 1980s. In 1993 the market for its products began to look different, and the company announced its first early retirement package. Vince knew it was only a matter of time before the layoffs began; because the average age of the employees at his company was only 42, few would be taking early retirement. In addition, almost all of the major pharmaceutical firms were announcing layoffs. Vince took a look at the economics of the industry, along with his company's competitive situation under the Clinton health care plan, and decided the future was not bright. The large buying groups and the new generics, along with new over-the-counter-drugs, were slowly eroding the entire price structure, which meant the profits and margins the company had realized in the past were not likely to be seen again. Instead, profits would be getting smaller and smaller. The national debate on health care reform was not yet over, but the direction was clear: It would mean even less profit for most pharmaceutical companies.

Because Vince had been working for the same company for ten years, he realized he would only be able to obtain a similar compensation level in a company that also was in the health care industry. Vince had spent the last two years working in the marketing area handling government accounts (Medicaid and Medicare), and also many of the managed-care customers. He decided the time to start looking for a new job was before he lost the one he had.

Vince's job-search plan

1. Research Stage at the Library

Vince went to the largest regional public library (the one in his town was too small and didn't carry the magazines he needed; he had called and checked) as it was opening one Saturday morning, when it was not crowded. He went to the service desk and waited for the most serious-looking librarian to be finished talking to another person.

Vince: Hi. I was wondering if you could help me.

Librarian: Yes, what do you need?

Vince: I would like to find the fastest-growing companies in the health-care field. I was told to look in the last two years of business magazines such as *Forbes, Fortune, Business Week, Inc.* and *Financial World*, which all have periodic listings of the top, growing companies. I would like to look particularly for those issues. Then once I find some company names, I need to find out where their headquarters are located if it's not mentioned in the magazine.

Librarian: Okay. Over here are the periodicals themselves from the last two years. Just look at the covers for your specific issue. They are arranged in alphabetical order, so begin with *Business Week*, or you can find the location by looking them up by title on the card catalogue or computer, just like any other book. The last couple of months are in the magazine section, which is over in that room, arranged alphabetically. The index of *Directory of Corporate Affiliates* will give you the location of the headquarters, and a page reference for a brief summary.

Something else that might interest you—we have a book called *Hoover's Handbook of Emerging Companies*, which consolidates those lists and also lists the companies that are increasing their new hires the most rapidly in the United States. But, you have to remember that its information is about a year old; you still should review the magazines to find the most recent lists.

Vince: You know, it's been years since I've done research in a library; and I've got a lot of research to do. Could you possibly show me how to find the company headquarters in that book? By the way, could I ask your name?

Librarian: (smiling) Certainly. It's Sue. And I'll be glad to help you. (She shows him where the magazines, and the *Directory of Corporate Affiliates*, are and looks up a sample company name.)

Vince wanted to know the location of the companies for two reasons. The nature of his work meant he would likely be located at the corporate headquarters in any new job he would find, as he was at his current position, and he wanted to stay in the South. In addition, he needed a location to call to ask for more information, in order to help him further evaluate the company and the likelihood of being able to find employment there. He knew that the best way to find out whether a company was growing and hiring was to call and ask for a recruitment package, a press or public-relations packet, and, if the company was publicly owned, an investor package.

Vince spent two hours finding all the specific magazine issues he was looking for, then turned to the section that listed the best small companies—Business Week's "100 Best Small Companies," Fortune's "100 Fastest-Growing Companies," Forbes's "200 Best Small Companies," Inc.'s "100 Fastest-Growing Public Companies," and Inc.'s "500 Most Rapidly Growing Private Companies." Vince wrote down the names of companies he found related to the health care industry. He was amazed at how many different kinds of companies in the industry there were whose sales were growing, while his company and most other pharmaceutical companies like it were downsizing and looking at every opportunity to save even a little money. He was happily surprised: There seemed to be great prospects in the new companies that were making generic drugs as well as those providing in-home health care services and cost containment services.

Monday morning Vince called several of the mutual funds listed and asked whether they had any small company funds, aggressive-growth funds, or select funds focusing exclusively on the health care industry. The first one he called had all three kinds of funds. Vince asked to be sent an annual report from each of these funds. He knew these reports would list all the companies that the funds had shares in—companies that financial analysts had obviously decided were likely to prosper. Two other mutual fund companies had funds devoted exclusively to health care companies. Vince asked to be sent those annual reports as well. After he received all the annual reports, he added all the companies he had never heard of (the smaller companies) to his list of possibilities.

By the time he was finished, Vince had a list of about 200 company names and a brief note about each one, as the following list shows.

COMPANY	LOCATION	SOURCE
A.L. Laboratories, Inc. Class A		Fidelity Health Care Portfolio
Abbey Healthcare Group, Inc.	CA	Fidelity Health Care Portfolio
Alkermes, Inc.	MA	Fidelity Health Care Portfolio
Allergen, Inc.	CA	Fidelity Health Care Portfolio
Allied Healthcare Product, Inc.	St. Louis, MO	Fidelity Select Portfolio
ALZA Corp.	Palo Alto, CA	*Hoover's Handbook* & G.T. Global Health Care Fund
AM Care Physician Services	Durham, NC	Durham, NC, Chamber of Commerce
American Home Patient	Franklin, TN	*Ward Business Listing*
American Medical Electronics		*Business Week's* 100 Best
Applied Analytical Industries, Inc.	Wilmington, NC	*News & Observer*
Applied Immune Sciences, Inc.	CA	Fidelity Health Care Portfolio
Ares Serono		Fidelity Health Care Portfolio
B & V Technologies	Idaho Falls, ID	
Ballard Medical Products	Draper, UT	*Forbes's* 200, *Financial World's* Best 200, *Business Week's* 100 Best
Bard (C.R.), Inc.	NJ	Fidelity Health Care Portfolio
Baxter ValueLink	Morrisville, NC	Durham, NC, Chamber of Commerce
Bergen Brunswig Corp. Class A	CA	Fidelity Health Care Portfolio
Biocraft Laboratories, Inc.	NJ	Fidelity Health Care Portfolio
Biomet	Warsaw, IN	*Forbes's* 200, *Financial World's* Best 200
Blarron Group Inc.	Raleigh, NC	*News & Observer*
Blessings		*Forbes's* 200
Bolar Pharmaceutical Co. Inc.		Fidelity Health Care Portfolio
Boston Scientific Corp.	MA	Fidelity Health Care Portfolio
Cabot Medical Corp.	PA	Fidelity Health Care Portfolio
Callagen Corp.	Palo Alto, CA	Fidelity Select Portfolio
Cardinal Distribution	OH	*Financial World* & Fidelity Health Care Portfolio
Carolina Physicians' Health Plan	Morrisville, NC	*News & Observer*
Carter-Wallace, Inc.	NY	Fidelity Health Care Portfolio
Chiron Corp.	CA	Fidelity Health Care Portfolio
CIS Industries	Tulsa, OK	
Coastal Healthcare Group Inc.	Durham, NC	Durham, NC, Chamber of Commerce & GT Global Health Care Fund
Coherent Inc.	Palo Alto, CA	Fidelity Select Portfolio
Columbia Hospital	Fort Worth, TX	*Fortune* 100
Command Medical Products	Ormond Beach, FL	*Inc.'s* 100
COMNET Corp.	MD	Fidelity Health Care Portfolio
Complete Health Services	Birmingham, AL	*Inc.'s* 100
Continental Medical Systems	Mechanicsburg, PA	*Fortune's* 100
Cordis Corp.	FL	Fidelity Health Care Portfolio & *Forbes's* 200
Cortech, Inc.	CO	Fidelity Health Care Portfolio
Coventry Corp.	Nashville, TN	*Fortune's* 100 & *Hoover's Handbook* & Fidelity Select Portfolio
Critical Care America		*Fortune's* 100
Curaflex Health Services	Ontario, CA	*Inc.'s* 100
Cygnus Therapeutics Systems, Inc.	CA	Fidelity Health Care Portfolio
DAMON	Needham Heights, MA	*Fortune's* 100
Danek Corp.	Memphis, TN	*Forbes's* 200 & *Hoover's Handbook*
Danels Group		*Business Week's* 100 Best
Diagnostic	Albuquerque, NM	*Fortune's* 100
E2Corp.	Austin, TX	*Hoover's Handbook*
Enzo Biochem Inc.	Farmingdale, NY	Fidelity Select Portfolio
Enzyme Tech Research Group Inc.	Durham, NC	*Ward Business Listing*
Ethix	Beaverton, OR	*Inc.'s* 500

COMPANY	LOCATION	SOURCE
Express Scripts	MD Heights, MO	*Business Week's* 100 Best
Family Health Plan	Miami Lakes, FL	*Inc.'s* 500
Florida Infusion	Palm Harbor, FL	*Inc.'s* 500
Forest Laboratories		*Financial World*
Foundation Health Corp.	Rancho Cordova, CA	*Hoover's Handbook*
FoxMeyer Corp.	Carrollton, TX	Fidelity Select Portfolio
Franklin Quest Co.	Salt Lake City, UT	*Hoover's Handbook*
Fresenius USA Inc.	Concord, CA	Fidelity Select Portfolio
Gendex		*Financial World*
Gensia Pharm	San Diego, CA	*Inc.'s* 100
Genzyme Corp.		*Hoover's Handbook*
Gran Care Inc.	CA	*Hoover's Handbook* & *Fortune's* 100
Greonery Rehabilitation Center	Durham, NC	Durham, NC, Chamber of Commerce
Hanger Orthopedic Group	Bethesda, MD	Fidelity Select Portfolio
Hauser Chemical Research Inc.	Boulder, CO	*Hoover's Handbook*
HCFS	Dallas, TX	*Inc.'s* 500
Health Images	Atlanta, GA	*Ward Business Listing*
Health 1st	Atlanta, GA	*Ward Business Listing*
Health Infusion Inc.	Miami, FL	*Hoover's Handbook* & *Business Week's* 100 Best
Health Management Associates Inc.	Naples, FL	G.T. Global Health Care Fund & *Ward Business Listing*
Health O Meter Products Inc.	Oaklawn, IL	Fidelity Select Portfolio
Health Source Inc.	Concord, NC	The *News and Observer*
Health South Rehabilitation	Birmingham, AL	*Fortune's* 100 & *Inc.'s* 100
Health-Chem Corp.	New York, NY	Fidelity Select Portfolio
Healthcare Compare	Downers Grove, IL	*Financial World's* Best 200 & *Inc.'s* 100
Home Healthcare Resources	Bensalem, PA	*Inc.'s* 500
Homecare Management	Ronkonkama, NY	*Business Week's* 100 Best
Homedco Group, Inc.	CA	Fidelity Health Care Portfolio
Hospital Staffing Services	Fort Lauderdale, FL	*Fortune's* 100
HPSC Inc.	Blue Bell, PA	Fidelity Select Portfolio
HTI Bio Services	Santa Ziabel, CA	*Inc.'s* 500
Intect Inc.		*Hoover's Handbook*
Integrated Health Service	La Jolla, CA	*Fortune's* 100
Intergroup Healthcare		*Forbes's* 200
Intramed Lab	San Diego, CA	*Inc.'s* 100
Isomedix		*Financial World*
IVAX Corporation	Miami, FL	*Fortune's* 100, *Business Week*, Fidelity Select Portfolio, The New York Times & *Hoover's Handbook*
John J. Lee & Associates	Durham, NC	Durham, NC, Chamber of Commerce
Johnson & Johnson	NJ	Fidelity Health Care Portfolio
Jones Medical Industries Inc.	St. Louis, MO	Fidelity Select Portfolio
Komag Inc.	CA	*Hoover's Handbook*
Lumex Inc.	Bay Shore, NY	Fidelity Select Portfolio
Manor Care		*Financial World*
Marsam Pharmaceuticals Inc.	Cherry Hill, NJ	*Inc.'s* 100
Maxxim Medical	Sugar Land, TX	*Fortune's* 100
MDT Corp.	Torrance, CA	Fidelity Select Portfolio
Medchem Products		*Forbes's* 200
Medco Research	Los Angeles, CA	*Inc.'s* 100
Medi-Mail	CA	*Inc.'s* 100
Medical Care America Inc.	TX	Fidelity Health Care Portfolio
Medical Diagnostics	Burlington, MA	*Business Week's* 100 Best

COMPANY	LOCATION	SOURCE
Medical Marketing Group Inc.	NJ	Fidelity Health Care Portfolio
Medical Technology Systems	Clearwater, FL	*Financial World* and *Forbes's* 200
Medicine Shopper		Financial World
MEDIQ Inc.	Pennsauken, NJ	Fidelity Select Portfolio
Medscribe	Pittsburgh, PA	*Inc.'s* 500
Medstat Systems	Ann Arbor, MI	*Financial World's* Best 200
Medvisit Inc.	Durham, NC	Durham, NC, Chamber of Commerce
Melaleuca	Idaho Falls, ID	*Inc.'s* 500
Meridian Diagnostics Inc.	Cincinnati, OH	Fidelity Select Portfolio
Merit Medical Systems	Salt Lake City, UT	*Inc.'s* 100
Mid-Atlanta Medical Services		*Inc.'s* 100 & *Fortune's* 100
Mylan Laboratories	Pittsburgh, PA	*Financial World*
Nabors Industries,	TX	*Hoover's Handbook*
National Intergroup Inc.	Carrollton, TX	Fidelity Select Portfolio
Natures Sunshine Products Inc.	Provo, UT	Fidelity Select Portfolio
NC Mutual Wholesale Drug Co.	Durham, NC	*Ward Business Listing*
Norrell Health Care	Atlanta, GA	*Ward Business Listing*
Nova Care	Valley Forge, PA	*Fortune's* 100, *Hoover's Handbook*, *Financial World's* Best 200
Optical Radiation Corp.	Azusa, CA	Fidelity Select Portfolio
Owens & Minor Inc.	Glen Allen, VA	Fidelity Select Portfolio & *Financial World*
Oxford Health Plans	Darien, CT	*Fortune's* 100 & *Hoover's Handbook*
Pace American Group Inc.	Middlebury, IN	*Hoover's Handbook*
Pharmaceutical Marketing Services Corp.	Phoenix, AZ	Fidelity Health Care Portfolio
Pharmaceutical Resources Inc.	Spring Valley, NY	Fidelity Select Portfolio
Pharmacy Management Services	Tampa. FL	*Fortune's* 100
Physician Corp of America	Miami, FL	*Fortune's* 100
Physicians Clinical Laboratories	CA	*Business Week's* 100 Best
Preferred Health Care Ltd.	Research Triangle Park, NC	Durham, NC, Chamber of Commerce & Fidelity Select Portfolio & *Hoover's Handbook*
Premier Anesthesia	Atlanta, GA	*Inc.'s* 100
Protocol Systems Inc.	Beaverton, OR	Fidelity Select Portfolio
PSICOR Inc.	San Diego, CA	Fidelity Health Care Portfolio
Q&E Software	Raleigh, NC	*Inc.'s* 500
Qual Med	Pueblo, CO	*Fortune's* 100's & *Inc.'s* 100 & *Hoover's Handbook*
Quantum Health Resources	Orange, CA	*Inc.'s* 100 & *Business Week's* 100 Best
Ramsey HMO	New Orleans, LA	*Fortune's* 100
ReLife	Birmingham, AL	*Hoover's Handbook* & *Business Week's* 100 Best
Repironics		*Forbes's* 200
Research Industries	Midvale, UT	*Financial World's* Best 200
Rhone Poulenc Rorer Inc.	Shelton, CT	Fidelity Health Care Portfolio
Rotech Medical	Orlando, FL	*Forbes's* 200 & *Financial World's* Best 200
ROW Sciences	Rockville, MD	*Inc.'s* 500
Scherer Healthcare Inc.	Atlanta, GA	Fidelity Health Care Portfolio
SCIMED Life Systems	Maple Grove, MN	*Fortune's* 100 & *Hoover's Handbook*
Sequal Care Affiliates	Nashville, TN	*Financial World's* Best 200
Sierra Health Services	Las Vegas, NV	*Financial World's* Best 200
Spacelabs Medical Inc.	WA	Fidelity Health Care Portfolio
Sphinx Pharm.	Durham, NC	*Raleigh News & Observer*, Durham Chamber of Commerce
St. Jude Medical Inc.	MN	Fidelity Health Care Portfolio & *Financial World*
Steris Corporation	OH	Fidelity Health Care Portfolio
Sterly Health Care Group	Coral Gables, FL	*Inc.'s* 500

COMPANY	LOCATION	SOURCE
Stryker	Kalamazoo, MI	*Financial World*
Summit Care	CA	*Business Week's* 100 Best
Summit Tech	Wachum, MA	
Sunrise Medical	Torrance, CA	*Financial World*
Superior Pharmaceutical	Cincinnati, OH	*Inc.'s* 500
Symantec Corp.	Cupertino, CA	*Hoover's Handbook*
Synergen Inc.	Boulder, CO	Fidelity Health Care Portfolio
Synetic Inc.	Montvale, NJ	Fidelity Health Care Portfolio
T^2 Medical	Alpharetta, GA	*Fortune's* 100 & *Hoover's Handbook*
TakeCare Inc.		G.T. Global Health Care Fund
Techne Corp.	Minneapolis, MN	Fidelity Select Portfolio & *Financial World's* Best 200
Teva Pharmaceutical Industries Ltd. ADR		Fidelity Health Care Portfolio
The Innovative Health Group	Cary, NC	Durham, NC, Chamber of Commerce
Thermedics Inc.	Woburn, MA	Fidelity Select Portfolio
Thermo Cardiosystems Inc.	Woburn, MA	Fidelity Select Portfolio
Tochne		*Forbes's* 200
Tokos Medical Corp.	CA	Fidelity Health Care Portfolio
Universal Std. Medical Labs	Michigan	*Business Week's* 100 Best
US Homecare	Hartsdale, NY	*Business Week's* 100 Best
Utah Medical Products		*Forbes's* 200
Vencar	Louisville, KY	*Fortune's* 100
Ventritex	Sunnyvale, CA	*Inc's* 100
Vestar	San Dimas, CA	Ref?
Vital Signs		*Forbes's* 200
Vitalink Pharmacy Services Inc.	Naperville, IL	Fidelity Select Portfolio, *Hoover's Handbook, Forbes's* 200
Yinlinx Inc.		*Hoover's Handbook*
Zenith Laboratories Inc.	NJ	Fidelity Health Care Portfolio

Then Vince returned to the library and started looking up the names of the companies whose location he didn't know in the *Directory of Corporate Affiliates*. If a company was based in the South, he circled it and added more information from the directory: product information, as well as names of key officers in the company. Several companies on his list were not in the directory, so he went back to the librarian, who had some other suggestions about where to look. Vince still had eighteen companies with no known addresses. The librarian showed him two other location sources, and he found all but ten headquarter locations. At that point Vince narrowed his list to include only small, fast-growing companies in the South.

After getting names from these sources, Vince obtained phone numbers from the phone book, an 800 directory, and a local directory.

In another effort to track down any fast-growing health care companies he might have missed, Vince contacted the Chambers of Commerce in the area. He focused not only on his city but also on several other cities close by. He asked to speak with someone knowledgeable about the local health care industry, an industrial re-

cruiter, if there was such a person. If there was not such a person, he asked for the receptionist's help and advice. He sometimes had to press for specific information in order to be transferred to someone knowledgeable.

Vince:	I hope you can help me. Do you know who could tell me about any local businesses in the health care industry that are rapidly growing? Do you have a recruiter or an industrial recruiter?
Karen:	Well, that would be John Sampson.
Vince:	I think you have a listing of major employers in the area. It would be great if you could fax a copy of the health care listings in addition to any company names you get from your colleagues.
Karen:	Yes, let me find out who you need to talk to.
Vince:	Thank you for your help, I really appreciate your time. My fax number is 350-4539. My phone number is 350-5862. Thanks again.
Karen:	No problem. I will send you some information.

Next Vince started calling each company headquarters located in the South. After explaining what information he wanted to the receptionist, he was usually transferred to someone who could help. He would ask first for an annual report and then for employment figures for recent years, growth rates in sales volumes, and whether they had PR or marketing packages. Often this information was not readily accessible, and many asked who Vince was and why he wanted the information. Sometimes Vince said he was evaluating possible investment in the company; other times he said he was evaluating them as a potential employee. Some contacts were helpful, but others transferred him to other people. He was persistent and explained what he wanted to each person he spoke with. Because he was polite yet persistent, asking each person for help (gaining their sympathy), he was hard to refuse. Vince received information from nine out of ten companies he called.

He told each person exactly who had referred him to her, or where he had obtained the name of the company: "The Chamber of Commerce referred me to you when I told them I was looking for successful, rapidly growing health care companies," or, "I saw the glowing write-up you got from the News & Observer saying what a great company you are." Some contacts were suspicious, especially if they had not had this type of request before. In general, publicly traded companies gave information more readily. If they took down his address, they usually sent him something, and a follow-up call ensured they sent what he was looking for. Also, following up dispelled any lingering doubts or suspicions, and also made his request a priority.

If Vince had not found enough companies using these methods, another way he might have found more was by going back to the phone book and looking under state or local government, through which he could have found bureaus for advancement of small business or employment divisions, or agencies for business/industry or economic development. Also, most areas have business organizations devoted to development or advancement of a certain industry or small business in general. These can be found either in the phone book if you have the name, or by looking through the business section of your area newspaper, scanning for meeting times or announcements accompanied by an informational phone number.

Or if you choose to widen your search geographically, go to a research desk of your regional or university library and ask for business listings or indexes that would contain phone numbers and some additional information such as revenues or employee numbers. One to consult, for example, is the Ward Business Listing of Private and Public Companies. To identify companies in one specific industry, you can utilize the SIC codes. An SIC code is a four-digit number assigned to each company in most business listings. The first two digits are the general industry, and the second two indicate the specific nature of the company's business.

Vince had found his search to be very effective for identifying promising companies in the South. He now had a list of possibilities from all his sources; the next step was to find out more about them. He went back to the librarian for help, hoping there was a way to avoid leafing through every magazine and newspaper again for relevant articles.

Sue suggested Infotrak, a computerized database of many newspaper and magazines that can be searched using keywords, such as the name of a company. It gives the titles, locations, and dates of the articles. Another method she suggested trying was the on-line database NEXIS, which contains the full-text articles from a wide variety of publications. This was available at the library of several large universities in the area, including the University of North Carolina at Chapel Hill and Duke University. Infotrak was available at the regional library.

Vince called the UNC library and learned that the public was permitted to use these resources, although it required reserving a time slot in advance. He also learned that the reference section had full-text versions of many national newspapers on CD-ROM, and that he could either read them on the computer and print them out there, or download stories from the computer onto a PC-compatible disk. The library also had indexes for the local newspapers, so he could look the companies up by name and then read about them on microfilm or microfiche.

     Vince went through all the information he had collected and began ranking the companies he had found information on as:

    A. *a hot prospect*
    B. *need more information later*
    C. *eliminate*

    He tried first to focus on each company's growth in sales (revenues) and profits. If they were consistently increasing sales and profits by 20% per year, he ranked them an A. If their growth was good, he went on to read more! Vince found that the easiest and fastest way to get this information was by calling the company directly. In most cases he already had an annual report, and simply reading the first two pages gave him a better feel for the company's future growth potential and new products. If he could not tell anything about employee growth from the information he had collected, he called the company back and asked. Only one company on his list was not growing. Another could not tell Vince their employment growth numbers, because they had grown so much through acquisition, no one really seemed to be "in charge" of those numbers. After spending three days reading and consolidating the information, Vince came up with his ranking list. Many decisions were subjective. For example, if Vince really didn't like a particular location, he moved the company down to a B or a C. He did the same if he decided that a company with less than a hundred employees was too small. The specific reasons Vince qualified or disqualified each company are listed at the end of this case study. Vince's rankings are a subjective evaluation of factors pertaining to the information Vince could find on each company. These might be incomplete or inaccurate, based on Vince's ability to scan and read the on-line information correctly along with his limited financial background. The rankings in this section are arbitrary based on Vince's personal criteria and do not represent a financial or any type of analysis of the company.

Health Infusion

Miami, FL
Rate: B (merging, so check back in six months)

The following information is from NEXIS/LEXIS on-line system:

Income Statement Data (in thousands, except per share data)

		1992	1991	1990	1989
[good]	**Revenues**	49,749	29,248	10,500	5,807
[good]	**Net income**	6,322	4,241	2,174	1,657
[good]	**Net income per common share**	.67	.54	.38	.33

The following information is excerpted from T^2 information obtained by calling the company:

T^2 Medical, Inc., announced on Feb. 7, 1994, that it had entered into an agreement concerning the combination of T^2, Curaflex Health Services Inc., Health Infusion Inc., and Medisys Inc. to form Coram Healthcare Corporation.

Ren Corporation

Nashville, TN
Rate: B [only because it's a one-product business—kidney dialysis treatment]

The following information is from NEXIS/LEXIS on-line system:

Ren Corp. reported record revenues, net income, and patient treatment in 1992.

REN's balance sheet was the strongest in the company's history. At year end 1992, the company had $15.6 million in cash, only $458,000 in long-term debt and shareholder's equity exceeded $98 million. *[good]*

		1992	1991	1990	1989	1988
[good]	**Total revenues (in thousands)**	81,426	53,865	36,894	16,764	7,205
[good]	**Net income**	5,809,682	2,374,902			

Danek Group Inc.

Memphis, TN
Rate: A
Hulbert Guide to Emerging Companies

The following information is from NEXIS/LEXIS on-line system:

		1992	1991	1990
[good]	**Net sales**	75,488	41,429	25,923
[good]	**Net income**	18,082	6,598	3,058

Substantially, all of the company's increased revenues during the past two years have resulted from the increase in *the volume of spinal-implant product sales*. The company generally attributes the increase in sales to a combination of the growth in the overall market for spinal-implant products as well as increased market penetration. In 1991, approximately 94 percent of the company's net sales were derived from spinal-implant products.

Foxmeyer Corp.

Carrollton, TX
Rate: C

The following information is from NEXIS/LEXIS on-line system:

Financial Highlights

		1993	1992
[bad]	**Net income (in thousands)**	220	38,861

Includes $42.8 million unusual charge, consisting of $41 million charge against amount owed by PharMor Inc. and reserve for anticipated legal and collection costs; and $1.8 million charge for the write-off of.... *[in a lawsuit]*

Summary of Operations (dollars in millions)

		1993	1992	1991
[good]	**Net sales**	4,505.4	3,077.7	2,879.1

Pharmacy Management Services Inc.

Tampa, FL
Rate: B [get more information]

The following information is from NEXIS/LEXIS on-line system:

Annual Report (in thousands)

		1993	1992	1991
[good]	**Net sales**	109,934	106,116	81,686
[OK]	**Net income (loss)**	2,782	(2,011)	1,893

[The nature of this business has bright prospects—get more info]

"PMSI is the country's largest independent national provider of medical products and cost containment services to workers' compensation payers and claimants.

Having pioneered a unique and effective approach to controlling the dispensing of medical products to the long-term, high-cost, work-related injury claimant, the company has expanded its business to offer a more comprehensive array of services. The company markets its products and services nationally through field representatives who call..."

Owens & Minor, Inc.

Glen Allen, VA
Rate: A

The following information is from NEXIS/LEXIS on-line system:

Medical, dental/hospital equipment, and supplies
A 3-for-2 stock split was distributed March 22, 1993 *[good]*
Number of Employees, 200 *[right size]*
A 3-for-2 stock split was distributed July 16, 1991 *[good]*

Consolidated Statements of Income (in thousands)

		1992	1991	1990
[great]	**Net income**	20,392	12,027	8,775

Financial Highlights (in thousands)

		1991	1990	1989	1988	1987
[good]	**Net sales**	1,320,438	1,219,617	952,935	731,565	576,805
	Stock price at year-end	20.25	10.00	8.50	9.58	5.89

Owens & Minor Inc. is headquartered in Richmond, VA, where it was founded in 1882. The company is a wholesale distributor of medical and surgical supplies to hospitals and alternate medical care facilities. These supplies are distributed in 37 states and the District of Columbia. Pharmaceuticals and other products are distributed in south Florida.

Balance Sheet Data

		1991	1990	1989
[going down, good]	**Long-term debt**	67,675	71,339	85,324

The following information is excerpted from the May 11, 1993, edition of the *Financial World*, "Owens & Minor: No. 2 in Health—and Loving It":

You don't have to get a preview of the Clinton's health care reform proposal to spot one likely winner—$1.2 billion-in-sales Owens & Minor. Second only to Baxter International in supplying hospitals with everything from sutures and surgical gowns to rubber gloves and diapers, O&M is a just-in-time-delivery specialist....

Enter Richmond-based Owens & Minor, a high-volume buyer that delivers these products as often as three times a day at competitive prices, so hospitals no longer have to buy a huge amount up front from manufacturers to get a good deal on what they need....

While hospital supply profits more than doubled in 1988 through 1991, drug profits had dropped nearly 50 percent....

O&M is bidding for part of the contracts to distribute U.S. Surgical's noninvasive operating instruments. That could add $200 million of new business. Another contract might result from the federal government's decision to stop using supply depots to order products for U.S. military and veterans' hospitals. That could mean $70 million in new just-in-time sales.

Says Lawrence Marsh of Wheat First Securities: "Health care reform will continue to accentuate a significant shift in power away from the manufacturer and the physician and toward the buyer and the agents of the buyer, which is what Owens is...."

The following information is excerpted from The *Wall Street Journal*/p. A6/Oct. 20, 1993:

Owens & Minor, Inc. said third-quarter profit grew 21 percent as new distribution centers bolstered sales. *[good]*

The following information is excerpted from The *Wall Street Journal* p. B5A/ Jan. 10, 1994, "Sees Acquisition Stirring Growth": *[Bad—based on product; it doesn't appear they have a real "niche" product or a lot of value added. Chances are they compete mainly on price. Maybe OK with health care reform.]*:

For the past 20 years, sales growth at Owens & Minor has averaged about 18 percent to 20 percent a year. *[good]*

The companies distribute such items as dressings, needles, syringes, and surgical packs and gowns, mostly to hospitals.

The way Mr. Minor sees it, unlike No. 1 medical distributor Baxter International Inc., which also manufactures medical supplies, both Owens & Minor and Stuart Medical have a "pure distribution mentality." But in the past, unlike Baxter, neither company could cover the whole country. "Now, with the combined distribution network, we can really create a more serious alternative to Baxter's distribution," Mr. Minor said.

Both companies emphasize low-cost distribution, Mr. Minor said. "We both understand we are in a pennies business," he said, referring to thin profit margins. "We don't have any margin for error in our business dealings," he said. He added that because of the expected increase in sales volume, both the company and its suppliers should benefit from economies of scale.

With this in mind, Mr. Minor's strategy will be to continue to focus on the needs of its hospital customers, which are under increasing pressure to reduce costs. "They're starting to feel they don't need to own any inventory because it's a capital investment that's taking away from other services," Mr. Minor said.

Mr. Minor sees technology as the key to winning in this market. "The products are pretty boilerplate; we're selling systems and information," he said. He believes the combination of Owens & Minor and Stuart Medical "will help propel us along that line faster than either one of us could alone." Both companies are in the process of re-engineering their computer systems, helping to put inventory information directly in the hands of sales representatives, customers and even suppliers.

The following is from the Annual Report for the period ended Sept. 30, 1993:

To Our Shareholders
Detroit...New Business

Last quarter we announced the opening of a distribution center in Detroit and the purchase there of A. Huhlman & Co. On July 19th, the Detroit Medical Center (DMC) selected Owens & Minor as their prime distributor for its seven hospitals and 2,500 total licensed beds in the Detroit area. The DMC is affiliated with the Wayne State University School of Medicine, and accounts for 17 percent of total in-patient days in the area. The agreement is for five years and should generate up to $225 million in sales over the life of the contract.

New Locations

As planned, we opened a new distribution center in the Boston area on Aug. 2. On Sep. 28, we announced that we would open a Custom Distribution Center in Seattle by the year's end.

A Look Ahead

A number of factors are influencing the medical supply marketplace. The uncertainty of health care reform tops the list, but a slow economy and a relatively high rate of unemployment are factors as well. We have been able to gain market share and grow by acquisition, and we expect to continue to do so.

About the Company

Owens & Minor Inc. was founded in 1882 in Richmond, VA, from which eight generations of leadership have continuously operated. The company is a national wholesale distributor of medical and surgical supplies, and other related products to hospitals and alternate medical care facilities. The company also distributes pharmaceuticals to hospitals in south Florida. Serving health care providers from 34 distribution centers coast-to-coast, Owens & Minor offers low-cost delivered health care products by supplying innovative solutions to customers' individual inventory management needs.

Throughout its history, the company has adhered to an aggressive growth strategy, through acquisitions and internally generated expansion, becoming the nation's leading low-cost distributor of healthcare products. Approximately 1,640 teammates are responsible for Owens & Minor's enduring quality and performance.[1]

The following is excerpted from "Owens & Minor to take inventory management concept and technology to the hospital level," *Health Industry Today,* October 1992:

Minor: We have partnerships with 15 of our major suppliers. Principal partnerships in place are with Kimberly-Clark and Proctor & Gamble. All of our distribution centers will interface with Kimberly-Clark by Oct. 1.

We are in various stages of development of the continuous inventory replenishment process with J&J, 3M, Sherwood Medical, Becton-Dickson, Kendall, Davis and Geck, C.R. Bard, Aladan, Abbott, DeRoyal, Devon, and Welch-Allen. We expect all of these initiatives to be solid in the next 12 months. We have begun to work with a number of other manufacturers on this same concept.

HIT: How do your manufacturer partners benefit from participating in your asset management programs?

Minor: The team takes the commitment made at the highest level and turns it into reality through both organizations. We blend our goals and objectives, and the customer is the clear winner in that scenario.

I believe it gives our manufacturing partners a competitive advantage in the marketplace. Hospitals want the same advantages

---

1 Owens and Minor Annual Report.

we have been able to generate for ourselves when it comes to inventory management.

Our goal is to take the technology and concept of continuous inventory replenishment to the hospital level.

RoTech Medical Corp.

Orlando, FL
Rate: A

The following information is from NEXIS/LEXIS on-line system:

Consolidated Statements of Income

		1993	1992	1991
[good]	**Operating revenue**	48,383,021	37,122,270	26,321,451
[good]	**Net income**	5,127,350	3,686,254	2,169,094

The following is excerpted from the 1993 Annual Report:

Year Ended July 31

	1993	1992	1991
Operating revenue	48,383,021	37,122,270	26,321,451
Net income	5,127,350	3,686,254	2,169,094

The following is excerpted from *Value Line*, Feb. 11, 1994:

RoTech Medical TIMELINESS   1 (Highest)

We have raised the company's Financial Strength rating one notch to a B+, in light of the firm's strong balance sheet and good returns on capital and net worth. RoTech's Safety rank has also been improved to a 3 (average).

The following is excerpted from Wheat First Securities: Butcher and Singer, Oct. 5, 1993:

Lawrence C. Marsh, CFA (804) 782-3611
Michael J. Weber (804) 782-3617:
Rated 1/1

INVESTMENT OPINION: BUY

We continue to recommend purchase of shares of RoTech for aggressive investors seeking capital gains. We view RoTech as a small but rapidly growing, well-managed, diversified home health-care company that focuses in smaller towns and rural areas mostly in the southeastern part of the United States. We believe health care reform will accelerate efforts by health payers to push users into progressively lower-cost treatment alternatives. Home health care, given to the absence of facility costs, will be an obvious source of more care in the future, due to (1) cost advantages vs. institutional treatments, (2) delivery advances that have increased the types of therapies that can be administered at home, and (3) an increased target market with gradual population aging. We think highly of RoTech's share prospects for the following reasons:

- Excellent Revenue and Earnings Growth Continues— We are estimating about 30% gains in both revenues and earnings per share this fiscal year and 25% gains in fiscal 1995.
- Internal Growth Supported by Acquisitions—The company has grown from 14 branches in one state in 1988 to more than 70 in 17 states at fiscal year end. We are estimating that the number of branches will be more than 100 by fiscal 1995.
- Diverse Home Care Provider—Not dependent on one particular home-care segment or geographic region.
- Medicare Payer Consolidation A Catalyst—Improved receivable collection and additional opportunities to acquire small home-care dealers not adapted to new Medicare reimbursement environment.

The following is excerpted from Corporate Investor Relations, Feb. 2, 1994

Krishen K. Sud (212) 371-5300:

	Revenues (millions)	Operating Margin	E.P.S.
Price (2/1/94)-(ROTC/OTC)	$78.0	18.5%	$1.20

RoTech Medical Corporation is a diversified home health care company that provides home respiratory therapy, home infusion therapy, and other home medical services and equipment to patients referred by primary-care physicians in smaller cities and rural areas. By marketing principally to primary-care physicians in smaller cities and rural locations, RoTech addresses an underserved segment of the medical community that can benefit substantially from the trend toward home health care. RoTech is a marketing-driven organization whose sales force counsels physicians on new medical procedures and technologies, which they are not exposed to as primary-care physicians in rural communities and smaller cities. This enables the physicians to retain patients who otherwise would have to be referred to specialists in the local hospitals. RoTech is actively looking to expand its business in the area of physician practice management by acquiring the practices of some of the primary-care physicians to whom it provides home care services.

Investment Opinion: from Needham & Company, Inc.

We recommend purchase of RoTech. In addition to consistent 30 percent growth in its core business and a 1994 multiple 50 percent of its growth rate, RoTech has a major opportunity in the area of physician practice management that should result in higher earnings and significant multiple expansion.

Haner Orthopedic Group, Inc.

Bethesda, MD
Rate: C [Too small, not a great fit, losing money]

The following information is from NEXIS/LEXIS online system:

Selected Historical Consolidated Financial Information (in thousands)

		1992	1991
[bad]	Net loss	(854)	(623)

National Intergroup, Inc.

Carrollton, TX
Rate: C

The following information is from NEXIS/LEXIS online system:

Results of Operations (in millions)

		1992	1991	1990
[fair]	Net sales	3,077.7	2,879.1	2,404.5
[not good]	Income (loss) before extraordinary items and cumulative effect of change in accounting principle	25.1	(279.5)	23.5

[no increasing revenue stream]

Ramsay Health Care, Inc.

New Orleans, LA
Rate: C

The following information is from NEXIS/LEXIS online system:

Net Income Before Extraordinary Loss (in millions)

		1992	1991	1990
[fair]	**Net sales**	3,077.7	2,879.1	2,404.5
[not good]	**Income (loss) before extraordinary items and cumulative effect of change in accounting principle**	25.1	(279.5)	23.5

Health Images, Inc.

Atlanta, GA
Rate: C

The following information is from NEXIS/LEXIS online system:

Consolidated Statements of Income

		1991	1990
[not much growth]	**Revenue**	12,299,400	12,132,000

Medvisit, Inc.

Henderson, North Carolina
Rate: C [too small]

The following information is from NEXIS/LEXIS online system: SOURCE—MedVisit, Inc.—"Bringing Care and Comfort Back Home"

Sales Information

Total Sales $1,193,000

Capital Home Therapy, Inc.

Raleigh, NC
Rate: C [too small]

The following information is from NEXIS/LEXIS online system:

Sales Information

Sales $421,000
Share of Market—7 percent

Applied Analytical Industries

Wilmington, NC
Rate: A [Need more info: difficult because it's privately held—
this is the most a job hunter could expect from written sources.]

The following information is from the Jan. 13, 1994 edition of the *News and Observer*, "Drug Firm opening near RTP"

> Applied Analytical Industries Inc. of Wilmington plans to hire 74 laboratory and office workers for an office it is opening near Research Triangle Park, the Greater Durham Chamber of Commerce announced...
>
> Tom White, chief industrial recruiter for the Durham chamber, speculated that Applied Analytical is opening a local branch to be closer to one of its customers, Glaxo Inc. ...
>
> The company employs more than 375 workers at its headquarters in Wilmington and has sales offices in New Jersey, Illinois, Puerto Rico and Italy....

The following information is from a March 9,1994, AAI News Release received after calling the company:

> AAI was founded by Frederick D. Sancilio, Ph.D. in 1979 to work as a partner with pharmaceutical companies, providing the expertise and technology to develop quality health care products. Designed to be more than a contract testing laboratory, AAI offers a fully integrated complement of pharmaceutical development services, affording clients the benefit to complete project management. AAI is committed to working with pharmaceutical companies to gain rapid approval of their products by the Food and Drug Administration with a high degree of quality assurance. AAI's laboratories are recognized within the industry for their strict compliance to current good Manufacturing Practices and good standing with the FDA.
>
> AAI offers pharmaceutical companies assistance with Analytical Testing, Stability Services, Formulation Development, Biotech Pharmaceutical Services, Clinical Supplies manufacturing and packaging, Microbiology Services, Regulatory Affairs Consulting, Quality Assurance Training, and Computer Validation Services.
>
> AAI is headquartered in Wilmington, NC, and just opened an additional laboratory facility in Research Triangle Park, NC. AAI also has sales offices in New Jersey, Illinois, Puerto Rico and Italy.

The following employee growth is from information faxed by the company in March of 1994:

> January 1, 1991—294 employees
> January 1, 1993—305 employees
> March 16, 1994—420 employees

Bladen In-Home Health Svc.

Elizabethtown, NC
Rate: C [too small]

The following information is from NEXIS/LEXIS online system:

Number of employees   35

J E Hanger, Inc.

Raleigh, NC
Rate: C [too small]

The following information is from NEXIS/LEXIS online system:

Number of employees   4

IVAX, Corp.

Miami, FL
Rate: A

The following information is from NEXIS/LEXIS online system:

> The company presently markets several brand-name pharmaceutical products and a wide variety of generic and over-the-counter pharmaceutical products primarily in the United States, Canada, the United Kingdom and Ireland. The company also markets a line of skin-care products in the United States and Canada and a line of veterinary products in the United States.
> The company has a number of pharmaceutical compounds and devices under development that, if approved by the U.S. Food and Drug Administration (FDA) and foreign health regulatory authorities, are expected to contribute significantly to sales growth in the next several years.
> Snaplets® consist of several products that utilize a unique delivery system developed and patented by the company for the administration of primarily pediatric and adult patients who have difficulty swallowing tablets or capsules. *[Concern: growth through*

acquisition generally difficult. Not a business they've "grown-up" themselves.]

Approximately 71 percent of the company's consolidated net revenues are attributable to sales of generic products. *[This is a concern. Difficult to compete only on price in the long term. Only a matter of "how long" before someone else introduces at an even lower price. Can be investigated further through conversations.]*

High and low stock prices as reported on the American Stock Exchange for each of the quarters indicated:

		1992		1991	
		High	Low	High	Low
[positive]	**First quarter**	40.87	31.25	12.17	5.15

[The stockbrokers are recommending this stock. They think it's going to do well.] This was sourced from one of Fidelity's Mutual Funds.

Selected financial data (in thousands, except per share data)

		1992	1991	1990	1989	1988
[great]	**Net revenues**	451,033	223,285	117,739	150,104	127,136
[great]	**Net income (loss) per Common Share: Primary**	.65	.21	.04	(.09)	(.06)

The following information is from the April 19, 1993, edition of *Business Week*, "Give the Shorts Some Aspirin. Here Comes a Headache."

The stock has two things going for it, says this pro. Sometime soon, the Street will realize that Ivax' "supergenerics" are starting to produce "impressive" sales, he says. And when the Clinton health care plan is unveiled, Ivax should attract more attention as investors start to see it as a major player in low-cost drugs. Generics, says this pro, "will be the cornerstone of national efforts to reduce healthcare costs, and Ivax is in an excellent position to benefit from that."...

NEW NICHE. Clinton's health care package is expected to mandate low-cost drugs as well as widen medical overage to include the 35 million Americans currently without health benefits. Already generics have boosted their share of the drug market, from 9 percent in 1980 to more than 20 percent last year.

"Although we are producing more generics than any other in the business, Ivax has been wrongly lumped together with the major drug companies," laments Dr. Phillip Frost, Ivax chairman and CEO. One reason, he believes, is that analysts who cover Ivax are longtime followers of the giant pharmaceuticals. Frost has taken advantage of the stock's drop by raising his stake to 20 percent from less than 19 percent.

One drug expected to pay off big this year is Verapamil, which is taken once a day to treat hypertension. In the four months that it was on the market last year, Verapamil had sales totaling $38 million. For 1993, Ivax expects Verapamil sales to come in between $75 million and $100 million. "At its current rate, the drug will hit $100 million, barring the entry of new competition," says Rick Pfenniger Jr., Ivax' chief legal counsel.

[good] Thanks to Verapamil, a future earning stream is now more certain, says analyst Sharon Dorsey Wagoner at Argus Research, who calls the new product Ivax' "first major supergeneric drug." If it does well, analysts may raise estimates of $1.10 to $1.20 a share in 1993 and $1.40 to $1.80 in 1994. Ivax earned $.65 in 1992.

The following information is from the June 28, 1993, edition of *Business Week* in the Top of the News Section, "A Compulsive Buyer—or a Master Builder?":

Phil Frost adds Johnson Products to Ivax' diverse stable of companies:

Veterinary products, industrial chemicals, pharmaceuticals for everything from hypertension to Alzheimer's disease, and now, Johnson Products Co. Will the combination produce the "world class health care products company" that Ivax Corp's chairman promises?

Since 1987, dermatologist Dr. Philip Frost has cobbled together more than 15 acquisitions, boosting sales of his Miami-based Ivax by 250 percent to $451 million. The latest addition: Johnson Products, a maker of personal-care products for African Americans, which Ivax said on June 14 it would buy in a stock deal valued at up to $73 million. Shares of Johnson Products surged $5 5/8, to $24 5/8, on the announcement.

Certainly, though, the deal making has brought results: Ivax' net income last year reached $44.6 million, up from a 1988 loss of $3 million. And Frost says the strategy is clear enough: Build the core pharmaceutical business by selling generic pharmaceuticals, making hard-to-copy generics from products coming off patent, and developing proprietary products.

Sales have grown at a 12.6 percent compound annual rate since 1989. Pretax earnings before extraordinary items totaled $5.7 million last year, from a $2.5 million loss in 1988.

The following information is from the Jan. 6, 1994, edition of The *New York Times*, Company News Section/p. D4, "Ivax to Acquire McGaw in $440 million deal."

The Ivax Corporation, a generic drug maker based in Miami, said yesterday that it would acquire McGaw Inc., which specializes in intravenous therapies and services, for $440 million. In the merger, expected to be completed by midyear, shareholders of McGaw will receive $16 worth of stock in Ivax for each McGaw share. McGaw will become a wholly owned Ivax subsidiary.

Shares of McGaw, which is based in Irvine, Calif., fell 12.5 cents, to $10.75, in Nasdaq trading yesterday, while shares of Ivax rose 50 cents, to $28.125, on the American Stock Exchange.

Cordis Corp.

Miami Lakes, FL
Rate: B [because it's in Miami; not enough growth]]

The following information is excerpted from the 1993 Annual Report, Letter from the President:

Fiscal 1994 got off to a strong start. Benefiting from growing strength in angioplasty operations, Cortis achieved sharply improved results for the three months ended Sep. 30. Income before the cumulative effect of an accounting change was $7.9 million, a 3-percent increase *[not enough growth]* in the corresponding period a year ago. Earnings per share were up 30 percent to 54 cents, our strongest percentages increase in eight quarters. The required adoption of a new accounting standard FAS#109 resulted in a $10.1 million *[one-time income only]* one-time earnings benefit, boosting net income to $18.0 million of $1.24 a share. *[not good]*

Worldwide sales increased 11 percent to $69.1 million notwithstanding significantly adverse currency exchange rates. For example, had rates remained constant, net sales for the period would have been up 22 percent.

[good, new markets] The effects of our new angioplasty products, in particular balloon catheters, were very much in evi-

dence outside the United States. Cortis continued to make solid gains in angioplasty while maintaining strong growth in the diagnostic portion of the business. As a result, foreign angiography sales were up 12 percent for the quarter, or a very strong 33 percent constant currency. In the US, where many of the new products are still in an early phase of release, angioplasty sales more than offset the continued sluggishness in the diagnostic segment *[not a good market today]* of the business, pushing overall angiography revenues 12 percent higher, their strongest gain in a year. As a result, worldwide angioplasty revenues ended the quarter up 12 percent, 23 percent at constant currency.

[good] Several of these products, in fact, were introduced during the first quarter. Additionally, we are continuing to pursue promising new business opportunities in coronary and peripheral stents, neuroradiology, electrophysiology and intravascular ultrasound. We have made encouraging progress in several of these efforts in the past several months, and we expect the year to be productive on each of these fronts.

	1993	1992	1991
Angiographic products (sales)	$238,334	$206,202	$181,787
Neuroscience products (sales)	$17,124	$16,757	$17,120
Total (good)	$255,458	$222,959	$198,907

Angiographic products *[good]*:

The company manufactures an extensive line of angiographic devices for the diagnosis of various cardiovascular diseases and for use in interventional angiography. The diagnostic devices include catheters and related equipment that are inserted into a patient's circulatory system to allow introduction of contrast media, enabling a physician to study the heart, blood vessels, and other soft-tissue organs for the purpose of determining the proper treatment of patients exhibiting disorders of such tissues. The interventional devices include balloon accessory products which are used to treat such patients.

As of June 30, 1993, the company and its subsidiaries had approximately 2,650 employees.

Following is excerpted from Jan. 21, 1994, PR Newswire Association Inc.:

Cordis Corporation announced that it has entered into a definitive agreement to acquire Webster Laboratories, Inc., a privately held California corporation, in a stock-for-stock transaction. Webster Laboratories is a pioneer and leader in the market for electrophysiology catheters.

"As one of healthcare's fastest-growing markets," *[Cordis' president/CEO Robert C. Strauss]* continued, "electrophysiology offers us a unique opportunity to expand our coverage among both cardiologists and electrophysiologists...."

..."Cordis's leadership in catheter technology and strong presence in cardiac catheterization labs worldwide will help to open new horizons and opportunities for our technology and people."

Cordis Corporation manufactures and markets a variety of medical devices and systems for the angiographic and neuroscience markets. CONTACT: Chick McDowell, vice president, corporate relations and assistant secretary of Cordis Corporation, (305) 824-2821.

Following is excerpted from Reuters, Copyright 1991:

Cordis Corp jumped 4 1/4 to 31 3/4. It received approval to market its Helix angioplasty catheter. *[good]*

	1993	**1992**	**1991**
Net sales	$255,458	$222,959	$198,907
Income from continuing operations	$29,060	$24,014	$119,332

[good]

Scherer Healthcare

Atlanta, GA
Rate: C [not fast enough growth]

The following information is excerpted from Standard & Poor's Research Report prepared March 21, 1994:

Business Summary
    Scherer Healthcare Inc., founded in 1981 as the successor to Aloe Creme Laboratories. Scherer Healthcare focuses effort in specialized types of health care products and services including services for health care providers, such as medical-waste disposal, surgical disposables and pharmaceutical research.

    [Overview: Scherer Healthcare was founded in 1981. Sales growth has been approximately 5 percent per year in the

last five years with sales of $20.94 million in 1993, $20.74 million in 1992, and $18.44 million in 1991. Net income was –1.46 million 1992 and –1.47 in 1993.]

ReLife

Birmingham, AL
Rank A

The following is excerpted from the May 24, 1993, edition of *Business Week*, "The Best Small Companies."

Three-Year Averages	Increase Percent Sales	Increase Percent Profits
[good]	65.9	174.9

Total Employment Figures

	1993	1992	1991
Total employment	20,80	1,431	1,664

The following information is excerpted from Wessels, Arnold and Henderson research, dated Oct. 18, 1993:

Positioning in relatively low managed, care-penetrated locations in the country, RELF is taking advantage of the opportunity to structure itself as a managed care provider:

1) With the rapid evolution of managed-care payers underway, RELF is strategically positioning itself with the core element of acute care, the hospital facility, and those hospitals that can provide broad, high-quality services—particularly lower-cost-of-care alternatives such as rehabilitation.

2) RELF specializes in more classical rehabilitation, treating more severe cases, such as traumatic brain injuries, spinal cord injuries, and work-related physical complication. In contrast to one of its leading competitors, HEALTHSOUTH Rehabilitation Corp. (NYSE-HRC), RELF focuses on this specialized niche as well as its continuum of care alternative so it can shift its patients to the lowest-cost appropriate-care alternative in the shorter time. In reality, the two are targeting different patient markets.

3) The majority of RELF's markets are still underserved in the rehabilitation area, allowing RELF the opportunity to position itself as a lead, if not sole, provider in the community.

4) RELF's plans to step down into other elements of related rehabilitation care, including subacute care, specialized nursing home care, and home health care.

Anticipating a 25 percent *[good]* compounded earnings and revenues growth rate, RELF's core growth currently emanates largely from its acquisitions *[a concern]* as same-store revenues run at approximately 8 percent. By the end of fiscal 1994, we expect that distribution to reverse as today's acquired facilities become more integrated into the cost-efficiency strategies behind RELF and become classified as same-store operations. We continue to rate RELF a "Buy—Aggressive Growth" opportunity.

The following is excerpted from *Forbes's* Dec. 20, 1993, issue, "WHY ME, WHY ME?"

Fate dealt young Mike Stephens a terrible blow. It was the inauspicious start of his rise to fortune.

On a muggy June afternoon in 1970, Michael Stephens, then 26 and a marketing rep for Prentice Hall, was hanging out at the pool at the Cliff Terrace apartment complex in Birmingham, Alabama. "I went to dive in," he recalls, "slipped on the concrete and slammed into the bottom. My hands hit first, then I smacked the top of my head."

Stephens broke his neck, paralyzing him from the chest down. His doctors told him he'd never walk again and if he was lucky, he might regain partial use of his arms.

The doctors were wrong. Today the only visible reminder of his accident is a slight limp. That and ReLife, Inc. a $57 million (1992 revenues) rehabilitation firm he started in 1987.

After three weeks he began wiggling his toes. Three months after entering the hospital, he hobbled out. But his troubles weren't over. He was weak, irritable, angry and unable to work. "No one guided me," he recalls. "There was no social or psychological counseling." His marriage soon began to fall apart. He forced himself to go back to school at the University of Alabama at Birmingham to study hospital administration. After earning his master's degree in 1975, he was named executive director of the hospital. A short five years after his accident, at 31, Stephens was in charge of a rehab center. Remembering his own difficulties coping with a return to normal life, Stephens introduced dozens of rehabilitation services, including speech therapy, a recreation program, and psychological counseling. He also started, in 1984, a for-profit subsidiary with outpatient services like job training to help ease the transition for rehab patients.

Stephens wasn't simply an altruist. Realizing there was money to be made from rehab, in 1987 he raised $1.6 million from local investors, borrowed $100,000 himself, and bought out Lakeshore's growing for-profit subsidiary. He retained a management contract for the nonprofit side.

Now Stephens was really rolling. He began taking on management contracts at rehab centers in Alabama and surrounding states, and by 1990 he was running 11 rehabilitation centers with a total of 401 beds. That year the firm took in revenues of $17 million and turned its first profit.

Today ReLife runs 40 rehab facilities, primarily in the Southeast, providing services that will take a patient from a comatose state back to a normal life.

ReLife flourishes in good part because its rehab programs are cheaper than hospital rehab programs. That's because as the patient progresses in his rehabilitation—and requires less care—the daily cost drops.

ReLife's tight focus on rehabilitation has also yielded treatment programs that speed the rehabilitation process. A ReLife patient with a traumatic brain injury, for example, is released, on average, after about 25 days—almost two weeks faster than the national average. Result: ReLife is among the lowest-cost providers in rehabilitation today.

Mike Stephens has all this simply because he refused to surrender to self-pity or to give up after fate struck him a blow that might have destroyed another man.

The following is from *Fortune*, Feb. 21, 1994:

A former Shearson broker, Klaskin, 33, started Oak Ridge Investments in 1989 and now manages $50 million in private accounts. Most of his clients are in his growth portfolio, which returned an annual average of 51.2 percent over three years, vs. 15.6 percent for the S&P 500. He recently launched a mutual fund, the ORI Growth Fund. He tells *Fortune*'s Shelley Neumeler what he likes.

Shelley Neumeler: Any smaller health care plays?

Klaskin: ReLife Rehabilitation Systems has had a tumultuous existence, but it's a good deal now. The company went public more than two years ago, and the stock got ahead of itself; it rose quickly from an offering price of $11.50 a share to $23. Now it trades for $17 and will earn at least $1.30 over the next 12 months. That gives it a P/E of just 13. I think the stock can explode. The growth rate is 20 percent a year. I'm looking for its candidates. Mid Atlantic Medical Services, which operates in Maryland and Virginia, is a good stock on its own. In addition, it could be an attractive acquisition for a larger company trying to get into that market. Earnings are growing by at least 25 percent a year, and at $29 it sells for 24 times next year's earnings.

Coastal Healthcare Group, Inc.

Durham, NC
Rate: A

The following is excerpted from the company's *News Release*, obtained by calling Investors Relations at corporate HQ.

Durham, NC. Feb. 28, 1994—Coastal Healthcare Group, Inc. (NASDAQ: CGRP) today announced record net operating revenue and net income for the fourth quarter and full year ending Dec. 31, 1993, as well as the completion of the acquisition of two primary-care networks previously announced Jan. 27, 1994.

For the year, net operating income rose 38 percent to $15,442,000.... Income from operations rose 50 percent to $28,474,000 from $19,028,000 in 1992.

Coastal Healthcare Group Inc., the largest medical group management company in the United States, provides a broad range of healthcare and administrative services to hospitals, managed care programs, physicians, and other health care providers. As a network system integrator, the company provides physician management services and administrative-support services to hospital based, community based, and alternate-site physician practices in a variety of settings. With more than 580 practice settings, Coastal continues to be a catalyst in the physician services industry, and today is the largest fully-integrated provider of these services.

The following is exerpted from Smith Barney Shearson:

March 16, 1994

◆ Initiating coverage of CGRP, one of the largest medical group management companies in the United States.

♦ Existing business relationships with virtually all partici-
pants in the health care delivery system uniquely positions CGRP to create physician-driven integrated-
delivery systems, thus driving strong growth in revenue
and earnings for the foreseeable future.

♦ Analyst's Opinion: 1 Buy

♦ Given the growing desire to manage health care costs
among private and public purchasers of health care
services (consisting of insurance, managed-care, and
self-insured companies as well as local, state, and federal agencies and governments), the demand for services provided by high-quality, low-cost integrated health
care delivery networks is likely to increase dramatically
in the coming years. This growth prospect, in combination with the sheer size ($1 trillion in annualized health
care spending) and high degree of fragmentation of the
health care delivery system (roughly 600,000 providers), in our view, represents an enormous growth opportunity for companies that are organizing health care
delivery networks. Efforts to organize high-quality and
cost-effective delivery systems are coming from the
payer community (health maintenance organizations
and other managed-care organizations are the best examples), the hospital community (as illustrated by Columbia Healthcare Corp.) and, more recently, the
physician community. Coastal represents one of the
leading players in the physician community that is actively organizing integrated health care delivery networks. While the jury is still out, the physician
community might have a leg up on organizing health
care delivery networks because physicians, as a rule,
would rather work with their peers than for managed
care/insurance companies or hospitals.

The following is excerpted from Alex, Brown & Sons, Inc., March 1, 1994:

COASTAL HEALTHCARE GROUP, INC. (NASDAQ: CGRP)
INVESTMENT CONCLUSION: BUY

We are initiating research coverage of Coastal Healthcare
Group Inc. with an investment rating of "buy." Coastal is a diversified physician services company and a leader in the formation of
integrated health care networks. We expect that both providing

physician services and forming integrated delivery systems will become major factors shaping the health care delivery system in the next two to three years. We believe that Coastal's experience and expertise will be competitive advantages in exploiting opportunities in this emerging market sector.

The following is excerpted from Institutional Investor, September 1993, Steven Scott of Coastal Healthcare Group, "Controlling health care costs."

As both a physician and a businessman, Dr. Steven Scott brings a rare perspective to the problem of health care costs. Coastal Healthcare Group, of which he is president and CEO, took in $278 million in revenues last year, providing a variety of services—among them staffing emergency, obstetrics and pediatrics departments in hospitals, running medical clinics for the military, and providing administrative services.

In this interview with Staff Editor Clem Morgello, Scott discusses some ways to stretch the health care dollar and other issues CEOs will have to deal with in providing health care for their employees.

The following is excerpted from the Robinson-Humphrey Company, Inc., December 28, 1993:

John R. Runningen (404) 266-6148
Pamela H. Memefee (404) 266-6163

Recommendation: long-term—buy
RECENT DEVELOPMENTS

We believe Coastal will benefit from health care reform, which stresses increased access and cost containment. Coastal helps hospitals save money by managing various segments of a hospital's operations more efficiently than the hospital can alone.

On Nov. 28, *60 Minutes* ran a story implying that emergency room physicians hired by contracting companies such as Coastal are poorly trained and underpaid.... We believe that at Coastal, such stories are the exception, not the norm, and exert little or no impact on the stock. In fact, that stock traded higher on the Monday following the *60 Minutes* story.

The following is excerpted from Company Report, a publication of the Investment Research Department, December 9, 1993:

Lawrence C. Marsh, CFA (804) 782-3611

Michael J. Weber (904) 782-3617

INVESTMENT OPINION: BUY

CONCLUSION

We reiterate our purchase recommendation of shares of Coastal Healthcare for investors seeking long-term growth of capital. We believe that the combination of a rapidly changing health delivery system, a push by hospitals to partner and save costs, a proactive and experienced management team, a strong financial base that can support significant expansion possibilities, an excellent history of demonstrating above-average growth, and an expanding role in key markets provide for excellent future prospects. The company's expansion plans make shares appropriate for more aggressive investors.

The following is excerpted from *Modern Healthcare,* Weekly Business News, Feb. 7, 1994, by Jay Greene.

Coastal Emergency Services has signed a multiyear capitated contract to provide emergency and primary care to Humana Health Plans of South Florida enrollees in Miami.

Coastal, like California Emergency Physicians, has combined primary-care and emergency physicians into the capitated contract so patients can be directed to the least expensive setting.

Following is information excerpted from the 1993 Annual Report:

Income Statement

		1992A	1993A	1994E	1995E
[great]	**Operating revenues, net**	341.1	446.5	691.6	948.9
[great]	**Net income**	11.2	14.1	26.1	35.8

Coventry Corporation

Nashville, TN
Rank: B

from 1992 Annual Report

Company Profile

Coventry Corporation, headquartered in Nashville, Tennessee, is a managed health care company that provides a wide range of health care benefit options to a broad cross section of employer groups through three market leading regional health maintenance organizations ("HMOs").

The company's regional HMOs are located in Pittsburgh and Central Pennsylvania, and in St. Louis, MO. The aggregate enrollment at Dec. 31, 1992, was approximately 327,000 members. The company emphasizes the "staff model" HMO and uses an "open panel model" to provide services in areas where enrollees are more geographically dispersed, or in conjunction with the company's staff model HMOs as additional primary-care locations.

Year Ended December 31 (in thousands)

	1992	1993
Operating earnings	28,245	18,414

Forecast for Future Growth: Favorable Climate with Significant Potential.

The climate for growth in managed care is arguably more favorable now than at any time since its inception. The traditional fee-for-service payer system, with its inherent disincentives to control costs, is becoming increasingly archaic. Pervasive acceptance of true concept of "managed competition" by both the public and private sectors bodes well for managed care in general and for HMOs in particular.

The three regions in which Coventry operates offer tremendous potential for HMO growth. By region, the respective market shares not yet served by HMOs are:

Pittsburgh

♦ 87 percent market share growth potential

Central Pennsylvania

♦ 89.3 percent market share growth potential

St. Louis

♦ 83.7 percent market share growth potential

Genzyme Corporation

Cambridge, MA
Rank: C [due to location]

from *Hoover's Handbook*

OVERVIEW:

Genzyme is a leading supplier of diagnostic enzymes and substrates for clinical diagnostic kits. The company operates in four business areas—biotherapeutics, diagnostic products, pharmaceuticals and fine chemicals, and diagnostic services—and develops many of its products through partnerships. In 1991 the company began marketing Ceredase, an enzyme used to treat Gaucher disease that generated 43 percent of sales in fiscal 1992. Overseas sales accounted for 16 percent of revenues in 1992.

Debt ratio: 24.8 percent [fair]

	Annual Growth	1987	1988	1989	1990	1991	1992	
Sales ($mil.)	67.2%	16.8	24.6	32.8	50.1	109.5	219.1	[good]

CHAPTER 6

A New Approach to Getting Your Foot in the Door

Do you want an insider's perspective on issues such as...

♦ ...when you should send your resume?
♦ ...what we want in a resume or cover letter?
♦ ...what managers want to hear from a candidate?
♦ ...how to find the hiring manager's name?

Are you...

♦ ...unable to get three to five interviews or meetings a week?
♦ ...unsure of the role of the initial phone screen or interview?
♦ ...sending resumes and getting no responses?
♦ ...sending your resume and getting a phone call but not a follow-up face-to-face meeting?
♦ ...finding that search firms are not as effective as they were in the past?
♦ ...reading all the books, talking to a lot of people about your search, and overwhelmed by the possible options to pursue?

Now that you have defined your mission and learned which companies to target, your next step is to learn how to approach these companies. It's vitally important to begin this portion of your job search with a new, positive attitude.

The 180 Degree Principle Revisited

Before you try contacting any companies, you must make a 180-degree shift in your thinking. In the past, career counselors encouraged job hunters to focus on their achievements and hit any potential employer with both barrels of "Why I'm so great." This approach is characterized by the two-minute summary: a memorized two-minute speech detailing your entire job history, strengths, and achievements. When contacting someone from a company, you are expected to launch into your script before he or she has a chance to stop you. This approach typifies the old "Me, Me, Me" mentality, which ignores the needs of the company you contact—and it won't make a hiring manager want to talk with you.

Today, managers want to talk with candidates who understand what their company or department needs. *Therefore, you have to learn to focus your entire approach—from your initial phone contact, resume and cover letter to your interview—on learning what the manager/company needs and how you can meet those needs.*

Because every great company is always trying to improve, your job is to find their challenges—either current or upcoming—and then find a way your talents can help meet those challenges.

In order to make a manager want to talk to you, you first must know your own strengths and have the necessary confidence to contact the hiring managers and learn their needs. This doesn't mean you focus on yourself; it means you learn where your talents lie so you can identify how you can add value.

You must know how to convert seemingly unrelated experience into concrete value to the target company; you also must know what characteristics hiring managers want today. You must do this self-examination before you pick up the phone. When you're talking to a manager, you don't have time to think about *you*, because you must then concentrate on their needs. All great job hunters are, like Donna in Chapter 3, able to define their skills and strengths concisely as if they were a "product on the market." They know that the title of their last job and its responsibilities explains nothing. These job hunters are ready to describe their accomplishments and times when they went beyond what was expected of them and how they can contribute significantly to the company's future success. By sorting out different problems they have been able to solve over the years, they figure out how they can apply what they've done to a new job.

Perhaps your work experience doesn't reflect your interests or real talents. Maybe you've been underemployed for some time and are ready to go for a great job. For instance, many people take jobs beneath their skill level for family or financial reasons and later have trouble breaking out of that low-level mold. *How can you communicate your talents to a potential employer beyond your work experience?* After you have asked and understand clearly what they are looking for, bring out these characteristics.

Example 1—What Hiring Managers Want to Hear

Even if you are seeking a much different, "better" position than you've had in the past, there are certain characteristics and kinds of experience that will transfer to any company. These are traits that most hiring managers look for regardless of the position.

    a. Your proven track record of extraordinary hard work: how you paid most of your college cost, for example, or how you're always willing to work anything to completion even if it's working to midnight every night for a month.

    b. Your tenacity and persistence; you'll figure anything out. Successful job hunters always provide examples of how quickly they learned and put something new to use. They have quick minds and can think on their feet.

    c. Your work ethic and high level of energy and enthusiasm for *any* job. You're a "roll up your sleeves" person. You do whatever it takes.

    d. Examples of how well you work as part of a team and as an individual contributor.

    e. Your creativity and idea generation capabilities.

Here are some examples from *Team Mapping: A New Approach to Managerial Leadership*, by Charles Margerison & Dick McCann. These are shortened descriptions based on the Margerison-McCann Team Management Index and include the kinds of characteristics important for any position.

1. *Creator-Innovators.* I am usually imaginative and good at initiating new ideas or concepts.

2. *Explorer-Promoters.* I like to take new ideas and see how they can be pushed forward. I enjoy introducing new ideas, contacts, and resources into the organization from outside. I usually work hard at communicating new initiatives and opportunities to any person inside or outside the organization. I am excellent at finding resources and promoting new ways of doing things.

3. *Assessor-Developers.* I have a strong analytical approach and will enjoy developing prototypes. I like to look for new markets and test to see how, when, and where the product or service will work. I am best when given several different possibilities to analyze and develop before a decision is made. I like to organize new activities and respond well to such challenges. I can push an idea forward and organize it into a workable scheme.

4. *Thruster-Organizers.* I can make things happen. I can produce action out of ideas, discussion, and experiments. I enjoy organizing and will always "thrust" forward to make sure results are achieved. I press for outputs and decisions. For me, action is the name of the game.

5. *Concluder-Producers.* I am concerned with results and am a very practical person. My strength is in setting up plans and standard systems so that output can be achieved on a regular basis in an orderly and controlled fashion. I keep to deadlines and am usually punctilious. In a team role I can be counted on to follow through and get the job finished. I will ensure that any action agreed on will be taken to conclusion. I have a "common-sense, feet-on-the-floor" approach.

6. *Controller-Inspectors.* I am good at examining details and making sure inaccuracies do not occur. My contributions are usually well thought out. I check facts and details and bring up key issues that could prevent the team from making mistakes.

7. *Upholder-Maintainers.* I will work tirelessly and unselfishly to assist you.

8. *Reporter-Advisors.* I am an excellent listener and am often well liked because I do not press my point of view on others.

9. *Linkers.* I try to understand all views and make decisions on the basis of facts. I implement decisions with due regard for other people's ideas and values. I also have a wide appreciation of individual work preferences and abilities and distribute tasks accordingly.

As we talk to dozens of hiring managers in the fast-growth environment, there is a common response. The traits listed above fit the kind of individual they are looking for to ensure a continued high growth rate. Adjectives such as flexible, creative, enthusiastic, and high energy are the words we use to describe potential new employees for star companies. These are the characteristics of successful people in a corporate environment. Make sure you have concrete examples of each of these if asked in depth about a particular characteristic.

Example 2—How to Make College Experience Relevant

Many employers don't automatically equate classroom experience with work experience, so you have to do it for them. If you always get outstanding grades on your term papers or long written projects, you can think along these lines: "I can research, find, sort, and communicate vast amounts of information in a concise, efficient and timely manner."

Example 3—How to Make Volunteer Experience Relevant

Think about the volunteer organizations with which you've been involved. What professional skills did you develop and use? Were you an officer or project leader? Highlight your people-management skills. Did you write copy for mailings, design flyers, give tours, or serve as a representative to other groups? Highlight your public relations know-how. Were you responsible for a budget or involved in fund raising? Highlight your financial skills. Did you provide market research, generate membership prospects, or find sponsors? Highlight your sales skills. Even though you weren't paid for your time, you might still have gained valuable experience.

Example 4—How to Make Previous Unrelated Job Experience Relevant

"I am a person who works every task to completion given any deadline. I had an assistant-teaching job at a preschool, and when the main teacher was in the hospital for a month, I jumped in and worked until midnight for two weeks creating new projects so the children would not see a difference in the quality of their time spent at preschool. I can initiate new projects with little direction or limited supervision. I can run with an idea and bring it to fruition."

Remember, smaller companies need people who can wear multiple hats. You need to demonstrate an attitude of "can do" and avoid talking about what you can't or won't do.

Consider Yourself a Valuable Asset, Not a Pest

Before successful job hunters send a resume or start making phone calls, they have already put their daily action plan together, as discussed in Chapter 2, and have a good general understanding of the company they want to pursue. Many job hunters are fearful of doing any more than sending a resume and cover letter because they don't want to bother busy people, make a pest of themselves, or face polite rejection or outright hostility on the other end of the telephone.

However, you must be able to accept that risk in your quest for a great job. Think back to other times when you took a calculated risk that really paid off. How did you feel before you took the plunge? You were probably nervous and a little unsure of yourself—much the way you're feeling now. But after your risk paid off, how did you feel? Excited, proud of yourself, even inspired! Contacting your target companies is no different. Once you remember the rewards you've gained by taking risks in the past, it's easier to make those phone calls and find the information you need.

Successful job hunters realize that the worst thing to do is become paralyzed by fear and, by relying on blind, generic resumes, in effect give up. The successful job hunters keep three important things in mind.

1. They are determined to succeed and know the best, most effective way to do so.

2. They see themselves as competent, knowledgeable experts in their field, with information and ideas that will benefit prospective employers.

3. They realize that their value is determined by what they think it is.

We have found that people who see themselves as of little value tend to search passively, relying on mass mailings, search firms, and ads—anything but themselves. Those who value themselves highly search more effectively and obtain the best jobs with the best companies—even if they don't really have, in all cases, more value to offer than the other sort of person.

The best way to communicate belief in one's abilities is by demonstrating a relaxed, confident air and an enthusiastic attitude. Warmth and friendliness are desirable voice characteristics. *When you speak on the phone, smile—it will show in your voice.* Another important characteristic is the sound of confidence, which is based on the conviction that you know what you're doing.

Remember, you can't sound confident when you think you're "bugging" people. Look at it this way. If you've done your research properly, you are calling only thriving companies, those with a great new product or service who, you hope, are hiring people. At this point you are just trying to obtain further information, to decide whether this company should be one that you really pursue. *You* are evaluating the company at this point, not the other way around. What do you have to worry about? Remember, this is a *calculated* risk. You've done enough research to know that this company needs people. You just need to find out whether they need you and you need them.

At this point you're over halfway though the Focus Method. You've developed and narrowed your list of great companies and have decided which few to start targeting. Now you're ready to start using the telephone to find out the hiring manager's name and understand his or her needs first by talking to others inside the company.

Why Find the Hiring Manager?

Why find the hiring manager? Finding the hiring manager is a waste of time, right? If the company is hiring, Human Resources will know of all the available positions, not just the ones in a single department, right? Wrong. Human Resources doesn't create jobs; the managers do. Successful job hunters we know give the following reasons for finding the manager:

♦ *That's where the jobs are—with the least amount of competition.* Jobs are created because a manager with hiring authority needs a problem solved. If he or she can find a person to solve that problem, that person is hired, no matter how many people are interviewed. No manager in a growth company wants or has time to interview hundreds of applicants. The fewer candidates she has to talk to, the better. Therefore, if you can find her before everyone else does, understand her problems, and show that you're the best person to fix those problems, you'll get the job. In most companies, by the time a job gets to Human Resources, if there is a Human Resources Department, and they post it, the competition has increased from about one in four to about one in 100 to 2000. After all, how much competition do you want?

- *It's the fastest way to land the job.* Successful job hunters don't wait until a job is requested by the manager, sent to Human Resources, and posted in various places, then send their resume to someone without hiring authority, wait to hear back from them, and spend an hour in their office only to get a "Dear John" letter two weeks later. They go right to the source! They take the time to find the best companies, learn what that manager needs before they talk to her, show that they are the answer to the problems, and get the job.

- *Successful job hunters get the position of their choice.* When companies recruit on a college campus or at a career fair, their recruiters usually have a list of the positions they want to fill. If you want to work for that company but don't fit those particular jobs, you probably won't get the interview, and your resume will make it into the "for general distribution" pile.

The same is true of want ad postings. If you send your resume in response to a job listing you don't want and aren't qualified for, hoping you'll be passed along to the right department, you could wait a very long time. Decide what job you want and contact the manager responsible for that position. For example, Jill, an MBA student we know, wanted to work for a certain company. When that company recruited on campus, she couldn't get the interview because she wasn't qualified for the specific position the recruiter wanted to fill. Instead of giving up, she found the hiring manager for her ideal job. She called company headquarters, found out the name of the local manager, tried to understand his business, and ultimately got the job of her choice, not someone else's choice.

Calling the receptionist

Once you have determined that the company is hiring, you need to continue your quest for information about the company before contacting the hiring manager. When calling a company for the first time, speaking confidently to the receptionist builds momentum. Following are actual conversations from a job hunter starting the process. Included are examples of her first try on the telephone. Notice she gets a much better response when she is just looking for information. The dialogues show the wrong way to approach the secretary and the right way. The job seeker starts out slowly and is transferred to human resources. When you say you're looking for a job, you'll always end up in personnel. Look how much further she got when she asked for advice.

1. O & M Inc.: secretary/receptionist.

Job Seeker: Hi. I would like to ask some questions about your company if you have time.

Receptionist: I don't have time now. I'll transfer you to someone else. Got voice mail.

2. Applied Pharmaceutical: secretary/receptionist.

Job seeker: Hi, I have heard great things about your company—how fast it is growing and that it is a great place to work.

Receptionist: Yes.

Job Seeker: I am currently job hunting and was wondering if you were hiring?

Receptionist: There are always positions available for the right people.

Job Seeker: I would really like an opportunity to apply. What is your advice to get my resume some attention?

Receptionist: Send an excellent cover letter and try to place yourself in the context of the company.

Job Seeker: What do you mean?

Receptionist: Well, make yourself sound like you would fit here. What is your forte?

Job Seeker: General pharmaceuticals. (Vague.)

Receptionist: You need to be specific…if you can talk with Bob…"

Job Seeker: Bob who?

Receptionist: Bob Nelson in personnel. He is the best, and he's very funny.

Job Seeker: In your opinion, what does your company generally look for in a new employee?

Receptionist: The most important thing is commitment. It isn't always an easy place. Your job has to be a priority. Competence is also impressive.

Job Seeker: Do you have any final advice?

Receptionist: Um, don't describe yourself as a people person. Bob hates that phrase.

Job Seeker: Thank you so much. You have been extremely helpful.

Receptionist: Oh, you're welcome. No problem.

3. Biotec Pharmaceuticals: secretary/receptionist.

Job Seeker: Hello, I am job hunting, and your company came up in my

search, and it looked great. I wonder if you have time to answer some questions about it?

Receptionist: I don't know very much. I am a temporary. Let me transfer
you to someone else.

Job Seeker: Thank you.

4. Star Pharmaceuticals: personnel

Job Seeker: Hi, I am currently job hunting, and I've heard what a great
company Star is, and I wanted to find out more about it.

Personnel: Well it is a good company, but right now we are under a hiring freeze.

Job Seeker: Oh. When do you expect it to be lifted?

Personnel: No time soon.

Job Seeker: I've heard about how fast you were growing. What aspect of
business is booming?

Personnel: As I said, we are a good company, but we are downsizing
right now. If you are still looking in a year, you could get
back to us.

Job seeker: May I keep in touch with you as long as I am not a pest?

Personnel: (Laughs.) Sure, and I'll let you know when the freeze lifts.

Job seeker: Thank you very much.

Personnel: You are welcome.

5. Innovative Health Group (president answers the telephone after 6 p.m.):

Job seeker: I've heard a lot about your company…about how you've
been growing. I wanted to learn more about Innovative
Health Group. I'm evaluating the fast-growth health care
companies in the area. What exactly are you involved in?

President: Actually, we are part of the health care initiative to control
costs, and we help organizations streamline.

Job Seeker: What is your customer base?

President: We work for hospitals, HMO's, service producers, and insurance companies.

Job Seeker: What do you look for in the people you hire?

President: We are industry focused and look for individuals with strong
backgrounds in health care administration. It's a growing
company, but we are small and quite specialized. Why don't
you send your resume so I can better predict if we can use
you?

Job Seeker:	Great. The way your company is growing...by leaps and bounds...
President:	Yes, we probably will have places for the right people. What was your name again?
Job Seeker:	Laurie Day. Could you send me some information about your company?
President:	Sure, what is your address?

The information was received two days later. Notice how being persistent, asking questions, and complimenting made a difference. You can do it too!

Prior to talking to the hiring manager in a specific company, you should have personally evaluated the company's products or services and talked to competitors or suppliers of the company to determine whether this is a company you should pursue.

How to Find the Hiring Manager

The process of gathering the information to write a customized resume and cover letter and make your first phone contact with the hiring manager goes something like this:

1. Learn the hiring manager's name.

2. Find out whether any hiring is occurring or will occur in the near future.

3. Determine who else works for the hiring manager.

4. Discover what are the crucial issues and challenges facing the department you wish to work for—finding the "hot buttons."

It might seem counterintuitive to do all this before you send a resume and talk to the manager, but if you rush your contact with the manager and aren't prepared, you can significantly damage your case. Managers in high-growth companies are busy; they don't have time to waste giving you information you could have found yourself.

If the company is doing well, not cutting expenses or downsizing, then they are probably hiring. However, small companies typically hire a lot of people in one quarter and then freeze the next—to make sure sales and profits continue to go up. Don't be too discouraged if you are told, "We're not hiring anyone." Just ask, "Is that for the short-term [a month] or for the long term [a year]? When do you think you'll be looking for bright, aggressive, new people?" If the answer is "Not in the foreseeable future," then this is not a place you want to pursue.

The process of finding out the hiring manager's name is much easier than people believe. Simply ask for the name of the person you desire to speak to in a natural, confident voice. As a future potential employee, think of yourself as a potential customer, which you are in many respects.

Following are some simple scripts to use for *getting managers' names* in your targeted companies:

Receptionist: Hello, this is XYZ Company. May I direct your call?

Job Hunter: I'm sending a fax to your manufacturing manager. May I get the correct spelling of their name? OR —

I think I spoke to your manufacturing manager in the past and I can't recall the name. OR —

May I speak to your manufacturing manager, and could you give me the correct pronunciation of their name (or their direct number[1])? (At this point, if you get the manager on the phone and aren't prepared to talk to him, hang up).

Here is another sample script to follow:

Job Hunter: May I speak to the secretary for the manufacturing department?

Secretary: Manufacturing Department, this is Sally Jones.

Job Hunter: Hello Sally, this is Joe Smith from ABC Company. I'd like to send a fax to the manufacturing manager and I need the correct spelling of their name.

Secretary: Could you tell me what this is in regard to?

Job hunter: Yes—I'm sending some information I thought would be of interest.

If a live person is not available to answer your call, you've reached the company's voice mail system. This new productivity tool can be a big time saver for you, too!

How to Use Voice Mail to Your Advantage

Secretary: Hello. This is Sally Hill. I am away from my desk right now. Please leave a message.

Job Hunter: (At this point you can hit "0" for an operator.) —OR— This is Joe Smith of ABC company. I'd like to send a fax to the Manufacturing Manager. Could you please return my call and leave me the correct spelling of their name and the fax number? I can be reached at 555-555-5555. Thank you.

---

1 The best way to reach the hiring manager is on his or her direct line before 8:30 a.m. or after 5:00 p.m.

If you call a company and find the receptionist unable or unwilling to give you the names of either the manufacturing manager or the manager's secretary, call the president's office and enlist the help of the president's secretary.

Again, you have information, ideas, and insight. Call the president's administrator, saying:

Job Hunter:	Hello, may I speak to the president's administrator and could you please tell me his or her name?
Receptionist:	Yes, his name is Bob Gordon.
Bob:	President's office.
Job Hunter:	Hello, is this Bob? This is John Jay of NTI.
Bob:	Yes, this is Bob Gordon.
Job Hunter:	Hi, Bob. I would appreciate your assistance. I've been trying to send a fax to your manufacturing manager. Could you please give me the fax number and the correct spelling of the name?

The key to success in obtaining information to these questions is to remember that you are in control. Obtain information without feeling compelled to explain to the receptionist who you are and why you need these facts. If you do, the receptionist will probably refer you to Personnel or Human Resources. This is not what you want. You are evaluating the company. They are not evaluating you!

Your best tool is a well-controlled voice. We've already mentioned the importance of confidence and warmth, but there is another important quality too. In cold calling, you must show no fear. Any hint of nervousness or hesitancy is immediately picked up by an administrator. Secretaries and receptionists become suspicious of people who sound like they're not sure they should be calling.

Find Out What is Going On inside the Company

To be effective in your approach you need more information. *This process involves talking with at least two people before contacting the hiring manager. Secretaries and assistants are gold mines of information and usually the best place to start.*

The secretary or administrative assistant should be treated as an equal partner in your attempt to get to the boss. Although assistants don't make the final hiring decision, their knowledge and influence are significant. Ask for their opinions; probe intelligently about the company, the organization, or the boss. Such questions as these can lead to key information, which will position you favorably with the hiring manager.

> *Job Hunter:* Jane, you must have a lot of knowledge and insight on your department. What do you think makes XYZ such a great company? or How did you get started here?

Asking open questions to administrators or assistants builds rapport. A question demonstrates your respect for their position and knowledge. The rapport you develop with *all* the people you speak to helps set you apart from other job hunters. Soon these assistants are helping you find ways to meet their boss, learn more about he company, and identify what other opportunities may exist at the company. Following is a script to help you uncover the real needs of an organization.

Sample Script: The Key to the Kingdom Is the Administrator

> *Secretary:* XYZ Company, this is Susan Mitchell. How may I help you?
>
> *Job Hunter:* Hello, Susan. I understand you're the assistant for the manufacturing department. Is that right?
>
> *Secretary:* Yes.
>
> *Job Hunter:* Hi. My name is Joe Smith of ABC Company. As the support for the manufacturing department for your company, you must have a good idea about what makes your company and your department such a success. I could really use your advice. Could you spend a few minutes of your time with me?
>
> *Secretary:* I have a couple of minutes, I guess.
>
> *Job Hunter:* I've spent a good deal of time trying to understand your company and its industry. It seems to be a team with winning strategies and great people. I need help trying to figure out how my skills might fit into your organization. Susan, what do you like at XYZ Company?
>
> *Secretary:* It is changing all the time. Nothing stays the same way long, and I love the hectic pace.
>
> *Job Hunter:* I've heard some positive comments about your boss, Barbara Jones. What do you believe are some of the most significant accomplishments of her department?
>
> *Secretary:* Barbara has developed a cohesive team which works together to solve problems and make the whole process work more effectively.
>
> *Job Hunter:* What factors do you think have made her successful?
>
> *Secretary:* She values the contribution of each team member. She expects a lot and she receives it.
>
> *Job Hunter:* What kinds of things does she look for in people she hires?
>
> *Secretary:* She hires committed team players who aren't afraid to look

	at a new way to do things, even if it means changing the way we work.
Job Hunter:	I would be interested in understanding how your quality assurance is handled. Could you tell me who handles quality assurance? Does that person report to the manufacturing manager?
Secretary:	Yes, quality assurance is handled by John Davis, our production control manager.
Job Hunter:	Can you think of any other people I should talk with in the manufacturing area so I don't bother your boss prematurely?
Secretary:	You may want to speak to the Operations Supervisor, Mary Decker, or to Pete Johnson, Materials Manager.
Job hunter:	All right. That's great. Thank you so much for your help, Susan. I really appreciate it!
Secretary:	Sure. No trouble.

Sample Script: Successful Conversation with a Potential Peer

How else do you find out whether the department is hiring someone like yourself? A potential peer in your prospective company probably has the answer. Included are potential questions to ask a peer. Remember, in a small company, everyone is loaded down with more work than they can complete. Your future peer might be just holding his breath for the department to hire someone else. You may be totally overwhelmed with how much information

---

QUESTIONS TO ASK A PEER

- What do you like about the company / department?
- How did you come to join the company?
- What do you see as the company's and department's strategic goals?
- What must go right to achieve those goals?
- Is this department hiring or thinking about future positions?
- What are the biggest obstacles to meeting the departments goals?
- What are your biggest competitive challenges?
- How large is the market and what will differentiate you in the future?
- How does the company view the long term?
- What is their attitude toward their employees?
- What do you think of the company culture?
- What is your perspective on future growth?
- If you were me, how would you approach the boss?

and coaching they can potentially provide. They might be dying for you to join the company!

Script: Conversation with a Potential Peer

Peer:	This is John Davis.
Job Hunter:	Hi John, this is Joe Smith of ABC Company. Susan Mitchell, your associate, suggested I give you a call. She indicated that, as the Production Control Manager, you understand a great deal about XYZ and the strategic importance of manufacturing. Do you have a minute? I would greatly appreciate your advise.
Peer:	Sure, what do you want to know?
Job Hunter:	I've been researching your company and am very impressed with your philosophy of TQC in manufacturing. I'm evaluating becoming part of the team. John, how did you join the company? Do you like working here?
Peer:	This is a great company. Sales have increased 1,200% in four years. Our ability to ship low-cost, quality products keeps us competitive.
Job Hunter:	The company has been growing, and I understand there has been considerable hiring taking place. Is that true in the manufacturing department?
Peer:	To grow as fast as we have, we are always on the lookout for good people who can contribute to our growth rate. We run lean and mean, and that is a significant reason for our success.
Job Hunter:	You've been very helpful. I'm planning to speak to your boss, Ms. Jackson. Is there any insight you can give me on what she's looking for in the people she hires?
Peer:	She looks for flexibility, a strong work ethic, a can-do-anything attitude. You won't get as much training as you might elsewhere, but we look for people who can make their own way, who are proactive and take initiative.
Job Hunter:	John, do you have any further advice?
Peer:	Be persistent, but be patient in some ways too. Susan Jackson is handling a lot of balls at once. She desperately needs to hire another quality engineer, but she just has not been able to take the adequate time to find the right candidate.
Job Hunter:	What would you recommend I do?
Peer:	Learn about what we're trying to do here and then leave her a voice mail on what you could be able to do help us right now. But you might need to make multiple attempts. If you don't catch her when she has a moment to think about this issue, you won't get her attention.

> *Job Hunter:* Would you recommend I speak to anyone else in your department?
>
> *Peer:* You might want to talk to Pete Johnson, the materials manager, or Mary Decker, the operations supervisor. And our division across town might be hiring too. Talk to Sam Light, the manufacturing manager.
>
> *Job Hunter:* I really appreciate your time and all of your suggestions. Maybe we could get together and I could buy you lunch. You could share with me your ideas on TQC and the manufacturing process issues.
>
> *Peer:* That sounds great. And if you have any more questions, feel free to call.

The best approach now is to call the other managers you were referred to—the direct reports of the hiring managers, those who would be your peers. The knowledge they might share could be invaluable in your quest for information. As you'll learn, knowledge yields power. You learned in the last scenario with the hiring manager that the department is desperate to hire someone like yourself. But a lack of a return phone call might lead you to a different conclusion. Remember, managers in fast-growth organizations are busy.

Calling a Sales Representative at Your Target Company

To find the sales rep's name, you need to specify the *location* and the *kind of product* he or she would sell.

Most companies divide the sales organization by product and geography. Because companies know many people call into their organization trying to find the name of the sales rep for their location, salespeoples' names are the easiest to obtain. And because most job hunters don't take the time to ask their opinions, sales representatives aren't being inundated with similar calls and will be glad to help most of the time.

Sample Scripts to Obtain Sales Representatives' Names

> *Receptionist:* Hello, Growth Co., Inc.
>
> *Job Hunter:* Hi, I'm trying to reach the sales representative who represents North Carolina—could you please tell me who that is?
>
> *Receptionist:* Yes, we have two reps. Bill Barlett handles Raleigh and Eastern North Carolina, and Sue Wilson handles Greensboro and Western North Carolina. To which person would you like to speak?

(Write down both names—you might want to speak to both.)

Or you might be told that there are multiple sales reps. In that case, be as specific as possible. For example:

Job Hunter: Hello, I'd like to speak with the sales rep who handles North Carolina.

Receptionist: What location and product are you interested in?

Job Hunter: Well, I'm in Chapel Hill and I'm looking to speak to someone who handles your industrial product line.

Receptionist: OK, that's John Dunn.

Job Hunter: Is there a sales rep for this area who handles consumer products?

Receptionist: Yes, that is Linda Griffin.

Job Hunter: Thank you. Could I speak to John, please?

Sample Script with a Sales Rep

Job Hunter: John, this is Sue Long with Health 2. I understand you've done a great job representing ABI in North Carolina.

John: Well thank you. How can I help you?

Job Hunter: You must know an awful lot about ABI. I've been following their great progress, and I'm trying to understand more about the company. I'm in the process of evaluating the company for a possible career change.

John: I'd be happy to help you, but I'm going to a meeting in just a few minutes.

Job Hunter: I can understand how busy you are. As a successful rep, I'm sure your knowledge about ABI is one of the most insightful in the company. Could you just spend a couple of minutes before your meeting?

John: OK. What do you want to know?

Job Hunter: What do you like best about ABI?

John: Oh, it's the fast pace. The benefits are great, and our customers love our products.

Job Hunter: What makes your customers so receptive?

John: Innovation has set us apart. We put together programs to match our customer's exact requirements. Our competitors do not do that. We try to make it easy to do business with us. A great company remembers who the customer is! We try to say yes—even if it means working on a request for 15 hours straight.

Job Hunter: What are some of your biggest challenges?

John: Making sure no one takes our market after we've done all the R&D, which keeps our products and services the most unique in the industry. We need to create enough barriers to make it difficult for others to grab market share. Sometimes it is not the company who does something *first*, but the one who can get the message out and market it—I'm sure you know what I mean. I'll tell you, I've got more information I'd be happy to share. Why don't I get in my car, and you can call me while I'm driving. The number is 967-1286.

Yes, **it is that easy**, as long as you remember to...

♦ ...compliment the person.

♦ ...expect initial resistance; usually job hunters pay a second compliment or repeat the first compliment and ask for help a second time.

♦ ...listen and ask good questions.

♦ ...be respectful of time pressures.

Actual Conversation of a Successful Job Hunter Who Tried First to Understand What the Company was About

(Called company and asked receptionist for name and phone number of the sales rep who handles territory where job hunter lives)

Sales Rep: Hi, this is Suzanne Bay, can I help you?

Job Hunter: Hi Suzanne, this is John Harrison, and I am calling to ask for some advice. I have been following ABI's success over the years and I am trying to decide if I should contact them regarding possible positions. I wanted to get your opinion of how you like working for them first.

Sales Rep: Sure. What company do you work for now?

Job Hunter: I'd rather not say because I'm just in the preliminary stage, but it is in the same industry. Could you tell me how long you've been at ABI?

Sales Rep: I've been with them only six months.

Job Hunter: Great. You must have a fresh, fairly unbiased opinion then. How did you get your position?

Sales Rep: Well, I replied to a want ad for another position I didn't end up getting. I was so impressed with the company that I kept following them in the news and through our industry meetings, and I just kept in touch, and they ended up opening a new territory for me and basing it out of this area. You see, the company is just booming, and when you keep in touch and seek out opportunities, a job will eventually be created if they're continuing to grow and hire as this company is. In fact, they really don't advertise positions much at all.

Job Hunter: You know, I notice from the news they sort of struggled along the first few years and then have been doing well the last three years. What has happened? Is Fred Johnston still the CEO?

Sales Rep: Yes, he is. He came from the NAC Company and started this eight years ago, just focusing on one product, really. Then he brought in two other partners—James Cornell, who was a great sales person and had a lot of contacts, and Susan Kemp, who had a lot of ideas for several new products, and things just took off.

Job Hunter: That's fantastic, Suzanne. What do you like best about the company?

Sales Rep: I like the energy and enthusiasm and the concrete vision of the company.

Job Hunter: What is the vision?

Sales Rep: To be the best in our business. With services and products such as we have now, we are the best, and the company is working hard, filling the line in with a full set of products and services for our whole industry niche.

Job Hunter: What do you see as their competitive advantage? Why are they the best?

Sales Rep: Our research and development laboratories do a better job than anyone in the industry, and the quality of our services ranks second to none. You know, I wish you could tell me a little more about your background. How did you get my name?

Job Hunter: I just called corporate and asked for the sales rep's name in this area. Well, I work in the quality assurance area of company ZBA—one of your customers, actually. Based on what I've told you, who should I contact at corporate? Do you think they need people with my background?

Sales Rep: You need to contact Dr. Peter Lyson.

Job Hunter: What is his title?

Sales Rep: Director of Quality and Standards.

Job Hunter: Great. Do you know anyone who works for him that I might talk with more about the department before I contact him directly?

Sales Rep: You could talk to Davy Tate or Ann Dixon; they could give you some good insight into this area.

Job Hunter: You know, I'd love to meet you. Could we meet for lunch one day? Maybe I could share some information that might be helpful to next time.

Sales Rep: Yeah, let's do that.

(Go on and set a date)

Notice the flow. The successful job hunters who relate their stories back to us always say the secret is to give as little information about yourself as possible up front so you don't bore people. Then give the other person an immediate opportunity to talk. Don't allow yourself to say something negative such as, "I've been laid off," or "I have no experience because I'm a new graduate." Press the point that you are in the evaluation stage only and are looking for advice and opinions. Very often these contacts end up getting the job hunter's resume and putting it in front of the right person. Always follow up directly with that person when this happens.

How to Call a Competitor

What do you say? Why is the information a competitor tells you significant?

All managers like to know what their competition thinks about them. This is value-added information. If you as a job hunter proactively seek out your target company's competition, how does that add to your credibility? It puts you with the elite 1 percent of the job seekers who today look for *all sources* to add to their knowledge base. Ultimately they become assets, not pests.

Evaluate the competition as if you are a future customer—and who knows, someday you might be. To find out who is a key competitor, look in articles, trade journals, the annual report—anything that mentions your company's targeted products. Next, call your target company's key competitor and ask to speak to the sales representative, dealer, or distributor for your part of the country. Salespeople are the best source of information on their competition. If they don't know much about your target company, it might indicate a lack of market presence for your target company.

Med-X Company is a key competitor of Superstar, one of your three focus companies. Here is a sample role play to follow when finding the name of the sales representative.

> *Receptionist:* This is Susan.
>
> *Job Hunter:* Hello. My name is Jane Bell of CTL. May I speak to your sales representative who handles the hospital accounts for the state of North Carolina? (It is important to be as specific as you can be when asking for sales representatives.)

Sample Script for a Competitor

In this role play you are calling the sales rep from Med-X to see what she thinks of Superstar's new product, the 1248B. Med-X has a product, the H2L, which competes directly with the Superstar Product.

Sales Rep:	Hi, this is Sally Smith.
Job Hunter:	Hi Sally, this is Jane Bell of CTL. Sally, I've heard a great deal about your product offering, especially your new H2L product.
Sales Rep:	Market acceptance has been great. What can I help you with?
Job Hunter:	I wanted to know specifically how you thought it compared with the 1248D from Superstar?
Sales Rep:	The 1248B is a good product, but it has been known to have quality problems and is not nearly as well known as the H2L.
Job Hunter:	Oh really, what do you mean?
Sales Rep:	Well, the brand recognition of the H2L means we have more sales volume and a larger revenue base for future R&D. Additionally, we believe our ability to stay ahead is based on our shorter R&D cycle time to bring products to market.
Job Hunter:	I see. And what product do you think will ultimately dominate the market?
Sales Rep:	That's hard to say. What else can I help you with?
Job Hunter:	You seem very enthusiastic about your company—what do you like about it? How did you come to work for Med-X?

(It is fine not to reveal why you are calling if the rep doesn't ask and is willing to give you the information, but most good sales reps will want to know why you're calling and who you are. Never be untruthful; just use persistence with charm!)

What to Say when the Sales Rep Asks, "Why are You Interested in Our Product?"

Job Hunter:	Sally, I've admired your company's products and ability to compete in this market. I wanted your advice on which company's future looks the best. I'm evaluating companies in this market and I am in the process of making a career change.
Sales Rep:	Well, I'm not sure I'm the best person to talk to about this.
Job Hunter:	Sally, you have been an outstanding representative for your company, and I hear you know more about the HZL than just about anyone. I'd just appreciate your advice.
Sales Rep:	OK, where do you want to start?
Job Hunter:	What are the future strategies for your company?

If you indicate that you are evaluating both companies and they are competitors, you might find that the sales rep will start selling you on why you should come to work for her company. She might be willing to take your resume and give you names of people hiring within the organization. Don't feel compelled to tell them all about yourself. You'll lose your advantage. Stay in the driver's seat and let them do the talking!

Now that you're completely prepared to contact the manager, the next step is faxing a customized resume and cover letter. If you've ever wondered what happens to your resume after you've sent it out, read on.

How to Avoid the Island of Lost Resumes

Most resumes are "filed," for one of two reasons: Either they are sent to a company not hiring many people, or they land on the desk of a person at a high-growth company who doesn't have time, at that moment, to give it a close look. In either case, it's wasted effort to send a resume without considering to whom one is sending it, and what to do after sending it.

In other words, you need a preliminary and follow-up plan. Less than one-tenth of one percent of the thousands of people in the job market that we've talked to in the last four years have gotten jobs based on sending unsolicited resumes to people or companies without any other follow up. Fast-growth companies use resume database products. The resumes are inputted and are not retrieved unless someone has a search on specific characteristics. Most companies simply file a resume without a hiring manager ever having a clue of your interest in working for their company.

All of the resumes that we receive from ads placed by Silicon Graphics or from direct employee networking referrals are reviewed. Ninety percent of these are filed, with a subsequent "Dear John" letter being generated. The most common resume mistakes:

- ◆ All general fluff; too difficult to tell whether the person's background fills the needs for the particular openings the company has. Because most companies receive many resumes, "weeding them out" is the first step. If the "buzzwords" and job description aren't there, they're filed.
- ◆ Lack of industry or related experience.
- ◆ No specific accomplishments.
- ◆ A resume that is too different, such as a long functional resume describing specific skills and competencies in a general sense without clarifying in chronological order what you did at each specific job. Such a resume is too hard to compare to others and suggests that the job hunter is hiding something. (The only exception to this would be for a new graduate—someone with less than five years of experience. Then a functional resume is appropriate.)
- ◆ Too long. More than one page is too much in most cases, and you should never have more than two pages. If you've been working

for 30 years, only include the last 15. That's all most hiring managers are interested in at this preliminary stage.

♦ Listing references, salary, hobbies, or any personal data. This "dates" your resume.

So how have savvy job hunters convinced us to take their resume out of the "file" and give it a real review? Remember, if the resume is sent to a small, fast-growing company, chances are good that in the next six months, somewhere in the company they'll need someone like you. Job hunters who realize this *call back again and again* to make sure that the resume got a real review by someone with the potential to hire him.

A Great Resume

In contrast to a resume sent "cold," a solicited resume is one sent in response to an ad or a short conversation that ended with, "Well, send me your resume, in case anything comes up."

We don't recommend spending a lot of time trying to get such a solicitation. A solicited resume, if it's sent out without research beforehand and follow-up afterward, is nearly as ineffective as an unsolicited one.

What *is* vital, as we've said, is to do your research first, before you talk to the hiring manager, so that you can tailor your resume and cover letter specifically to his department's needs. In order to do that, you must first identify the manager and his subordinates and then gather information on the challenges facing that department.

What We Look for in a Resume:

1. One that's customized to the job and company you're applying for, so we know we're not just a "shot in the dark."

2. Accomplishments above and beyond a job description such as:

    ♦ Finished job or project in 50 percent of the time specified
    ♦ Increased company revenue by $x
    ♦ Saved company $x
    ♦ Discovered a way to improve something and followed it through
    ♦ Solved great problems; list specifically
    ♦ Performed in the position more efficiently and effectively by reducing costs, improving productivity, increasing revenue, and improving customer satisfaction
    ♦ Special awards and recognition
    ♦ Key player in a successful project

♦ Self-financed your education—a sign of a hard worker, something everyone wants.

3. Evidence of how your capabilities satisfy our job requirement.

4. One that meets the requirements for today's resume databases with key word-search capability and buzz words pertaining to the industry and position you're seeking.

Read the following resumes. Mr. Milan and Ms. McNeal do an excellent job of meeting these four requirements.

Donald D. Milan
23 E. Main Avenue   Charleston, CA 03330   912-555-9080

CAREER OBJECTIVE

A senior sales or management position in the indirect channel, requiring business acumen, analytical and conceptual skills for strategic planning and business development.

EXPERIENCE

Compubit, Inc.—Sunshine, California (1990–present)
Manager, Strategic Accounts OEM Division

- Sold software technology to all of the major independent software vendors in the PC, MAC and Unix environments.
- Key liaison between OEM and Retail accounts and coordinated engineering, marketing, manufacturing, finance and legal resources.
- Successfully negotiated several $1M contracts between domestic and Asian companies.
- Assisted Retail division in account penetration and developed business strategies to enhance sales.
- 70% of revenues were gained from new accounts.
- **Top producer for last three years. Exceeded revenue targets for the past eight years.**

Autotech, Inc.—Blueskies, California (1986–1990)
Northwest VAR/OEM Marketing Representative

- Represented the Strategic Partners Marketing division and sold high-performance graphic workstations, X windows terminals and high-end color printers in selected vertical markets exclusively through resellers/OEMs.
- Negotiated volume purchase agreements with major OEM accounts. Established a $2M account within a year.
- Responsible for VAR/OEM recruitment, coordinated technical training, and helped promote business development.
- Signed 18 new accounts in 20 months.
- Developed marketing and promotional strategies between our end-user sales people and resellers sales staff.
- Achieved 140% of quota.

EDUCATION

B.S. University of Michigan
Hewlett-Packard's Strategic Selling Course, Xerox Professional Selling Skills

Danielle A. McNeal
5 Rock Quarry
Raleigh, NC 27606
H: (919) 555-1469
W: (919) 555-2344

PROFESSIONAL OBJECTIVE

Continue in object-oriented development with emphasis on designing high-level, distributed systems.

SPECIAL QUALIFICATIONS

- Extensive work with expert systems and fourth-generation development tools.
- Development of distributed database systems in Oracle and C++.
- Designing user-friendly applications and interfacing with non-technical users.
- Most noted for innovative ideas and learning aptitude.

SKILLS

Programming Languages:	C++, C, Jam, AION, Rexx, Pascal, X11 Windows
Screen Writers:	Jam, AION (Expert System), Oracle FORMS
Software Systems:	CBDS, CADAM, CATIA (Mechanical Drafting) GDDM, GDQR (Graphical Display Manager), Framemaker
Databases:	SQL/DS, Oracle
Operating Systems:	Unix, VM/CMS
Hardware:	HP 900 (389, 720, 840, 857 Series), IBM 3090

WORK EXPERIENCE

NETWORK INC, Research Triangle Park, NC
(November 1989–Present)
Senior Analyst—Customer Service: Responsible for Unix application development to improve DMS 100 switch software delivery efficiency.

- Designed a character and graphical scheduling system to automatically deliver patches and perform support functions for DMS 100 switches via X.25 communication protocol.
- Developed a manual patch delivery system, accessing DMS switches over phone lines. Constructed the front-end that utilized a client/server architecture and C++ communication libraries.

(continued)

WORK EXPERIENCE (continued)

(January 1987–November 1989)

Software Engineer II—Design Control: Responsible for development of information systems between the design and manufacturing community to reduce product enhancement life cycle.

- Designed and developed a Design Change Introduction System that reduced the implementation of critical hardware changes from 12 to 8.25 days, resulting in a cost savings of $825K per year.
- Administered the design and implementation of an Engineering Document Library system used by five manufacturing sites. This reduced the actual design change implementation by two months.
- Developed a graphical Shop Aid System for mechanical frames using X11 windows on a UNIX workstation.

EDUCATION

Michigan State University, East Lansing, MI —B.S. Computer Science, June 1985

Now look at the next resume. A lot of space is wasted describing Telcore and U.S. Sprint. We want to know what great things John accomplished above and beyond the ordinary job description. Many resumes refer to activities, duties, and responsibilities, and we are not very interested in that kind of information beyond a job title and the years in the job. We want to understand how your achievements will translate into "What you can do for us."

John Marsden
56 East Robinson St. #889
Dallas, Texas 02140
(214) 555-1232

SUMMARY

A seasoned marketing professional with a proven track record. Strengths in analysis of customer needs, marketing, creativity, and communication skills.

PROFESSIONAL EXPERIENCE

TELCORE INCORPORATED, Dallas, Texas   1992 to Present
A multi-million dollar company marketing communication technologies, combining conferencing system, groupware, and voice process systems.

National Account Manager

- Provide marketing of conferencing solutions to Fortune 1000 accounts based in the Chicagoland area.
- Establish and manage accounts utilizing innovative communication software and conferencing technologies.

U.S. SPRINT, Kansas City, MO   1991–1992
A $10 billion organization that is the second-largest long distance services company in the U.S., and the sixth largest network services carrier of international traffic in the world.

Senior Market Analyst

- Responsible for selected Fortune 1000 accounts; analyzed customer's current communication systems, and recommended network software services.
- Coordinated and managed remote account support teams.
- Evaluated and analyzed competitive information.

CELLULAR ONE TELECOMMUNICATIONS, Houston, Texas   1985–1990
A $2 billion leading independent telephone company providing comprehensive telecommunications solutions with digital switching systems and peripheral equipment.

Marketing Analyst—Client Base

- Successfully developed and implemented strategies for a new client base marketing program.
- Responsible for total project management of accounts, marketing complex network telecommunications systems.
- Provided marketing support to regional field offices.

EDUCATION

B.S. Degree, Illinois State University, 1979

How to Write a Cover Letter We Might Notice

The first thing to realize is that a cover letter is a stepping stone—a tool to ease you into that difficult but crucial first phone conversation with the hiring manager that you, as the job hunter, must initiate. It provides a reference point, a justification for calling. *Savvy job hunters know that a cover letter represents about 5 percent of the effort required to get into an interview.* A tenacious, active follow-up to the letter on the telephone is what will make the difference—not some magical arrangement of words on a page.

Having said that, does it really matter what you write in your cover letter? Yes. It still does. As we've said, successful companies receive thousands of cover letters. Your goal in writing yours is to generate interest, to set yourself apart from the crowd in a positive way.

The best way to accomplish this is to remember the 180 Degree Principle: Demonstrate superior knowledge of the targeted company, as well as the particular challenges of the position you want to fill, then define how you can meet those challenges. Use the information gained in your research and your conversations with the support staff to write a cover letter uniquely tailored to the needs of the company and the department. Mention your past achievements, but keep the focus of the letter on your reader, not yourself. You should include at least two positive statements directed to the manager that demonstrate your understanding of his or her goals.

What We Want to See in a Cover Letter

+ Three concise paragraphs totaling less than a page; otherwise it is skipped over.
+ A nice compliment or demonstration of some knowledge of the company and the reasons why you want to pursue a job there. Refer to specific employees you know at the company. Managers take notice when an internal reference is made.
+ Specific focus or a specific job. We don't like to talk to vague people.
+ Three bullets stating why you should be considered for a specific job. This should focus on how you can help us—not what *you* want.

The following cover letter successfully meets these goals.

September 1, 1993

Carl Morgan, Technology Manager
Donovan Technologies, Inc.
P.O. Box 13737
RTP, NC 27709

Dear Carl,

Congratulations on your company's recent public offering and the market's tremendous response to Donovan's innovative FLX system! Donovan's fascinating vision for the future is a tribute to the superb people you have hired.

I have recently spoken with two former co-workers now at Donovan, Chris Carbone and Drupti Patel, which leads me to bring my qualifications to your attention as a possible addition to your dynamic team. As Donovan begins ramp up for volume deployment of the Fiber Loop Access system, my experience in customer service and object-oriented development could be a great asset to your company.

As a software developer for Digital LEX, I have in the last seven years:

- Developed customer service systems that improved the quality of software delivery and maintenance for digital switches.
- Created an automated and manual patch delivery system that allowed the same number of downloaders manage an increase of 2,000 to 5,000 patches per software release.
- Designed and developed a Design Change Introduction System that reduced the implementation of critical hardware changes from 12 to 8.25 days, resulting in a cost savings of $825K per year.

I would like to understand what you are looking for in terms of qualifications in your new hires and what your time frames are for bringing new software developers into your organization. I will call you to set up a time that we can talk further. Thank you.

Regards,

Daniel O'Callahan

Ms. Jackie Samson
Vice President, Customer Support
Superstar, Inc.
344 Merelake Rd.
Durham, NC 26627

Dear Ms. Samson:

Congratulations on the new contract Superstar won in China. Your company's commitment to excellent customer support is driving Superstar's growth. Your organization's ability to react quickly and understand customer needs provides a significant competitive advantage!

In talking with Tom Avery and Anne Williams in your organization, I've learned that your department values people with high energy and good analytical skills who take a proactive approach in supporting your customers.

As support manager at Mertec, I face critical customer support issues every day and have learned the value of teamwork, customer focus, and strategic relationships. My achievements include:

- Our customer support department was named Department of the Year two years in a row,
- I received Mertec's "Difference Maker" award both those years.

I would like to learn more about your challenges, what you look for in new members of your team, and how I could contribute to your team. I will call you at 10:00 a.m. on March 31, 1994 to arrange a time for us to speak further.

Sincerely,

Sharon Long

As you can see, Dan and Sharon are specific about how they can help the company and demonstrate that they know what's going on within the company. Contrast this with Gerald's cover letter on page 149.

Gerald's letter is obviously a form letter mailed to 500 companies. He hopes someone will take the time to decipher his background and figure out the possible positions we might have to fit it. We won't; we don't have time. Also, we receive too many of the new, better kinds of cover letters such as Dan's and Sharon's.

43 Morningdale
Simon, IL 64905
Home: 613-555-4566
Office: 314-555-5635

February 19, 1994

Ms. Rachel Davis
Susan Anderson & Associates
514 Brookside Terrace
Chapel Hill, NC 27514

Dear Ms. Davis:

I am very interested in the sales position you had listed with Drake Beam Morin Inc. Please find my resume enclosed.

During my professional career I have had the opportunity to work with many large national accounts as well as smaller organizations, both as a salesman and as a sales manager. This experience has spanned all industries including all levels of government and educational institutions.

While in management, I was responsible for recruiting, training, motivating, and, when necessary, releasing marketing personnel. I have attended numerous marketing schools and seminars and have implemented these skills throughout my career.

Although my professional experience has emphasized the high-tech industry, I feel the skills I have can be easily transferred to almost any industry. I strongly believe that marketing is simply understanding the needs of potential customers and satisfying those needs to our mutual benefit.

My work location preferences are the midwest, southeast and south central parts of the U.S. I trust you will find my background of interest, and I look forward to hearing from you in the near future.

Sincerely,

Gerald Stuarts

Summary of Problems with Gerald's Cover Letter

+ No mention of the company he's trying to get a job with.
+ Obviously hasn't done research.
+ I as opposed to "you."
+ No focus for position or location.
+ No follow-up.

Cover Letters: The Biggest Mistakes

+ Rehashing what is on the enclosed resume.
+ Putting too many "I's" in your letter. Think about how boring and impolite it is when people talk about themselves all the time and never ask you how *you* are doing. Gerald's letter from the previous page conveys this "I" message.
+ Lack of focus to a particular position we might have.

We won't spend a lot of time on resumes and cover letters in this book because frankly, we don't think that this is a particularly important part of the job search. Of course, you need to have them, and you need to incorporate the research you've done, applying the 180 Degree principle, but if you obsess needlessly about a resume, it will simply distract you from the other, more important things you need to do, such as research and networking.

By now we hope you feel able to focus on the hiring manager's needs, call companies for information, and write a more effective, tailored cover letter and resume. This approach is different from that of traditional job-hunting guides; it is also much more efficient and productive. As a comparison, let's review some of the conventional wisdom:

Summary: The Biggest Time Wasters and Why They Aren't Effective

+ Any kind of mass-mailing: There's no way to know which companies are growing.
+ The two-minute overview: It focuses on the job hunter's delivery process, not the hiring company or manager's needs.
+ Elaborate, offset-printed cover letters and resumes; instead, tailor each to the job. In today's offices, faxes and scanners read laser jet high-quality output the best.
+ Writing many follow-up letters. One is plenty; after that, use the phone.

CHAPTER 7

How to Generate the Hiring Manager's Interest

Do you…

+ …wish you knew how to make a great first impression on the phone and in person?
+ …feel uneasy when you make an introductory telephone call to a hiring manager at a target company?
+ …wonder what you should say to make them want to talk to you?
+ …find yourself unsure how to proceed when the person resists talking?

Have you…

+ …had many phone calls following up on your resume but few face-to-face interviews, and you don't know why?
+ …tried to call key hiring managers in your target companies and been unable to get them to return your phone call?
+ …been nervous and unsure of what to say to a prospective employer?

Most job hunters are trained to focus on their resume and the delivery of their credentials. But the game has changed: A great delivery process and great resume aren't as important today as they were in the past. The tools that successful job hunters are using to get great jobs are advanced communication skills.

The greatest of great resumes sit by the thousands in our filing cabinets and data bases. Once successful job hunters have jumped into the great company funnel (after properly researching and focusing on a few great companies that are hiring people like them), they start using the phone *non-stop*. They are what we on the inside call "persistent with charm." They start calling around, and surprise! their resume is pulled out of the cabinet, and they get a phone screen. But, as we've mentioned, half of the people we talk to fail at the phone screen/interview. Why? Because they think it's a call where they need to 1) redeliver their resume, or 2) work with a secretary to set up a time for a face-to-face interview. Here's a startling statistic: Ninety percent of the people who send us resumes are unprepared for our phone call. Because they are not prepared, many are not moved on to the next step. This chapter illustrates in detail how to get from the resume in our mailbox to the face-to-face interview, dramatically increasing your chance of success to one in seven!

There are many great books out there on handling a face-to-face interview, but the ground that is not covered anywhere else is how to get through the process up to the face-to-face interview. If a job hunter is getting two or three face-to-face interviews every week, he doesn't need this book. He's figured it out, as have most of the people we've hired in the last four years. But what we find is that most job hunters are stuck somewhere at the start of the process without any idea what the problem is.

The key point to remember throughout your job search is that most of the time the "best fit" does not get the offer, because his or her resume and one or two phone messages into a busy, growing company get lost in the company's quest to meet its urgent priorities. Successful job hunters know their biggest challenge is to get and keep their resume in front of a potential hiring manager. They learn how to use the telephone, fax, and voice mail to do this. It might not be easy, because it involves telephoning people who usually have no idea why you are calling or who you are. Almost everyone feels awkward and uncomfortable doing this; they might even feel like a pest sometimes. But after all, that is the worst that can happen. Moreover, most job hunters we have brought on board at Silicon Graphics have gotten the job because they knew how to use persistence without being a pest—"persistence with charm."

Tools to Find the Hidden Jobs

Why is using the telephone so effective for most job hunters? Because they beat their competition to the job. This kind of calling, or cold networking, as some call it, thrusts the job hunter to the front of the list for the "hidden jobs," the ones that have not opened up yet. The jobs are not known to the general public, so there will be very few people calling for them.

When we started recruiting for Silicon Graphics in 1990, the company had about $400 million in sales and was growing by 50 percent a year. We received almost no calls, although we were involved in hiring for the central and eastern two-thirds of the country. The company now has more than $1.5 billion in sales—and we still receive few calls! Almost every hiring manager in companies with less than a thousand employees tells us the same thing. Not many job hunters make an effort to track down the right person to call.

We have a small file of job hunters who call regularly hoping for an opening in their particular area of expertise. This file represents less than 1 percent of the resumes we receive. Most people simply don't make the effort to stay in touch, and so we forget about them when, six months later, a job comes up in their area, and we have 300 new resumes to wade through. So to stay ahead of the competition, start calling, and keep calling every few months.

The second-greatest advantage of the telephone is the speed and directness with which the job hunter can reach the largest number of contacts. People throw mail away, but most of them still listen to their voice mail and read their faxes. By talking to prospective employers on the telephone, a job hunter can quickly separate the real prospective employers from those not worth pursuing and can decide the priority each company should take. Those who wait for people to call wait forever.

We are all afraid to call people blindly, even those of us who have done it as a career for more than ten years. We are afraid of rejection, of looking awkward or foolish. No one is born to do this, even salespeople. In our years as sales reps at Hewlett Packard, we saw thousands of top sales people in action, but we can count the "naturals"—people who easily and successfully cold call from "Day 1"— on one hand. For the rest it took hard work, practice, and a will of iron. There are almost no naturals at anything. The hardest part is making the first phone call. Successful job hunters learn to say, "I don't care what people think; I'm going to do it."

Now that you have a list of target companies, along with some general knowledge about each one, the starting point in making these uninvited phone calls to prospective hiring managers is to acknowledge your normal fear of rejection and to know that, with practice, you'll overcome it.

> *Successful people have the habit of doing things*
> *failures don't like to do. They don't like doing*
> *them either, but their disliking is subordinate to*
> *the strength of their purpose.*
> — ALBERT E. GREY,
> *The Common Denominator of Success*

Best Remedies for Nerves

The best solutions for nervous, uncomfortable, and awkward feelings about telephoning prospective employers are preparation, practice, and a positive attitude regarding one's capabilities. Preparing the groundwork involves all of Chapters 3, 4, 5, and 6.

Assuming you have obtained hiring managers' names and background information on prospective target companies, the next step in laying the groundwork for a telephone call should be one of two things—an introductory letter or a cover letter and resume. If you have talked to the hiring manager's secretary or peers and know the requirements for the particular position, go ahead and fax a *customized* resume. This is a great springboard to a conversation. Again, if the company or department is hiring, the resume will be welcomed when sent to a hiring manager. It will save her an extraordinary amount of time and money in conducting her own search, even if she won't have an opening for months. The key concept to remember is: *Think like the hiring manager.* Put yourself in her shoes. She is busy, part of a small, fast-growing company, probably without an extensive Human Resources department to help in recruiting and hiring. There is nothing more helpful for those of us involved in hiring in this environment than to receive an unsolicited resume from a job hunter who understands the company he's applying to, has researched it, has talked to some other people in the company, and has sent a customized resume specifically tailored to a job opening, or possible opening.

The best approach in calling is first to write a script of what you mean to say. If not written, your "opener" will tend to be too long and rambling. Writing a script allows you to be concise. Most people tend to say too much out of nervousness. They are bent on attracting interest in themselves, but talking about yourself never creates much interest. Most people who get an unexpected call from someone they don't know will not be in the mood for a long, friendly conversation—at least not at first. Writing down what you want to say lets you get to the point quickly. Think of the prospective employer. She does not have the patience to follow a long-winded, several-minute monologue. She will judge this kind of job hunter negatively from the start.

Another reason for writing your script is to eliminate "weasel words." Theodore Roosevelt is credited with naming this problem, describing it as "words that destroy the force of a statement by equivocal qualification as a weasel ruins an egg by sucking out its content while leaving it superficially intact."

Weak: I was wondering if you might possibly have a few minutes in the future to talk with me about a job?

Better: Could I have 15 minutes of your time this Thursday?

Weak: Maybe we might get together sometime, if you aren't too busy.

Better: Could I take you to lunch to talk with you about your company's phenomenal growth?

Weak: Perhaps I could send you my resume, if it's not too much trouble.

Better: I'll drop my resume by tomorrow afternoon.

Weak: Sorry to interrupt you—and I know you must get calls like this all the time—but could I have a few minutes of your time to talk about my job search? It has come to my attention that you might be a possibly good person to talk to about manufacturing?

Better: Joe Smith told me you were the best person to give me the inside scoop on the manufacturing industry in the Chicago area. Could I ask you for 10 minutes to talk with me?

You need to demonstrate your confidence and self-assurance. Using weak words destroys a good tone. Writing a script first helps to avoid making poor word choices. You also will be more relaxed, since you'll know exactly what to say.

Prospective hiring managers often reject an initial attempt to talk. This probably means that today or this week is not good, but a future time might be, so keep trying. Many job hunters think we view them as pests—and then they act that prescribed role. We can hear in their voice their lack of conviction and mission. A job hunter feels inferior because he is thinking hiring managers think he is. *Wrong! If you have followed all our advice, the hiring managers will be fighting over you.* Let us repeat: A well-informed job hunter who has taken the time to research the company and has a good case for what he "can bring to the table" is a welcome interruption. So don't think we think you're a nuisance. We know that if there is not an opening today, there will probably be one within six months.

How to Use Persistence with Charm

Hiring managers are impressed by job hunters who *really* want to come to work for their company. Calling back again and again over a period of months demonstrates this desire.

Some people are persistent but come across as a pest by…

♦ *…not giving us a chance to call back.* This includes calling back more often than every three days and not finding out from our assistant or secretary whether the person is out of town or tied up in a class before calling a second time.

♦ *…not leaving the reason for their call.* You should refer to your letter and give a compliment or share a reason as to *why* we should call back.

♦ *…including us as part of a resume blitz.* We get plenty of unsolicited resumes from people who are mailing to the masses and have not tailored their resume to a specific job. We file most of these. We do receive a few "Did you get my resume?" phone calls. And when we ask, "So why are you interested in a position with Silicon Graphics?" most stumble and fall with answers like, "I heard from Joe Smith SGI was hiring, and I thought I would call." Those resumes from ill-prepared, uninformed job hunters are filed again. Another point—don't use a weak opening such as, "Could I have a few minutes of your time?" If you've never talked to the person before, this question is irritating. You can ask for it later in the conversation, but not right off. Don't ask for anything without at least giving a compliment and a reason for calling first.

Never ridicule the validity of an objection. When someone is open enough to give you a reason for "no," even if they are wrong, agree with it and try to understand why.

Charming means being complimentary, polite, and *knowledgeable*. We want to hear some enthusiasm and knowledge about the company and its products. Don't insult us by sending us one of a hundred resumes as if you were throwing a handful of darts at a dart board and hoping one would hit!

Here are Some Examples of Using Charm

"I have admired your company for a long time and am interested in obtaining your advice about potential hiring needs in the future."

If you obtain some relevant information or news about the specific person you're calling, say: *"I have admired your work and some of the things you've accomplished as I heard from Joe Smith (or read about in an article in the local newspaper), and I was interested in learning how you've become so successful. Perhaps you can offer me some advice on my job search or input on my resume."*

or

"I understand you are one of the best people to talk to regarding the 'ins and outs' of this industry. Can you give me some advice regarding my career search? I am a recent graduate of the University of Georgia."

or

"I understand you know a lot of people in this area. Could I ask for your advice regarding my possibly changing companies?"

or

"You have been so successful in your area. My background is in advertising. If you were me, how would you pursue career opportunities in this company? Could you recommend anyone else I should contact?"

Continue:

"How did you get started in this business?"

"What are the aspects of this company that make it especially successful?"

"Could I take you to lunch to learn more about your company/industry?"

"Can you recommend any of your associates whom you think I should talk with?"

The ability to perform at your best when you introduce yourself in person or on the telephone is a learned skill. Successful job hunters practice over and over until they get it right. Using a cassette recorder, a camcorder (voice only), or a voice mail box is great for practice. Listen to yourself; smile when you talk. For practice, work on a company that's not one of the three you're focusing on and that you don't care as much about.

Voice Mail Secrets

Almost every company has voice mail now, but it can be very difficult to get people to call you back by leaving a voice mail. What do savvy job hunters do? They figure out a way to get a live person on the telephone. They press 0 or # or * or call back and say they want the person's assistant to arrange a time for a live conversation. Remember to find out whether the person has a direct-line phone number so you can reach him or her early or late when others are not in.

If, however, you can't arrange a live conversation immediately, voice mail can be a very effective method of introducing yourself to the manager and arousing interest by demonstrating your knowledge of his business. In order to make voice mail work for you, you must use similar techniques to those you use in your opening lines to the manager—because that's what voice mail is. Your message is your introduction and conveys the first impression the manager will have of you. In your message you should open with a specific compliment, be enthusiastic and responsive, display your knowledge of the company, and end with another compliment.

> *Job Hunter:* Hi Susan, this is Amy Hurring. Congratulations on the great press coverage HiGrowth, Inc. has had recently. The feature article in July's *Fortune* was particularly impressive. Susan, I've heard some good things about your department, could you spend a few minutes talking with me sharing what makes your team so successful. I'll call you again tomorrow morning at 9:30 to arrange a convenient time. Again, congratulations, and I look forward to talking with you.

Practice your voice mail messages and your introduction. If you make a mistake while you're leaving the voice mail, you might be able to erase it and start over. There are many different systems, and each one has different options, but there should be some way to erase the message. One of the most popular systems is the Aspen System by Octel. In this voice mail system you can erase the message by pressing 1 and then 3. In the Audix System, you can hear the available options by waiting for the automated attendant to give you the options after you stop talking.

When leaving your message, make sure your voice sounds relaxed and enthusiastic. Also, keep your message *short* and focused. If it's too long or unconvincing, your introduction will make a bad first impression and will get you no further.

Some of these requests—for advice, help, and job-opening leads to other prospective hiring managers—will create interest on the part of a growing, hiring company. It might take five or six telephone calls to get a busy executive live on the telephone, but the job at the end of the chase is worth it.

How to Obtain Help from the Secretary or Assistant

Secretaries and administrative assistants can either help or hinder your attempts to reach the hiring manager—the choice is largely yours. We all know part of their job is to protect their bosses from unwanted and unnecessary telephone calls. It is your job to be so prepared that you are neither unwanted nor unnecessary and to communicate that to the secretary. If you treat him as an ally, he can help you get in touch with his boss as quickly as possible. If you treat him as a mere minion or obstacle, he can make it very hard for you to get through to the manager. Never be condescending, rude, or impatient with the assistant. You might think that no one in his right mind would be rude to *anyone* during the hiring process, but you'd be surprised. We had a candidate not long ago who lost his chance at a position because he was impatient with the manager's assistant.

Secretaries quickly figure out whether they are being seen as a roadblock by the caller's tone and the words chosen. You should sound as if you *know* his boss will want to talk to you, rather than saying, "Is Ben Jones in?" or "May I speak with Mr. Jones please." This sounds like a vacuum cleaner salesman calling. In order to be helped you must convey the attitude that you have ideas, experience, or information Ben Jones would want to hear. If you view and treat secretaries or assistants as allies, they will do everything they can to see that their boss receives this important information from you. Work with the secretary to arrange a time to talk; this person should be your ally if you are asking for help. Make assistants feel important—they are a crucial cog in the wheel, and you won't get to a busy executive without their aid.

Work with the assistant to enlist help in getting in touch with the manager. Be persistent, show enthusiasm, and ask sincerely for their help and guidance. Try these approaches in teaming with the secretary to get you and the boss together.

> *Job Hunter:* Hi Jane, this is Susan White with ABC Co., and I've been playing telephone tag with John. Jane, you've always been so helpful. Could you please see what you could do to schedule a call with John?
>
> *Jane:* I don't usually make appointments for John. Why don't you call at 7:45 a.m.? He's usually here.

Or, try this:

Job Hunter:	Jane, this is Susan White, with ABC Co. Your organization is such a fast-paced group, and I realize you are incredibly busy. Could you help me to speak with John. Do you schedule his calendar? When would you recommend I call?
Jane:	You can call him at 10:30 on April 16.

Script: A Conversation with the Administrator to the Customer Service Vice President

The administrator opens new doors and provides a wealth of information. Here is another role play. Does the job hunter, Sharon, gain from the conversation? Does she move her job search closer to her goal?

James:	Superstar Company. This is James.
Sharon:	Hi James. The reason I'm calling is that I've heard so many great achievements about your customer service department. And I am evaluating Superstar as a possible future employer. James, I know you have a lot of insight about the department. Could you spare a few moments? I'd really appreciate your advice on Superstar.
James:	I'd really like to but I'm tied up right now. And that's really not my forte—perhaps you should speak with Linda in Human Resources.
Sharon:	I appreciate that you're busy right now, but I understand you have the real inside knowledge on the customer service department and you seem to make things happen. Could you spare a few minutes?
James:	Oh, OK. (Expect a rebuff, but make an informed compliment and ask again. It works!)
Sharon:	What do you like about Superstar?
James:	Superstar is a fast-growth company and there is always a lot going on at once. The people are very supportive, too.
Sharon:	How did you get to Superstar?
James:	Funny that you should ask. I had a friend who had heard that Superstar was a good small company. When I called to see if there were any openings, I spoke with Jackie and she set up an interview later that day. I started right after that! Superstar's not so small anymore.
Sharon:	That's great! How do you see Superstar in the future?
James:	We are growing so fast that this is the time that will make or break us. We are ahead of our competitors in technology, but if we don't keep our customers happy, we will be in trouble. Things have been pretty hectic (ring, ring)—can you hold one moment?
Sharon:	No problem.

James:	Thanks for holding. Now what were you saying?
Sharon:	I really appreciate your time—I only have a couple more questions. Have you heard of any hiring taking place?
James:	There is nothing formal, but I know that Jackie needs some help. You should really talk to Anne Williams who is the customer service manager and she should be able to give you more information.
Sharon:	Thanks a lot James. Is there anyone else in the department you would recommend I speak to?
James:	Try Susan Steele, the XYZ customer service manager.
Sharon:	Thank you again so much for your time. Is there any other advice you can give me?
James:	Sure. Why don't you send me your resume and I'll try to get it to Jackie.

Still, there may be some situations where you need to get right through to the manager and feel more comfortable asking directly for him or her. These sample scripts suggest ways to get in touch with the manager quickly. If they don't work, you need to ask for help.

"Hello, Jane, this is Sarah Shey. Joe Smith suggested I contact Ed regarding some competitive information."

"Hello, Jane, this is Luis Munoz of G.D. Goodsell. I wanted to congratulate Ed on the XYZ product introduction."

"Hello, Jane, I'm calling with regard to my letter of June 14."

"Hello, Jane, may I speak to Ed? We've been playing telephone tag."

The *most important trait is persistence.* It's easy to give up, but an enthusiastic, cheerful and humble attitude works almost every time. Seven or even ten phone calls might be necessary to achieve your objective.

Once you get through to the manager, you must show in the first things you say that you are a knowledgeable caller and worth his time. If you blow this first impression, you might not get a second chance. Your research should have yielded several concrete challenges or recent accomplishments that you can use in your opening.

Job Hunter:	I have talked to some people in your organization, and I understand your team is in the process of designing a new customer service system. I have had some experience at XYZ Co. designing and implementing quality systems, and I would like to understand a little more of your goals in that area.

Or, for someone with whom you have had some contact in the past:

Job Hunter:	I would like to ask for your help because I cannot think of anyone else who is a) better connected, b) more informed

about the industry, or c) who could point me in the right direction. (etc.)

Again, the secret of success is putting yourself in your prospective employer's shoes. Think about his needs, his ego—not yours. Pass along a sincere compliment. In your research, you came across some article or investment advice about this company—fax it to him. Take the time to try to do something nice for somebody else. You will gain more ground by being genuinely interested in someone and their needs than you ever will by trying to push yourself on someone without understanding them first.

Sample Script: How to Attract the Hiring Manager's Attention

Sharon: Hi Jackie. This is Sharon Long of Mertec. From my conversations with Bob Samms at Customer, Inc., and with your associate, James, I've learned that your customer service department has developed some of the most innovative and effective programs in the industry. I was wondering if you could give me a few minutes of your time so I can understand more about your business and see whether my background might fit in with your organization in the future.

Jackie: I'd like to, Sharon, but Human Resources handles these kinds of calls. You should probably contact them, and ask to speak with Jan Start.

Sharon: Certainly, I'd do that, Jackie, it's just that I've heard from customers and your associates that you know more customer service than anyone and I'd just appreciate a couple of minutes.

Jackie: OK, but not any more than that —I've got a conference call.

Sharon: Jackie, what are your most important goals for the customer service department?

Jackie: Our number-one goal is to keep our customers satisfied, but with our growth and shipping problems this has been almost impossible. You know, everyone waits until the last minute to order, and then they want it yesterday. We're just having trouble keeping up.

Sharon: How has that affected customer satisfaction?

Jackie: I've got the vice president of sales and the CEO checking with me daily to get products out on time. It's gotten so bad, we're allocating deliveries. The most frustrating part is that I like to run a proactive operation, but it's impossible with this kind of growth. I don't like being in the position of always reacting to everything.

Sharon: Have you had any way to get the customer's insight on the problem?

Jackie: We've tried, but there has not been equal access for everyone. If someone yells loud enough, then we spend extra time trying to mollify them—it's basically the squeaky wheel getting the grease.

Sharon: At Mertec, we ran into similar customer problems. We ran several very successful programs. I once put together a SWAT team of all our executives and then assigned each executive to a key customer.

Jackie: Well sure, that sounds great, but everybody is so busy around here. I don't know if I could get their attention. It's one thing for the VP of Sales to call me and complain about delivery time, it's another to ask her to spend an hour and a half at the customer site listening to them complain about it.

Sharon: What role has the Marketing VP played during this situation?

Jackie: He's interested, but he's working on new product launches for the new markets we're trying to penetrate. He doesn't have the time to work out customer satisfaction problems until they become marketing problems.

Sharon: That is a tough situation—maybe a plan for a proactive SWAT team, with all the logistics nailed down before you took it to the executives, could make the difference.

Jackie: That sounds good—it's much easier to get their buy-in if they don't have to tie up their staff in doing much of the up-front work. But then I'd have to pull someone from my staff to do it, and we're all stacked up with six weeks worth of work marked "Urgent."

Sharon: I see your point. Perhaps this is where my experience could help you. I was the person they always turned to for all the new ideas and plans in my department. I could do the groundwork to make the plan work. What do you think?

Jackie: You know, I'd like to talk about this further, but I've got to make this conference call.

Sharon: Sounds great, thanks for your time. I'll look forward to meeting with you.

Jackie: Sounds good.

Sharon: How about getting together this morning?

Jackie: No, I've got a meeting.

Sharon: How about lunch?

Jackie: Okay, meet me at my office at noon.

How to Make a Comeback from a Rebuff

We had many job hunters who were able to turn around a rejection and later get hired. Expect a rebuff! Compliment with knowledge and sincerity. If you get a rebuff (which you probably will), repeat your compliment and ask again for advice.

Here are a few examples of strategies they used. If the person seems hesitant to talk, then tell them how much time you need—five minutes on the phone or a thirty-minute lunch. Or ask whether you can schedule another time to talk for ten minutes if he seems hurried. If they try to pass you to Human Resources or personnel, say, "Great, do you think I could get a little background information from you first?" Then you can ask; "What do you like about this company?" or "Why do you think it's been so successful?"

Executive:	We aren't hiring anyone now; send your resume to personnel.
Job Hunter:	Susan, thank you for your help; do you think you'll be hiring in the next year?
Executive:	Yes, we will.
Job Hunter:	Well, I'd just like to come by and meet you, shake your hand, so you can match my face to the name, and personally give you my resume.
Executive:	Oh, that's not necessary.
Job Hunter:	You're right, but I've heard and read so much about Company X (or you) that I want to make this extra effort! It will take only a minute of your time.
Executive:	Fine, arrange a time with my secretary.
Job Hunter:	Great, I look forward to it.

You are making an extra effort, and people appreciate it, they really do. Now when you call and arrange a time with her secretary, tell her you'd like to bring Ms. Hiring Manager something to thank her for her help, and ask what her interests are. We know of people who bring a really special book, an article about a hobby or interest, or some gourmet coffee; something very small, but that shows you took the extra effort. It's not the gift—executives get "freebies" from vendors and customers all the time—it's the thought behind it. A truly thoughtful gift is a great compliment to the receiver.

How to Make Them Want to Talk to You

When you put yourself in your prospective employer's shoes and try to think what their wants and needs are instead of pestering people about yourself and your wants, you are 90 percent of the way there. Dale Carnegie, in *How to Win Friends and Influence People*, talks a lot about how to persuade other people to do what you want. It boils down to finding out about their needs, making them feel understood and important. The great successes in life are not the brightest or the hardest working. They are the ones who have learned how to deal with people and are great positive communicators. Always take the time to understand other people's needs, and give sincere, well-informed compliments about them or their company. No one cares about you; they don't know you. They only care about what you can do for them.

If you can reach a common ground of understanding with a hiring manager, you'll be perceived as an asset immediately. What are the things that must go right for the hiring manager, CEO, or specific department to be successful?

If you've taken the time to talk to other subordinates, customers, or competitors, you already have an idea of the "hot button" for a specific manager. You want to appear knowledgeable, but not as bossy or as someone who knows everything and can't learn anything new.

Think about the situation of your future employer. Visualize the scenario—write out their current situation. Visualize yourself being part of this team solving specific problems, creating new ideas on how to become more productive or competitive.

As an example, imagine you're targeting Super Services Co. Think about the challenges associated with high growth: not enough resources; difficulties in fulfilling customer demands and providing good customer service; difficulties in forging hard-working, committed and focused work groups.

You've researched the written material, and talked to assistants, competitors, and vendors of Super Services Co. Imagine you're a manager of customer service recently laid off from a competitor that lost market share. You know that the company (your hoped-for future employer) has been challenged to ship products before quality is at the level customers expect. John Jay is the hiring manager and V.P. of Customer Relations, and he just got another call from one of the largest customers complaining about quality. John knows he needs more help in this area, and you know it too, even though you've never talked to him.

You've written him a letter of congratulations on their opening offices in Asia and the new contract they won with Big Company, Inc. You know their objective is the highest customer satisfaction rating. You understand the challenge of the market because, under your management at the key competitor:

- You improved customer service by 50 percent and moved from 5th to 2nd place in industry customer satisfaction in two years.
- You chaired the group that achieved the "ISO 9000" quality award.

♦ You've spent hundreds of hours with customers and know how to turn around dissatisfied customers (you were the last resort before the lawyers were called in).

You haven't worked at Super Services, but you know so much about the company and its challenges, you feel like you have. On July 8, you call John, the hiring manager. It has taken about two weeks to reach him. Finally, with the help of his assistant, you have him on the telephone.

Job Hunter:	John, hello, this is Bob Smith of XYZ. I'm calling in regards to my letter of July 3, and wanted to congratulate you on the recent huge increase in Asian business. After talking to your associates, Bill Wheeler, Jane Snow, and some others, I understand your group was the major factor in winning this business.
John:	Thank you, but what can I help you with?
Job Hunter:	I've heard so many positive things about your company, and I'd like to learn if I might add any value with your team in the future. I'd be interested in learning more about your challenges. Could you take 15 minutes with me in the next week?
John:	I don't think that's possible. Can I give you five minutes now?
Job Hunter:	Thank you! You've got an impressive product and marketing strategy. What do you see as the main goals for your department? What do you think must go right to meet these goals? What are the biggest obstacles?
John:	Truthfully, as demand has increased, our yields haven't kept with the quality expectations of our customers. We need to turn this around, and we're working at it feverishly.
Job Hunter:	You've made a big impact already. From what I understand, though, if your demand remains at the same rate, you might actually be in danger of losing customers from a customer service prospective. Won't that have an impact on growth?
John:	Absolutely. I've got the CEO calling me twice a day asking about what our largest customers are saying and doing. The last thing we can afford is customers canceling orders!
Job Hunter:	As you might recall from my letter, my background is as customer service manager from XYZ Competitor Co. Our organization faced those same challenges. How about letting me take you out to lunch next week and we can discuss the solutions we came up with?
John:	That's a good idea. I'll tell you what; call my assistant and let her know I suggested an hour meeting. I've got to run, but it sounds like you might have some great insight for us.

Does this sound too easy? Not luck, but planning, preparation, and the power of knowledge brought the successful job hunter to this position. There are situations in which piquing the hiring manager's interest is more difficult, but if you can "peel the onion," as we call it, if you can ferret out the problem, you can position yourself to become the solution. "Peeling the onion" just means asking more probing questions. The more you can get people talking, the better chance you have of finding some niche that fits your background, or somewhere you can add value to the organization.

The telephone is one of the most valuable tools in your job hunt. It can help you find hidden opportunities and get you in the door ahead of those who are content to wait until their resume does the work for them. It can be the tool that gets you to the hiring manager and helps you communicate your knowledge and empathy for his challenges. It can be the best way to make the right first impression. But the phone is just a tool. It can't help you if you are too afraid to use it, and it won't help you if you don't do the necessary research beforehand. The next chapter will discuss the other important way the phone is used—as a more convenient interviewing space. Some of the techniques are the same, but we'll show you how to avoid the common mistakes of the phone interview and power on to the next step.

CHAPTER 8

How to Survive the Telephone Interview

Do you…

♦ …Wonder why you've received many phone calls from prospective hiring managers but no following interviews?

♦ …Feel ambushed by an interviewer and unable to move the interview your way?

♦ …Want advice on handling tough questions?

♦ …Need help presenting your accomplishments in the best light?

♦ …Find yourself rambling during the interview?

♦ …Need examples of good questions to ask the interviewer?

Small, growing companies can't afford to make mistakes in hiring; they must hire not just good, but great candidates each time to continue growing at the same rates. *This pressure to hire superstars has forced a change in hiring.*

As we mentioned in an earlier chapter, hiring practices have changed in the last few years. One of the most significant changes has been the rise of the phone interview. There are several reasons for this. First, the hiring manager does not have time to interview every possible candidate; he only has time to see the best. Second, in these leaner times, companies can no longer afford to fly people in for interviews based on a resume. Third, the hiring cycle is longer now, as each manager wants more and more people involved in choosing the best candidate. It might not be easy or practical to have each person meet each candidate, so companies increasingly conduct initial interviews over the phone. You might receive many more than just one phone interview, and you have to pass them all.

When you receive a phone call from a potential employer, don't assume it is an administrator calling you to schedule a face-to-face interview with the hiring manager. This initial telephone call might be the first round in an arduous selection process.

The person making this first call is not the hiring manager, in most cases. Rather, the hiring manager designates a Human Resources professional, a subordinate within the department, or an executive recruiter to do initial screening. Their role is to reduce the pool of applicants.

Many people find it difficult to be effective on the phone. Without the visual feedback available in a face-to-face interview, you can't rely on nonverbal clues to help you gauge the interviewer's response to you. Some people are much more impressive in person, but in the age of the phone screen, they might never get the chance to prove it.

There are many books available on interviewing techniques, and we have talked to thousands of job hunters who have gone through extensive outplacement training, but most of them never get to practice all these "techniques" in a formal interview because they are not trained in the right "first-impression" basics for the phone.

The most important rule to remember comes from Dale Carnegie. "If you want to win people over, let the other person do most of the talking." That means asking the right questions and answering questions in two sentences, no matter how much you think you have to say on the subject. We called one candidate who had a fairly good resume. We asked her one question—"So, what does your company do?" Thirteen minutes later (we timed it) she finished her reply—and we finished the interview.

A major mistake people make is to repeat the information on their resumes. *Remember, we have your resume; we already know your technical qualifications. A phone screen or interview is a process of further "weeding out."* Your interpersonal communication skills are much more important at this point. The interviewer usually makes up her mind in the first five minutes. The remainder of time is spent just confirming the initial impression.

Most job hunters get a call back either by maintaining a continuing dialogue over a period of months, or by finding an organization with a current job opening that fits the job hunter's background. All of a sudden the phone starts ringing, and it could be someone from Company X calling back, or it could be a search firm, or it could be a follow-up to a response to an ad. The ineffective job hunter handles them all in the same way—unprepared, but too afraid not to take the call. We remember one candidate who rushed to the phone dripping wet from a shower to catch a call. Her lack of preparation will cost her some interviews: It's hard to be confident and professional when you're wrapped in a towel.

If we call job hunters and catch them before they have researched the company, some are smart enough to rearrange another time a day or two later. Be sincere in your pleas. "This is not a good time for me, but I'm really interested in the position. Could we schedule this for tomorrow?" If you are at home or at your office, there are many reasonable explanations why this specific time is not appropriate for a telephone interview.

You should never have any kind of interview without a working knowledge of the company and its products or services. Don't think of us as fish at the end of a hook. If we have taken the time to call you, we are interested in your qualifications. *Our interest is your power.* While we're interested in you, and before we know whether you're a good fit or not, you are in the best possible position. By rescheduling the call to a better time, you keep your edge.

Successful job hunters always can explain why they want to work for the company and why their experience is something we need. Less successful job hunters tell us they were afraid that if they let us off the phone, we wouldn't call back. Don't worry. If we took the time to call once, we'll call again. Your ranking in the candidate pool will not change one iota if you change the time to talk. Just tell the caller that it really isn't a good time to talk, and ask whether another time can be set up. Have a sense of urgency in your voice, and the interviewer will understand. It is important, however, that you are enthusiastic about the position, so that the interviewer doesn't think you aren't interested.

We estimate that we have spent approximately 3,500 hours conducting phone screens. We can say without a doubt that most of the job hunters are eliminated because of a poor phone screen. Let us share with you what works.

There are many techniques for conducting a successful phone screen or interview. If you can only remember the things listed below, you'll do better than 95 percent of the people we call.

1. Be informed about the company and its products.
    Example: "You must be excited about the stock split last week," or "The 'Good Morning America' spot showcased not only the great products the company makes, but also the spirit of the organization."

2. Be enthusiastic and positive.
    Example: "I'm glad you called. HiGrowth, Inc., is the best company in the industry, and I'm excited about the chance to be a part of your team!"

3. Ask questions in a proactive manner without waiting until the end of the interview to be asked, "Do you have any questions?"
    Example: "What do you see as the major challenge facing your team?" or "What are the most important attributes the person you plan to hire should possess?"

4. Limit your responses to two sentences.
    Example: "Probably the thing I'm most proud of from my time at Downturn Co. was the 45-percent drop in defects I was able to achieve by instituting work teams and quality circles on the production line. We were able to increase orders by decreasing returns." or

"My biggest challenge is to realize that my level of enthusiasm might frustrate others who do not have the burning desire I have to make my company or department successful."

We have heard it all: all the mistakes, all the successes, all the ways to pass and fail a phone screen. Following is a sketch of *the right way to handle the first minute of a telephone interview.*

1. When we call, the person answers the phone with a happy, upbeat voice. We have called hundreds of people who answer with a grumpy hello, and then perk up upon learning it's someone calling in regard to a position at Silicon Graphics. This turns us off right away—it sounds fake. It's a negative trait that we might assume you would demonstrate to a customer, an employee, or someone you don't consider worthy of putting your best foot forward.

2. The job hunter is in a quiet place with time to talk. She sounds composed, confident, and enthusiastic and knows all about the company.

3. She takes the lead in the conversation. She opens with some sincere appreciation—so glad you called, etc. She is enthusiastic and positive about an accomplishment, a newspaper article, a new product, financial results, a new building, a contribution to the community, reputation, or has personally tried or seen products or services in use.

4. She continues to take the initiative after we say why we're calling. She doesn't sit and wait for the assault. She doesn't let us put her on the defensive by allowing us to launch into some quick screening questions. If you don't ask questions first, you'll get trapped into rambling on about details of yourself without getting to the results you can bring to the table. Additionally, if you're asking questions, you're less likely to come across as desperate for the job. Remember, the best thing to do is to find out the needs and requirements of the company.

As an important side note, if you are ever told you're being too aggressive or are asking too many questions, don't get defensive and don't be embarrassed. First, respond by thanking the caller for his feedback. Then apologize and say that you're just so excited about the opportunity that your enthusiasm runs over. Whatever happens, don't stop asking questions altogether—just be less intense. By asking questions in a friendly, upbeat tone, you will warm the interviewer up, and the strained conditions will evaporate quickly. Good questions will be focused on the interviewer's needs, not yours.

Examples:

"Sue, before I start telling you about myself, could you describe to me your ideal candidate for the position?" Many job hunters give up here because they don't meet the requirements; they shouldn't be discouraged at this point. Ask the interviewer whether the experience you don't have is a rock-solid requirement. If it is, ask why; if you dig around enough, you'll usually find that many requirements are not show-stoppers. But don't dwell on this; move on to:

"What are you looking for this person to achieve?" By finding out what achievements the manager wants, you will know which of your accomplishments to highlight.

"What is the long-term marketing focus of this company? What kind of growth do you foresee in the nineties?"

"What are your biggest challenges?"

"Is this a growth position? How did it come about?" Basically, you want to know whether someone was fired or whether this is a new position. This information should be filed away. If someone was fired and you get the job, you'll want to find out what they did wrong so you don't make the same mistakes.

By determining what is called the "critical success factors" of a manager, you unlock the power of knowledge. What must go right for the manager to be successful? Where and how can you contribute to that effort? Once you understand the problem, you've hit the jackpot, because now you know specifically how your experience and background solves the problem.

Find Out the Hiring Manager's Challenges or Problems

Job hunter: Which areas are not meeting profitability expectations?

Manager: Truthfully, we've not generated the profitability we anticipated in our customer-service repair program.

Job hunter: Bob, do you see this as a result of productivity or inventory control challenges?

Manager: Actually, it's a situation where both need improvement, but we're not sure which one to concentrate on first.

Job Hunter: We had some similar challenges at XYZ where I worked for the "No Growth" division. Inventories were not being tracked accurately. We implemented a simple incentive program with our field engineers. It improved inventory turnover and increased productivity by 25 percent. Is this a concern for you?

Manager: It sure is. Tell me more about it.

Suddenly it's no longer a phone interview. You're helping Bob solve his problem, which puts you right at the top of the list for coming in for a face-to-face interview. The manager is seeing you in action, and you're being evaluated as a team player almost immediately; the fact that you lack some of the key "must have" requirements doesn't matter nearly as much as it would have if you had played the traditional role of interviewer and interviewee.

If you can get a perspective on what is important to the hiring manager, you can present yourself in a way that will make you important and useful to the hiring manager right away.

Favorite Guerrilla Interview Questions and the Best Ways to Answer Them

As we said in Chapter 1, guerrilla interviewing is an aggressive style that tests your ability to analyze a situation and handle stress, and also shows how you think. Sometimes interviewers ask tough questions; other times they give you difficult situations for which you must devise solutions, and at other times they'll hit you with one reason after another why you can't do the job. Some interviewers might even be purposefully tactless in order to see whether you can keep your cool. In these situations you must not lose your temper or become defensive; you must be concise and articulate, and you must be ready.

Again, the golden rules are to ask for clarifications of questions you are not sure how to answer, and to answer briefly. Speak in short sentences, but don't make the interviewer feel like he's pulling the information out of you. Follow every answer with a question, so that you aren't doing all of the talking and can keep on an even par with the interviewer. The following questions aren't hard to answer if you know what to expect.

"So tell me, what do you know about our company? Why did you send us a resume?" This is easy if you've done your research. Compliment the products, sources, and market position, and say you want to be part of this winning team.

"Why were you laid off?" Be honest, but not bitter or defensive. If you were caught in a downsizing or restructuring operation along with almost everyone else in your group, say so.

"What do you 'bring to the table' for our company? Why should we want to hire you for this position?" This is where many job hunters stumble. If they have not taken the opportunity to find out more about the job requirements, they end up rehashing items on their resume that don't pertain to this particular job. In general, if the job hunter was unable to obtain specifics earlier, he should answer in terms of his outstanding personality characteristics, such as "I work harder and am more motivated to do a good job than anyone else I know." "I am bright and a quick learner. I always am working to be and do the best I can." "I am always willing to roll up my sleeves and do whatever it takes to get the job done right." "I work issues to completion and don't get easily discouraged." "I know this industry. I know your company's outstanding track record. My background, energy, and enthusiasm make me certain I'm

the person for this job." *These are things almost every manager wants to see in the people he hires, regardless of the company or position.*

"How would you describe yourself?" The best job hunters take this opportunity to demonstrate how brief and articulate they can be. A lengthy response always is wrong because it is boring, provides information that could hurt you by showing immaturity or lack of real achievement, and shows little empathy. Great job hunters outline their strengths as they relate to the job requirements and demonstrate these qualities throughout the whole conversation.

- I am a conceptual thinker
- I can think quickly on my feet
- I can assess a situation and take action quickly
- I am highly respected for openness and integrity
- I motivate people positively and effectively
- I am a good communicator
- I have high energy
- I can arouse enthusiasm in my people
- I am tenacious and persistent; I work until it's right
- I work well in a team environment
- I look for new ways to work more effectively and productively
- I try to understand the needs of my external or internal customers and react accordingly
- I am a self-starter
- I manage by walking around—I believe in hands-on involvement
- I am creative, not rules oriented

"What are your goals/ambitions?" Always align your goals with those of the company. "I want to work for a growing, dynamic company and make a real contribution toward its success." "I would like to be working in the industry with a company on top of the marketplace." "My goal is a position with one of the best companies in the industry." In outlining your goals, it's not wrong to show ambition for the future—so long as you don't give the impression you won't be happy in the job for which you're applying. We see many candidates who make it obvious that they're not interested enough in the open job to stay in it, but will be looking for the next position before the ink's dry on their contract.

"Why did you leave [or do you want to leave your last company?" Don't tell us! Just tell us again why you want to work for us. "It's not that I don't like Company J, but I see and hear such great things about Superstar Company and where they are going that I would like to see whether I can add to their success."

Many job hunters have an understandably negative attitude toward their most recent employer, particularly if they were laid off. Interviewers can "trap" job hunters into talking about their feelings, but you shouldn't share any of this with an interviewer. We all want to have positive, enthusiastic employees. We don't want to hire complainers or those who would rather dwell on the bad than work with the good. In growing companies there will be challenges. We look for people who will overcome the petty problems. It is always easier to find fault than praise, particularly if you've been laid off or might be, so take this opportunity to demonstrate how positive you are and say something good about your soon-to-be past employer.

Often after a job hunter has an interview, we hear from the potential hiring managers that the job hunter seems a little beaten down. As we said earlier, the job hunter is always surprised; he never thinks he is coming across badly. So just don't talk about anything negative at all. We speak to many job hunters who think it's okay to speak negatively of their boss or their company as long as the grievance is true. It's never okay. We don't care if your boss was unfair and your company cheated you. It doesn't make you look more virtuous by telling us how bad everyone else is. Your mother was right: "If you can't say something nice..."

"When things weren't going well (didn't make quota, had too many defects, etc.) what did you do to turn the situation around?" Here we're looking for signs that you're coachable, that you get help if you have to. No one wants people who require hand-holding; nor do they need someone who stubbornly refuses to ask for help. In addition, your ability to make a viable plan to overcome the difficulty is being addressed. If you get stuck when things are difficult, you might slow progress down and be a liability, not an asset. You'll notice we don't ask, "Has there ever been a time when things didn't go well?" We know everybody hits rough spots now and then, but we want people who can realize there's a problem, get coaching, develop a plan to fix it, and implement results.

"What do you think are the most important characteristics needed for this position?" If you've done your homework, you should have a pretty good idea of what the manager wants. We ask this question to gauge how well you understand the position and the company. If we're looking for a Human Resources manager who really understands the big picture, and you tell us the ideal candidate should have a micro-management style, we probably won't think you're a good fit. If you're not sure of exactly what we want, refer back to the list of qualifications in the section on successful phone screens. All growing companies want to hire people with these characteristics.

"What is the most monumental thing you've done?" This question has two purposes. First, we want to hear how effectively you can articulate your accomplishments. We've said it before and it bears repeating: *Be brief.*

The second purpose for this question is to determine your ability to achieve. Small companies need everyone to pull more than their own weight, so we want to find out what results we can expect from you. If the accomplishment was due to a team effort, be prepared for a follow-up regarding your particular contribution to the goal. We can determine very quickly whether you were a real factor in the success or just someone along for the ride. If your plant had an overall defect reduction of 50 percent but your division had only a 3-percent reduction, you might be in trouble. It's best to choose a situation that shows you as a strong individual contributor on a winning team.

"Describe an organization or program you started from scratch." This kind of question might require a slightly longer response than two sentences. Nevertheless, you should make your answer as concise and focused as possible. More than one minute is too long. This question also highlights your articulation and achievement skills. Your response also shows how you can take initiative and work with the available materials to build something important. In your response, briefly state the problem and why you chose to start the new process or whatever it was. Then give an overview of what you achieved, some of the challenges you faced, and how you overcame them. Finally, include results of what you built and how it solved the initial problem.

Ideally, you should pick something that matches the goals or challenges of the company with which you're interviewing. Because a phone screen can be a stressful situation, you might forget some of your best examples during the conversation if you don't think about them beforehand. You should take 30 minutes or an hour as part of your preparation to review your accomplishments, match them to the challenges you've uncovered in your target companies, and write out concise analyses of each situation.

"What do you see as the biggest challenge of this job?" Here we are looking for evidence of strategy and more understanding of the position and the company. We ask many questions to probe your knowledge of our situation because we don't have time to train someone who doesn't really understand the company culture or the job.

When we were looking for a Human Resources manager, we asked someone this question. We had described the fast-paced, entrepreneurial environment and the lack of a strict hierarchy. She replied that the biggest challenge would be to put all the rules and procedures in place to develop a proper structure. Wrong! The biggest challenge is to stay ahead of the game and remain flexible while everything is moving so quickly.

All these are general questions and answers. When the interviewer gets more specific to your background, describe your accomplishments in terms of requirements of the job for which you're applying.

Talk about your accomplishments parallel to the challenges the group, department, or organization faces today. Hiring managers want to know what you can do for them. Explore the problems and find out why they are challenges or why a specific attribute is critical to this position. Again: Think about your interviewer continuously. What has made her day go right, and what has made it tougher? Talk about what you can do for her by telling what you've done in the past. If asked for a specific example of an accomplishment, it sounds best if the job hunter describes a problem and then how he or she solved it. Again, the briefer the better.

> Job Hunter: We had a similar problem with an increasing number of customer complaints regarding service response time. (Remember to think of a problem the company you're talking to probably also has.) I worked with two other departments and we developed and implemented a new plan that decreased complaints by 50 percent in one year.

Describe the problem, the action you took, and the result, preferably in measurable terms. This formula keeps the job hunter from rambling on in an attempt to "say the right thing." *Successful job hunters are always able to tell prospective employers what they can do for them from the employer's point of view.*

Remember, if the interview takes on the wrong momentum, and you feel like you're being "grilled," don't let it go on too long. Always interject with your own questions, so that you're not talking much. Ask questions the other person will enjoy answering. Good questions allow the interviewer to talk about his or her accomplishments or background.

"What is your competitive advantage over Company X (a competitor)?"

"How long have you been with the company, and what do you like most about it?"

"How did you come to this position?"

The best way to end the conversation is to ask first, "Could you tell me where you are in your search for this position?" Or "Where would you rank me in terms of other candidates you've talked with?" Then, ask, "What is the next step in the process?"

"Joan, this has been most helpful for me, and I appreciate your insight on the company. You've made it even more clear to me that I'd like to be part of this team. Where do we go from here? How do you see my chances?"

Don't let the interviewer get off the phone without finding out if you're going to be passed on to the next step. Those who wait for the next call can wait forever.

Biggest Phone-Screen Mistakes (And How to Avoid Them)

We've told you the best way to handle a phone screen and the tough questions interviewers ask. In summary, we want to list the most common mistakes we see and how to avoid them. These are the show-stoppers, things that can knock you out of the running even if you look qualified "on paper."

Talking too much. Repeating your strengths to us or explaining a point of your background in detail doesn't bring you closer to the goal of winning a job. Dominating the discussion shows a lack of empathy and maturity. Ideally, you and the interviewer are on an equal level discussing mutual challenges facing the department, company, or organization. Give and take in the conversation reinforces your confidence and knowledge.

Using the conversation to rehash your resume. If an interviewer has your resume, assume they know what you've done. Don't repeat your background unless you're asked a specific question. By stating the obvious, you're wasting valuable time better used to emphasize specific experiences that fit what the company is looking for. (This is done after you've probed sufficiently to understand how you could fit into the organization.)

Selling yourself without taking the time to understand our needs. If you begin to speak without understanding what the company is looking for, you miss an opportunity to demonstrate your ability to listen and your knowledge of the potential employer. Step into the interviewer's shoes and find out what is most important to him or her.

Knowing little about the target company. This means you can't describe why you would be successful there. If you want to work for Northern Telecom, for instance, you need to be able to say why they should consider you for the position. Often an interview ends because the candidate cannot describe why he or she wants to work for the company.

Bad-mouthing or being negative about your former employer. Any negative discussion of your boss, your former company, or your industry puts the interviewer off. Instead of a detailed description of how your boss or company wronged you, express your enthusiasm for the company with which you're interviewing. Congratulate them on their successes and speak specifically about why the company is competitive.

Asking about benefits, vacation, or trying to negotiate salary before we're even interested in you. If you aren't sensitive to how a company perceives you for a certain job but start asking about benefits, you will make the wrong impression. Think how annoying it is when a salesman starts asking you how you want to pay for an item, or where you want it sent, before you have even decided to buy it. Be empathetic!

Being argumentative or defensive about a weakness. We have witnessed many talented job hunters lose their opportunity to turn a *no* into a *yes* by being defensive about a weakness. If they had listened, accepted the feedback, and then asked a clarifying question, they might have actually demonstrated why they should be selected for the position. Thoroughly understand the objection, state it, and dissect it. Many times the interviewer will learn how your "perceived deficiency" is actually a strength.

Insulting the interviewer. A job hunter can quickly see his chances diminish when he belittles or insults the interviewer. An insult can never be recovered from gracefully. This might seem obvious, but it is amazing how many times it happens. We might not come to terms today, but why ruin your chances for an opportunity in the future?

One candidate we interviewed had a second phone screen with someone else from our group. Not knowing the second interviewer worked with us, the candidate began by describing how he thought we had bungled the handling of his resume. He went on to deny the validity of the hiring manager's objections to his qualifications, suggesting that if she couldn't see his worth, she has a problem. [It's always a good idea to ask the interviewer's relation to those with whom you've already spoken.] Remember, though, that hiring managers don't want to hear negative comments about anyone, even if from a different organization.

Not realizing who all the decision-makers are. In our phone interviewing process, a job hunter might speak with two to five people before winning a face-to-face interview. Each person in the process has input and can put you in the "no fit" category. Be professional and courteous to *everyone* you speak to during the interview process. We see dozens of candidates perceive someone as "not important" and act accordingly. It's the off-the-cuff comment in a tense voice that can ruin an otherwise positive image, such as: "I've already received *that* recruiting package. You were supposed to send me something different" to an administrator, or: "I can't believe how long this process is taking. What is taking you guys all this time to make a decision?" to a peer of the job hunter. Or, "How your boss can't see that my kind of experience is just what you need is beyond me. She must be crazy to want someone who…" to a Human Resources staff person. Any hint of rudeness, or of a negative or condescending attitude will sink your opportunity fast—even if the comment isn't directed to the hiring manager!

In this chapter, we've showed you how to pass the phone screen with flying colors. In order to be successful you must be constantly aware of what is happening on the other end of the line. We've said it a hundred times, but we'll say it once more:

> **Be prepared,**
> **be focused,**
> **be brief,**
> **and ask questions.**

Visualize the interviewer's situation. He is probably in an office with many distractions vying for his attention. You can't bore him with extraneous details or you'll lose his focus. Managers might have six other candidates to call before lunch, so they'll be taking as little time as possible to weed you out. If you don't ask questions, the interviewer will assume you don't understand the company or the position. He wants to find out whether you'll be an asset to his company. You must demonstrate that you understand his business and have taken the time to identify its challenges. The interviewer doesn't have time to explain things that you should have learned on your own. Does all this sound heartless to you? It shouldn't, if you remember that every company making this effort to hire the best becomes a stronger company with more jobs to offer.

You can pass the phone screen and move on to the next step by using these techniques to put yourself in the interviewer's shoes. This is the step that all the research, networking, and practicing is for. You've done the work and you know the drill; now go out there and impress them.

CHAPTER 9

How to Turn a "No" into a "Yes"

Do you...

♦ ...sometimes think an interview or phone screen went well, but wonder why it never went any further?

♦ ...wonder what goes on after you've had an interview or phone screen?

♦ ...wonder why Joe Smith got the job when you were much more qualified for the position?

♦ ...ask yourself whether you should just sit and wait for "them" to get back to you after an interview or do something else?

♦ ...want to know what kinds of things interviewers of these hiring, dynamic companies look for in an interview?

♦ ...wonder whether (and how) you can get back in the running after being told "no"?

What the interviewers are looking for in a job candidate can be easily summarized. We would love a "perfect fit." What we usually get, however, is a less than "perfect fit" who demonstrates clearly superior communication skills. Most job hunters think they know what these skills are, but most never demonstrate them. We'll teach you how to prove that you can competently handle any job and demonstrate your outstanding personality characteristics. It's easier than most people think. Job hunting is not so different from other situations; people are simply being taught the wrong techniques. We know, because we hear the mistakes every day!

Everyone thinks that after they've had that first interview with the hiring manager, and it appears that it was a mutually positive encounter, the offer is in the mail. Not so! This is another strategic point where many job hunters get lost and end up with a "Dear John" letter a month later. Or, they are told, "We'll be in touch." They finally start calling back, but no one returns their phone calls. It's another important area that the experts rarely discuss. We'll talk about what goes on behind closed doors after the interview. We will discuss who gets the offer and why, and what the job hunter can do after the interview is finished to increase his or her chances of moving on to the next step.

Job hunters who make a great impression make people want to hire them. They know people hire those they like and feel comfortable with. They are aware of subtle opportunities to impress us and other hiring managers positively. The new rules we will share in this chapter have positive effects on a hiring manager's perspective of you. They are not our theories. They are simple "people skills" that most of us know, but may forget to apply in the quest for going after what we want. The job hunters who remember to use them see miracles happen.

We hear a short replay of most interviews with the job hunters we pass on to Silicon Graphics; a typical hire goes through about ten interviews. So we know what works with us and what works with others, too—and it's the same. We hear what impresses hiring executives and what doesn't. We have seen the application of the following principles turn around the progress of hundreds of job hunters. Here they are.

How to Make the Hiring Manager Like You

These needs have to do with being understood and feeling important. As Stephen Covey points out in his *7 Habits of Highly Effective People*, almost all of us want other people to understand us, and almost all of us want to feel important. Not many people try to meet these needs. The few who do we almost always like. So what generally happens in an interview is as follows:

Two total strangers engage in a brief discussion to decide whether one person (the job hunter) should become a part of the team and form a long-term relationship with the interviewer. It's rather like deciding in sixty minutes whether a stranger should be your wife or husband.

We find that most of these prospects for long-term relationships are trying hard to make sure we understand them, who they are, what they can do, and how incredible they are. But we're sitting here with our own unmet needs. If our needs are not met, we're not going to pick you for a partner, no matter how great your technical fit is. If both people in an interview are trying to be understood and feel important, the two never will desire a long-term relationship together.

It's just like a date. Have you ever been on one in which the other person constantly talked about himself, what he likes, what he does, how great he is? It's really unpleasant. An interview situation is no different. Many job-hunting books promote one-way communication skills—how to dump everything you can in the shortest amount of time into a hiring manager's head. They couldn't be more wrong!

In our four years of recruiting and hiring for Silicon Graphics, we have never had a hiring manager tell us that the job hunter asked too many questions or didn't talk enough about himself. More than half the time they tell us:

"John talked too much."

"Joe did a ten-minute monologue."

"She never asked me what I was looking for in this position."

We love people to be interested in us and to help make us feel important! So the job hunter needs to make sure he or she is trying to be interested in understanding his potential employer, not vice versa. So many job hunters tell us, when we tell them they talked too much, that they thought the hiring manager would want to know all about them. A resume provides the technical details; the rest of the interview is more of a mating game. Do I like this person? Do I want her to be a part of my company? Use your best tactics to get someone to like you instead of trying to sell your qualifications.

Being "understood" begins by understanding the person's company on the high level and works its way down to understanding the requirements for the particular job. Most job hunters describe their needs and their backgrounds before taking the time to understand the needs of the interviewer. We've read about lots of psychological strategies for figuring out the type of person you're interviewing with and customizing your approach. We believe it's too complicated, and therefore ineffective, to approach people in this way. Job hunters don't need to psychoanalyze anyone. They just need to ask enough questions so they are articulate about why their skills and experience match the requirements of the position.

The other way great job hunters make a good impression is by making the interviewer feel important. This is not shallow flattery, as many people might think. Asking good questions is one way to make someone feel important. The job hunter is deferring to "the higher authority," and it demonstrates that the job hunter respects and honestly desires this person's ideas and opinions. It all goes back to listening rather than talking first.

Another excellent way to make people feel important is to make them feel good about themselves. In an interview this can be done by complimenting the company, giving sincere appreciation for their time and attention, and acknowledging their success, good ideas, approach, or any other positive point that comes from the conversation. Make the effort to find out about the interviewer's accomplishments and successes. If the job hunter is busy harping on his own greatness, he'll miss important opportunities to make the interviewer feel important.

Just remember, we talk to hundreds of job hunters a week who are busy calling prospective employers every waking minute—and they haven't had an offer in six months. Why? After talking to them, we can say most of them are only interested in what they want; They have no idea how to communicate anything else to us. Savvy job hunters answer after taking the time to research the company, the job, and the interviewer, and they effectively demonstrate their interest in someone else's needs rather than only their own.

Why Some People Move to a Second Interview

Feedback from many interviews with other hiring executives led us to another interesting insight. Successful job hunters are patient; they listen and probe. Part of this patience involves probing any negative comments or "vibes." Many job hunters dislike probing hesitancies and negative comments because they are afraid of what they'll hear. But if the interviewer doesn't think the job hunter understands his possible concerns and objections, he or she probably will not be hired. The savvy job hunter knows everything needs to come out of the interviewer. All needs, concerns, problems, and objections must be aired for the job hunter to identify areas where they have even more to offer than they initially thought. Some tell us how great they would be for the job before they even understand what the job is. The best job hunters always make us feel understood and important by asking about our (or Silicon Graphics's) ideas, knowledge, goals, and needs. An interviewer shouldn't be "sold to." Most people don't like to be "sold to." They like to buy or choose something of their own free will. Potential employers are no different when choosing a new employee.

In summary, job hunters who get the interviewer to like them and want to hire them understand how the mating game works. It will be the person who represents the least risk in terms of probable success on the job. This is the job hunter who understands the interviewer's business and who wants to understand and meet the interviewer's needs. Obviously they also are a decent technical fit, an aspect that comes out primarily during resume screening.

Successful job hunters all have one thing in common: They take the temperature of the interviewer. In order to move to the next step, great ones always ask what the process is at the end of each interview, whether on the phone or in person. They are not afraid to find out where they stand. Here are two crucial questions all job hunters should ask. They are:

+ How many more people are you planning on talking with?
+ I know it's hard to remember one of the first (last/middle) people you talk to, but I am committed to doing everything I can to work for you (your company). Is there anything you can recommend for me to do in order to move to the next step?

They always find out exactly what the next step is. If it's another interview, they ask for some coaching. "Tell me about your manager, Ms. Frazier. What kind of person is she?"

How to Turn a "No" into a "Yes"

Great "doers" in life never really hear the word no. They know that "no," no matter how many times said, can be turned into "yes." We say "no" to people all day long—it's our job. But some job hunters can turn around our "No, we're not interested."

In order to turn it around, you need to learn what objectives the manager has for the person she is planning to hire. Unsuccessful job hunters seldom take a temperature. They don't ask what the next step is and whether they'll be moving on to it. They think that after we hang up the phone, we'll think about them more and reach a decision. *No—the decision is always made while we're still talking to them.* Successful job hunters tell us they know they won't get another shot to turn us around, so they will not say good-bye. Now they can at least try to turn it into a yes.

When you ask whether you are going on and have trouble getting a clear answer, assume that something is wrong and they don't want to tell you. At this point you can't be afraid to probe. Ask follow-up questions, such as, "I sense some hesitancy. Please share it with me; maybe there's an issue or question in your mind I can help clarify." Some job hunters will then, as soon as we get five words out regarding our concern, interrupt with their clarifications. They are sunk again. This is the wrong way to handle an objection.

> *Interviewer:* John, you seem qualified and talented, but I'm really looking for someone with more experience in the area of cost-basis accounting method because...
>
> *Job hunter:* No, you're wrong, I really have had...

If you assume we're wrong or challenge the validity of our objection, do you make us want to agree with you? Of course not; we might just dig our heels in deeper. Another typical response is anger, and then telling us we're wrong. Instead, listen to us fully. Ask clarifying questions such as "Why do you think that's important?" Always acknowledge that we have a good point, even if you believe we're stupid and dead wrong. Validate our opinion—make us feel important.

If you can uncover the reason for the negative response, you have a great opportunity. Agree with the interviewer's objection and ask qualifying questions. Following are several better follow-ups to objections.

"That's a good point. You must have thought about that. Could you share your reasoning with me?" or

"How did you come to your decision?" or

"Could you share with me what factors determined your decision? or

"Could you elaborate on that?"

"Do you have any concerns about me and my ability to do this job?"

Following is an example.

Job Hunter: Susan, thank you for taking time to share with me your ideas for new research methods. How do you feel my experience matches your requirements?

Interviewer: You have some good experience, but we might need someone with more specific experience related to statistical analysis in an industry setting.

Job Hunter: Could you share with me what specifically concerns you?

Interviewer: Sure. You have never worked in this industry environment.

Job Hunter: Yes, you're right. My experience has been focused in an educational setting—I can see how an industry focus has differences. What do you feel are the most important attributes of industry experience?

Interviewer: In industry, our situation changes constantly. We're directed by our customer.

Job Hunter: Yes, flexibility is very important. How do you see flexibility impacting the daily priorities? Do you see not only flexibility but also the ability to do what it takes to make the difference?

Interviewer: Exactly. You see why it is so important.

Job Hunter: Your customers expect the best and they want it now. My career has been built on my ability to be flexible, as we discussed in my handling of the XYZ situation. My managers always have pointed out my capability to get the job done with no questions and a willingness to do anything without thinking something was beneath me. Is that the type of flexibility and roll-up-your-sleeves initiative characteristics you're looking for?

Interviewer: Maybe it does make sense for John to talk to you also. I might have been hasty in my earlier assessment.

Don't get into an argument; you will never win. If you get a more personal objection, such as "I didn't think you did a good job talking about your strengths in...," apologize. "You're right, I want to apologize; it is helpful for you to bring that to my attention. Most people never take the time to review with candidates how they did." At this point, we're thinking we really liked the way you accepted criticism; you might be okay. You made us feel "important" by agreeing with us. If you disagree, you might end up with more "points" and you might even prove that you're right, but we interviewers won't like you any better for it, and we still won't want you to be part of the team.

Another example of a successful response: "Yes, you're right, I understand your concern about hiring someone who has changed jobs three times in the last seven years. I am now aware of where I went wrong in hastily taking the highest bidder that came along, and I am determined to do all my homework on a company and join the best, such as yours, this time. You certainly made the right choices. I wish I could have done as good a job."

Another crucial point: Never make excuses. It's always irritating to hear excuses. Just acknowledge the objection, try to turn it around, and move on.

> *Interviewer:* I'm concerned that you haven't been employed for more than a year now.
>
> *Wrong:* The economy has been terrible, my industry is in a negative spiral; no one wants someone with my experience or lack of experience (a new graduate).
>
> *Correct:* You're right: I would wonder too if I were you. I made some mistakes, such as relying on search firms to do the work I needed to be doing myself. I have finally figured out that people find their own jobs and have to work hard to find them.

One job hunter, Sarah Lanning, successfully used these methods to turn a rejection into an acceptance. The following case study and letter demonstrate how well these methods really work.

College Case Study: Sarah

Sarah, a liberal-arts major who was graduating in two months with honors from a prestigious college, had been continually rebuffed in her job-search effort to be a reporter. Sarah learned in her job hunting that experience was what counted most in finding a journalism job. Even internships were highly competitive—everyone expected a lot of examples of published work. She wanted to find at least a part-time job that would help her get more writing and editing experience, but her initial lack of experience made this impossible.

Sarah started working at the student newspaper, having finally understood the importance of experience to potential employers. From this and from part-time editing of a book about investments, Sarah concluded that she preferred editing to reporting. She decided to try to become a copy editor: The pay was the same or better as the pay for reporters, but the field seemed a little less competitive.

She applied for several newspaper positions all over the country in the fall of her senior year in school and received several rejection letters. Finally she was waiting to hear from the one place where she really wanted to work, the largest and best newspaper in the local area.

A friend and classmate of Sarah's who had done a reporting internship there the summer before and was currently working at the newspaper full time tried to find out how the selection process was going and to recommend Sarah, with whom she had worked on several writing projects in the past. The friend learned that Sarah was among the final three contenders for the position. Sarah soon received formal notification in the form of a letter from the hiring manager that she had not gotten the internship.

Sarah asked the advice of the authors of the investment book she was editing after she told them about her difficulties, and they encouraged her to keep trying. Sarah was feeling very discouraged at that point, and was not sure she was capable of doing this—after all, she was very shy. But the authors pointed out that she had nothing to lose.

On their own initiative, based on their desire to "help," the authors wrote Sarah a glowing letter of recommendation (attached) and faxed it to the hiring manager at the newspaper.

Sarah wrote a letter back to the hiring manager, thanking her for considering her. She also described how she had taken on new responsibilities at the student newspaper (becoming co-chief of the copy editors in an effort to get more experience and asked for the hiring manager's advice. Would this new experience make her a possibility for part-time work at the newspaper? If not, what papers in the area did she need to try first in looking for a job?

Sarah called the hiring manager a few days after she had faxed this letter and left a follow-up message on her voice mail, asking her to call. After a second message, the hiring manager called Sarah back. She was very encouraging, and suggested that Sarah call the head of the copy editors and ask him about work. Sarah really felt like a pest calling him, but she had two internal references now, and after a few days of getting her "nerve up," she finally did call and leave a message (for which she had written a script in advance). He called back the same evening and asked her to come in for an interview the next week.

Sarah went to the interview and was offered a job, starting "as soon as possible." She was surprised and happy—her career in newspapers had finally begun! She recognized at last the importance of persistence and flexibility and was determined to work as hard doing her job as she did getting one. Her only problem now is indecision. While she had been trying to get a job at the newspaper, she also had written, on the advice of her brother-in-law, to an old friend of his who was the managing editor of a magazine in the Washington area. She sent her resume and wrote asking for advice about where he thought she should look for work. When she called him to follow up, he asked if she would be interested in interviewing for a position at his magazine. It turned out that circulation had increased sevenfold in the last two years, and they needed more copy editors. Now she is trying to decide what to do—a beautiful predicament for someone who, only two months before, expected to graduate and be unemployed.

Jennifer O'Donnell
Catherine Sharrard
Home Financing
425 Main Street
Teaneck, N.J. 07666

January 27, 1994

Julie Jennings
Assistant Managing Editor for Hiring/Development
The Gazette
210 Flower St.
Hackensack, N.J. 07601

Dear Ms. Jennings:
First, we would like to say congratulations on the work you are doing at the Bergen Record. We have been impressed by what we've seen and heard about you.

We understand that you are considering Sarah Lanning for a position at The Gazette. After receiving the resume she sent you, we feel an enormous compulsion to represent more fairly Sarah's work for us over the last year. We owe Sarah a great deal of our success and we would like to help her in any way we can.

Investment Times is publishing an 80,000 word book titled *A Home Companion to Investments* in November of this year. Sarah has worked twelve-hour days and weekends doing all of the editing for this book. She has the ability to grasp mundane facts and turn them into a "must read on." Sarah has edited articles in several trade publications for us, including *Careers for the Investor*, whose circulation includes the top thirty graduate schools in the country and their students.

Sarah is truly an overriding force behind our success with all of our publications. Sarah has also edited many articles written by us.

In summary, we can't say enough about Sarah's skill as an editor and writer. As a person, she has a "can do anything" attitude. She works all hours to completion, and she is a true contributor and professional in every sense.

We will follow up with a phone call to cover any further questions you might have. Thank you for considering Sarah.

Sincerely,

Jennifer O'Donnell

Julie Jennings
Assistant Managing Editor
for Hiring Development
The Bergen Record

Dear Ms. Jennings,

Thank you for considering me as a copy editing intern. I sympathize with the difficulty you must have had choosing from so many able candidates.

Since I applied for your paper's internship program, I have become the co-copy desk editor of my university's student paper, The Brazen Bugle. This means overseeing other copy editors, reading every word of the paper two or three nights a week, and helping to write headlines. Mainly it means responsibility, hard work, and tireless devotion to detail. The opportunity to do this has sharpened my editorial eye, as well as my ambition to copy edit at the best paper in the state, yours. Therefore I write to ask your advice, in particular about the following:

Will this additional experience make me a possibility for any copy editing positions that might open up?

Are there any likely to do so in the next year?

What else can I do to improve myself as a candidate for such a position?

Are there any other obstacles I need to overcome to be considered as a serious candidate?

I will be calling in a few days to make sure you received my letter. I realize that you are busy; five or six minutes of your time to discuss these questions is all I need. Your advice would really be a great help to me. Thank you.

Sincerely,

Sarah Lanning

P. S. The authors of the book I edited feel I did not do justice to my editing experience in my resume, which they saw. Therefore, they will be writing you a letter also.

Following is a voice mail script that followed the letter that was sent.

Hi, Martin. This is Sarah Lanning. You may recall that I was one of the people who applied for the summer copy editing internship at your paper. Well, I wasn't chosen, but I admire your paper a lot and would still like to work for it someday. Julie Jennings suggested that I contact you about the possibility of working on the copy desk in the future. I would really enjoy talking with you about this. Please give me a call when it is handy for you to do so. My number is 555-9898 and I can be reached Tuesdays and Thursday nights at the Brazen Bugle at 555-6855. Thanks very much.

How to Go around a Roadblock or Obstacle

If, after you use all the appropriate ways of moving forward in the process, one individual is not allowing you to progress further, the best strategy might be to go around this person. You might need to go above or sideways to create interest. We have often told a job hunter, "You are not the right match for this position." Some people, instead of simply taking "no," have found other ways to get the hiring manager's attention. An easy way in most circumstances is to find out more about the position from the assistant or someone who works in the department. Sometimes a note and your resume faxed directly to another hiring manager with a follow-up phone call might get you the interview.

Strategies to Win the Offer

In the negotiation process, winning a job is not a matter of luck. Even when the decision is down to three people, coming in second place doesn't leave you with much. *You must focus to win.* It is easier to compete on an inside track.

To do this, you need inside information. *A "coach" can provide valuable information on what you need to do to secure the job.* Find out where you are in the competition. Your best coaches are the people you first talked to—the Human Resources manager, peer, or initial screener who supported you as a possible hire. Ask to have lunch with them if possible.

> *Job Hunter:* Susan, your insight has been most helpful. Your ability to articulate the needs of the department provided excellent background for me.
>
> *Coach:* Thank you. I'm glad it helped you out.
>
> *Job Hunter:* Susan, I'm meeting with John Jay, the hiring manager. Could we get together for lunch so you could share your ideas on the philosophy of finance for ABC?

Coach:	I only have 30 minutes.
Job Hunter:	How about Friday? We could meet at the company cafeteria.
Coach:	O.K.

At the next meeting, gain rapport and an ally. Ask for your coach's opinions on how the company does business. What is the orientation for customer satisfaction? What are the priorities of the business? What must go right for the company, department, or organization to be successful? After you have gained her trust and showed her that your objective is not only to secure the job but to understand the needs of the business, ask specific questions about your prospects for landing the job.

Job Hunter:	Susan, you've clarified for me why ABC is such a great company with the zeal for excellence in design, manufacturing, and customer service. No wonder they are leading the industry.
Susan:	Yes, ABC is an amazing company.
Job Hunter:	That is exactly why I am considering this team. Could you share with me what the decision criteria will be for selecting the candidate?
Susan:	We're looking for the best fit and for the person who can grow into this job and contribute to our 50-percent growth.
Job Hunter:	Susan, we've had some more time to spend together. How do you see my ability to fit this job?
Susan:	You seem to have a good grasp of our company, but it's tough competition these days.
Job Hunter:	How many candidates are you down to? Where do I fit in?
Susan:	It's down to three candidates. I'm not sure where you are, but I don't think you're the leading candidate.
Job Hunter:	Could you give me some clues as to why I'm not considered the best person for the position?
Susan:	Well, you don't have as much experience as one of the other candidates.
Job Hunter:	How important do you think this additional experience is? Is Mr. Jay the only one who feels this way? Is there any advice you could give me on what I need to do to demonstrate to Mr. Jay that I'm the right person for this job?
Susan:	You might want to get someone to give you a reference from your last position. Customer references carry the most weight with him.

By showing interest and asking for advice, you are getting clued in to what you must do to win the job. As you gain a coach, they become interested in your ultimate success. Nurture your coaches—be appreciative, and keep their time restraints in mind.

If your coach helps bring a new superstar into the organization, she is ultimately rewarded for her contribution. Both the organization and you will benefit. Let your coaches know that if they help you out, you won't let them down. Your future contributions will be further evidence of their own excellent decision-making abilities.

You must not only ask for coaches, you must also cover the other decision makers in the process. There might be as many as three kinds of decision makers in the hiring process. The rules have changed. Ten years ago, one or two people might have been involved in the hiring process. Today, up to a dozen or more individuals have input on who gets the job.

The hiring process includes both decision makers and influencers. A decision maker has the authority to approve. The influencer not only might suggest you be hired, but also might have sufficient authority to say "no." There is normally a hierarchy of decision makers. You can sometimes win if you can convince the hiring manager or even the hiring manager's boss you are the right person, but *a lower-level supporter can help (Fig. 9.1).*

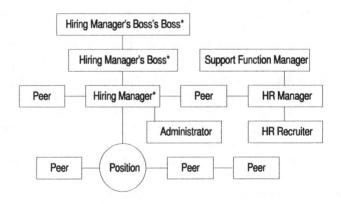

Fig. 9.1.
The hiring organization. An asterisk (*) represents an ultimate hiring decision maker.

This organization chart represents the actual number of individuals involved in a specific hiring process. As the job seeker, you must be prepared to ensure that each one of these decision makers is in favor of your joining the team. Be prepared to call each one proactively. Diagram the decision process.

Where do you see areas of caution? Is the hiring manager comfortable with you? What about her boss and the person in Human Resources? If you don't receive nearly unanimous support, you might not win the offer.

Take the Bull by the Horns

After the interview, have your references call the hiring manager on an unsolicited basis. Specifically ask them to address what the company might feel are your weaknesses. Try to identify someone you know who might have a former or present association with your potential employer, and have them act as a reference for you. A hiring decision is a business decision based on risk. Lower the risk factor by making yourself a known commodity rather than a complete stranger.

Call each person who might have any input in the decision and express your interest and enthusiasm for the position. Ask each person how you meet his or her perspective of the best candidate for the job. If you encounter negative feedback, take the opportunity to understand why this particular individual is not willing to give you a 100-percent endorsement. If you express appreciation for her concern and ask her more questions, you might demonstrate your ability to listen and be coached. If you understand the objection, you might be able to turn it around.

Consider Chris's situation. Chris was finishing her medical residency at the Mayo Clinic and applying for positions in private practice. She focused her efforts on a practice in Sacramento, CA, where she thought she had successfully negotiated an offer. There were five physicians in the group, and it was suggested that Chris keep communications directed to only one of the partners. The offer was made verbally, and Chris had two weeks to make a decision. At the end of the two weeks she called back to accept the offer—and found out that they had given the position to someone else because they perceived that she wasn't interested. It was too late, and there was no recovery of the position. The one partner was concerned, and because he hadn't heard from Chris until the last minute, he assumed Chris had lost interest in the position. After failing to get this job even though it had been offered to her, Chris vowed she would correct her mistakes the next time by being proactive in expressing her interest and by communicating with all the partners to let them know her intentions.

The second group she approached was a group of 16 physicians. Instead of relying on one or two partners to do her communicating for her, she called each of them more than once to ensure that her tenacity, enthusiasm, and interest were understood. Chris beat all seven other competitors (all with more experience) for the position. Her proactive style made the difference.

The ability to cover all the bases in the decision-making process makes all the difference when you apply for a position that has other contenders.

Keep the interest obvious, not obnoxious. Use the same approach as Chris to demonstrate interest in the company and the team you'd like to join. Excuse your enthusiasm, and restate why you want to join the organization. Sincere exuberance and high energy are always perceived as assets.

Examples of Great Endings

The end of a conversation is the last thing the interviewer hears. It might be the part most remembered. Make sure you go out on a strong note. "This is a great company; I'd like to work for you. If you choose me, I promise you, I won't disappoint you!"

Empathize with the hiring manager: "I understand bringing someone new into your organization is a risk. Making sure you hire the right person is a big decision. Going with me is a decision you can make with confidence." Stop talking here. *Once you make a closing statement, stop talking.* Even if there is a long silence, don't be the person to break it. The interviewer might be about to say, "You're right. Let's bring you on the team!"

How to Get Hired for the "Next Job"

You might not get the job this time, but you might be the top candidate in six months. Maybe they never end up hiring anyone right now. Of the open positions we've interviewed for, at least 25 percent are put on hold for various reasons. But 95 percent of the people we interviewed were never heard from again. The ones who were later hired (three months or one year later) learned where they were in the final list. They took the temperature of their candidacy, and if it was warm, they stayed in touch. Of the ones who called back and re-interviewed at a later date, many actually got an offer! Surprised? Successful job hunters like these keep their name in front of the hiring managers in a nice way. They look for articles or personal items that might be of interest and fax or mail them along over a period of months. They ask how often they should call and keep in touch. In short, they make a little extra effort and think of what the interviewer or hiring manager would like.

How (and What) to Learn from a Rejection

After you have reviewed all objections and concerns and you were not able to receive a commitment to move to the next step, you still can gather some valuable information, because the interviewer should feel a twinge of guilt about still saying no. Take advantage of this by asking for help and suggestions, with the objective of obtaining some more names of companies and contacts. No matter how "stung" you feel by the rejection, don't end the conversation too quickly. Ask follow-up questions like these.

"I would like to ask for your help."

"Are there any other small companies doing well that I should contact, based on my experience?"

"Where would you call if you were me?"

"Do you know any other people I should talk to?"

"Is there a trade association representing this industry? Is there someone at the trade association I should talk to?"

"Who would you recommend I talk with concerning other job opportunities in this company or others?"

Remember, these new names represent a return on investment. You've invested time and effort in this company. Don't end the conversation without gaining something valuable for your hard work.

How to Improve

Always ask, "How can I improve? Is there anything I should do or say differently?" even if the interviewer is moving you to the next interview. Perhaps you are passed on with reservations.

You can easily overcome these reservations if you know what they are. One candidate sensed a hesitancy in us when we told him we'd be passing his resume to the hiring manager. He asked us whether there was a problem, and we mentioned that his listening skills weren't great. He accepted the objection and spent the next ten minutes asking our advice and learning our perspective. He got the job.

This chapter has focused on what to do after the interview to make sure you're passed along in the process. By now you should be identifying a common theme in our approach: You get what you want by helping others get what they need.

In order to power on to the next step, you must create empathy with the interviewer, understand and overcome objections, keep your name in front of the managers, and always seek to improve. In this arena, there's no prize for second place.

CHAPTER 10

A Summary:
How to Beat Your Competition
(Or, How to Propel Yourself
over the Hurdles of
Today's Hiring Process)

In the last four years we have individually interviewed thousands and helped hire hundreds. Everybody knows how ineffective unsolicited resumes are, yet we're not sure why companies are still receiving so many uninvited resumes with no follow-up. We do know what happens to most of them and at what stage of the process the unsuccessful fall out. Our own hiring statistics look something a funnel. For every 10,000 resumes we receive, 58 people are hired. Let's take a look at what happens to the other 9,942 people.

There are essentially five steps to the hiring process in fast-growth companies today. These steps are:

1. Initial resume review
2. Second resume review
3. One to five phone interviews
4. Three to eight face-to-face interviews
5. An offer

How Many Stay in the Funnel?

The jobs we hire for include a broad mix of white-collar professional positions requiring recent computer industry experience, from a human resources manager to a regional sales vice president. For every 10,000 resumes reviewed, only 1,500 (or 15 percent) are passed on for the second step. We told you in Chapter 6 about great resumes and common resume problems we see.

Proceeding down the funnel, of the 1,500 remaining candidates, 750, or 50 percent, get a phone interview. About 400, or 53 percent of those who make it to the phone screening get a face-to-face interview. There is a tremendous lack of information in the available job-hunting guides about the whys and how-to's of a preliminary phone screening. Most "authorities" focus on the candidate's delivery of his or her credentials, instead of explaining the purpose and the process of the phone screen. You know differently now!

Finally, 14.5 percent of the people who get face-to-face interviews get offers. Using techniques we suggest and following the new rules should increase your chances of getting a job with a fast-growth company by about 1,000 percent!

How do the few who make it differentiate themselves? Many of the ones who don't get the job console themselves with the idea that the ones who made it to the bottom of the funnel are just lucky—in the right place at the right time. Our experience says that this could not be less true. Successful job hunters are systematic hunters who work hard and work smart. Those who wait for their luck to turn around will find that it usually doesn't—they will shortly be facing a significant drop in their standard of living. They are simply afraid to try new ways that we see really work. The successful job hunters who make it to the end of the funnel are determined not to follow the losing road. They already know, or learn through trial and error, that doing what the "experts" have taught only places them in a large, highly competitive pool of cutthroat job hunters where their chances of success are slim.

They pull out of the crowd and win the good jobs; they start with a mission. They learn about themselves, and they decide exactly what they want. They focus and act like detectives on a search mission. They put themselves in the hiring manager's shoes and make the manager like them.

Most Common Problems We See from Job Hunters and How to Solve Them

Problem 1: Sending Out Generic Resumes

Why is this a problem? When we receive a generic form resume and cover letter, we know that we are one of at least 100 recipients of this material. We would have to spend an inordinate amount of time deciphering this generic information to see if it can be matched to a position we might be trying to fill. In short, it will not get much of a review. We probably will not call the person because we know, based on our past experience, that he or she will know little about the company and therefore will not be a good fit. For any particular position we want to fill, we look for certain buzzwords in the re-sumes we review. If they are not there, we file the resume. Many fast-growth companies, including Silicon Graphics, use a computer-managed resume sys-tem. These systems store resumes, and can retrieve them through keyword searches. If the key buzzwords we look for are not in the resume, it never will be reviewed even once by any human.

Solution:
    After reading everything he or she can about the company and talking to some people about potential openings, the job hunter should then customize his or her resume to fit the hiring manager or the company's requirements for a position.

Problem 2: Using Ineffective Methods

For example: posted job openings/want ads, search firms, and mass mailings. Why? The competition for a job placed in a want ad or with a search firm is intense. The job hunter will be one of many applicants. We always try to hire without advertising, using search firms, or posting. We know that once the job is advertised, we get a lot of unqualified candidates who need to be weeded out.

Solution:
    We much prefer to receive a resume and voice mail from a well-researched and reasonably qualified job hunter. To us, this really demonstrates initiative, a quality we always look for in trying to fill any job position.

Problem 3: Talking Too Much

We thoroughly dislike receiving or making follow-up phone calls to or from job hunters who bore us with a chronological summary of their life or work history. We are interested only in what they can bring to the table in the future. We won't ask too many more questions if a job hunter's answers take more than a minute.

Solution:
    On the other hand, we enjoy giving our perspective occasionally, but not many people ask for it. They're too busy talking about themselves. Of course, every job hunter should be able to summarize his or her strengths and accom-plishments, but briefly. Ask questions to further define the requirements for the position, and answer questions as briefly as possible.

Problem 4: Having Mistaken Ideas About Networking

Many job hunters think that networking is contacting friends and associ-ates to ask about possible job openings they might know of. Why is this incor-rect? Calling us and asking us if we know of openings or of anyone hiring immediately puts us on the defensive. We ask ourselves, "Who is this person?" We don't know anything about her business qualifications, even if she is a nice neighbor. We certainly don't want to give out any names, because if we send her to the vice president of research and development and she's not an appropriate fit, this will reflect on us.

Solution:
Be humble, and only call asking for advice and help.

Problem 5: Doom and Gloom
The job hunter says something less than positive about:

1. His or her past employer
2. His or her difficulty in finding a job
3. The state of the economy and how terrible it is that companies are having all these layoffs
4. His or her current job or employer.

Why is that a problem? Many job hunters think that stating a fact about the economy or the difficult time new grads have obtaining a job is simply stating a fact. But prospective employers or someone you're trying to ask advice from should never hear any statement that is not enthusiastic, positive, and bright. Anything else will label you in their minds as "Negative." If you're unemployed and looking for a job, our antennas are way up, searching for any less-than-positive responses.

Solution:
No one wants anything less than an enthusiastic, positive outlook from people who are going to be part of the new team. If you had a terrible boss and everyone in town knew it, or if you feel that big corporate America has let you down, or that there are just far too many qualified people on the street— keep such ideas and thoughts among you and your closest friends. Smaller, high-growth companies have lean workforces. There are never enough resources. We rely on everyone to deal with adversity and overcome the challenges. By being positive during your job search, you show the company that you aren't easily discouraged. Instead of denigrating your luck or your last employer, say, "I am concerned about the financial future of my current employer," or "It's not that I don't like Company X, it's that I've heard so many great things about your company, and I want to be with a company that is on the fast track." Neither luck nor external factors determine your destiny; you do.

Problem 6: Making Excuses
Why is this unacceptable? It is another way of coming across negatively. Here are some excuses we often hear:

1. "My boss and I didn't get along; he practically cheated me out of a raise."

2. "I've left three different companies in six years because…" and five minutes later you are still discussing your problems.

3. "I've been looking for over a year because the industry is terrible." (Or other external factors.)

4. "I did that because…" and we hear a list of excuses for saying the wrong thing, having the wrong degree, leaving a company, etc. These add no value to our assessment of your suitability for the job, and they make us think you don't take responsibility for your own actions. No one wants someone who makes excuses for his or her own decisions and tries to blame other people or situations.

Solution:
Make every effort to take credit for your own actions and decisions. This attitude suggests that you are a person who can accept responsibility and is willing to work to improve.

Examples:

"I left company X to go to company Y two years ago, and it was a bad decision on my part. I am determined to do my homework right this time and join a star like you did."

"A better decision on my part would have been to major in computer science. However, I took a lot of those courses and I am positive that not having had it as a formal major will not be a hindrance because I can…"

Problem 7: Leaping Before You Look

Job hunters are focused on telling us about themselves. Many job hunters are taught or think that they need to provide a two-minute summary of their background, qualifications, and things they do well at every opportunity. Why is this a problem? There is nothing worse than having people take up our time without ever asking us about our needs and what is important to us and the other hiring managers. It's next to impossible to sell something to someone without figuring out if they have a need for what you're selling. Many job hunters think they can and should try to create that need, which is fine. However, usually they don't understand that the need is created by desire to know them further because they created a positive first impression.

Solution:
To create a positive first impression, you must be well-informed about the company. This demonstrates that you care and are not just shooting in the dark at anything that comes along. In order to make a good first impression, you should be complimenting some specific items you know about us or the company we're representing. Then you should be trying to ask questions to understand our requirements—what we're looking for. We sometimes think

job hunters don't want to know what we're looking for because if it doesn't fit their background, they'll be out. And if they have us on the phone, they don't want to let us go before they can tell us all about themselves. They forget that we usually have their resume, so we know all the biographical facts. We are just trying to figure out if we like the person and if he or she can bring something good to the organization.

Problem 8: Failing To Focus

We see many job hunters who don't concentrate on a particular type of job, industry, or set of companies. Why is this a problem? The longer you stay unemployed, the harder it will be to obtain a new job, because people such as us start to wonder, Why hasn't anyone hired this person in 18 months? And if the job hunter doesn't focus on a particular type of job in a specific industry and find a few companies at a time, he or she will waste months chasing down leads thousands of others are chasing too. Unless you walk on water, you're better off not competing for all the known jobs. We talk to so many unsuccessful job hunters who think they'll have a better shot if they look for both accounting positions in high-tech companies and marketing jobs in advertising. They think they're doubling their coverage, but in fact they're just diluting their efforts and wasting untold weeks.

Solution:

Figure out what you want to do, then find out what areas have the most growth. Call the Bureau of Labor Statistics in Washington and ask for information about which branches of a particular industry are doing well. Even if you're part of a shrinking industry, as Michael was, there usually are some rising stars within that industry or in some closely related industry. Many people choose dying jobs in a large company in a dying industry because that's what they think they want. It takes them a year of looking before they figure out that these guys just aren't hiring anyone. So, find your focus and stick to it.

Problem 9: Calling Off the Search Early

Many job hunters make a minimal effort to contact people. They feel that if they leave two messages and their call isn't returned, they are being a pest, and they give up. Or, if they are told that their resume was received, and that they'll be contacted if something comes up, they move on. Or, if they are given one objection, such as "You don't have enough experience," they give up. Or, if they get a no from one person in a phone interview, or if one hiring manager just never calls back, they give up and move on. Why is this a problem?

In today's marketplace, tenacity and the ability to "power on" are crucial to success. If you take a no at any point in the process and give up without trying an alternative route, you'll never land the job of your dreams. Only the job hunters who learn to fuse persistence with charm are getting the jobs. If a job hunter expects to obtain a good job today, he or she needs to try all kinds of different and new methods to get in front of a hiring manager—and that job hunter should stay in touch with them once he or she makes a contact in a growing, hiring company.

Managers in fast-growth companies receive calls, and voice mails and are sent resumes every day without any further follow-up. They don't usually have time to call back people who call them when they don't know what it is in regard to. The few that get called back have resumes that are customized for a known job and are well-informed candidates. We receive hundreds of resumes every month that are sent to us in error and should be going to other people in the company. The typical unsolicited resume never even makes it to the desk of someone who could be interested in it; the person who sent it never followed up to see if it was received by the correct person. This kind of mailing is a waste of time and money for the job hunter.

Second, often if we do get into a live conversation or interview, we'll throw out an objection just to see how the job hunter thinks on his or her feet. But many just say, "Okay; good-bye." We don't talk to very many people who are 100 percent qualified for any particular job. It's the job hunters who can push on even when we say, "What about X, Y, and Z?" who win the offers. Even if we say no and really mean it, there are dozens of other people in Silicon Graphics who are hiring, and they could be talking to you about a job. We have job hunters who are turned down by one manager today, only to be hired by another one two months later. You have done a lot of background work by the time you get a phone call. Use that knowledge with other possible hiring managers.

Solution:
Don't let an objection go by until you've understood the entire problem and tried to overcome it. A weekly telephone call several times along with a customized resume should be a standard plan. If you have trouble getting through to the manager, work with the secretary to get him or her on the line. In short, if you hit a roadblock, go over or around it. Don't let it stop you!

Problem 10: Looking In All the Wrong Places

We have noticed that many job hunters are unable to find and focus on the companies where the probability of getting hired is the greatest. Why is this such a problem? Many job hunters spend months sending resumes to, and trying to get a job with, companies that are not increasing their employee population. Many job hunters pursue companies that are decreasing the number of people employed. It is much more difficult to obtain a job with a company that had 10,000 employees last year and has 10,100 this year (1 percent growth) than it is to get into a company that has gone from 150 employees to 200 employees (a 50 percent increase). The 1 percent growth rate does signify an addition of 100 people, but chances are you're competing with a lot more people for those 100 jobs. And within a large company, finding all the hiring managers for the 100 jobs will be almost impossible. The job hunter almost always gets stuck in a file in Human Resources.

Solution:

If the company is publicly traded (issues stock), it is required by law to publish the employee population numbers in its annual report. You also can ask someone for this information. This is a question with which you can gladly be transferred to personnel or investor relations.

> *Receptionist:* XYZ Company
>
> *Job Hunter:* Could you help direct me to someone who can tell me your change in the number of employees from last year to this year?
>
> *Receptionist:* Who is this and why do you want to know?
>
> *Job Hunter:* Oh, I'm sorry, you're absolutely right. This is Joe Job Hunter and I'm just trying to get some background information for a job interview.

or,

> Oh, I'm sorry, you're absolutely right. This is Joe Job Hunter and I had talked to someone about a potential job there. I just wanted to get a feel for the company's growth. I'm at a shrinking company today, and I want to make sure I'm not going to the same kind of problem. Do you have any advice for me? (If the person has worked there for any length of time, or it's a smaller company, you'll probably get all kinds of good information.)

You can repeat the same script if you're transferred to personnel. Also ask them if there is any information on the company you could have sent to you. Successful job hunters send their resumes only to hiring managers at companies that they know are hiring and could have a possible use for their talents now, or in the future if there isn't an opening now.

In order to obtain a good job in a reasonable amount of time (six months is a good guess on the professional level), these job hunters focus only on the growing, hiring companies with hot products or services. They spend their time reading and talking to people to find these companies before ever sending a resume. They seldom spend time interviewing for and worrying about jobs in companies that aren't on the fast track, because they know that their chances of being hired are small.

In Conclusion

The rules have changed; no matter how much we'd rather fall into a job than rely on our own initiative, we have to adapt to survive.

To make the change, you must leave your comfort zone. You must develop a mission, so you know where you're going; make extensive preparation, so you know how to get there; and focus on your goal, so you don't get sidetracked.

Today's job hunter needs to engage in new research—really dig for the information in up-to-date sources. Your proactive search involves talking to multiple people—not only as information sources, but as decision makers in an increasingly complex process. It also involves focusing your time and efforts on only a few smaller, high-growth companies at a time.

Another part of the change from the old rules to the new rules is thinking the way the hiring manager thinks. As a hiring manager, you read faxes before you read mail; you take phone calls from informed, complimentary assets before you talk to a total stranger about a job; you're interested in building your organization, not filling a generic slot.

When you think like a hiring manager, you try to understand that manager's challenges and where your strengths fit in.

Remember, for any company today, a decision to hire someone represents a financial risk. You must be able to demonstrate how bringing you on board—your solution—will benefit the company and justify the risk.

CHAPTER 11

Commonly Asked Questions about the Focus Method

The following questions and answers came from live seminars conducted by our organization. We include this information to help answer some of the most common questions asked by job hunters today about the Seven Step Focus Method.

Why will using two knowledgeable compliments induce someone to spend time with me? That seems impossible.

Logically, it does seem impossible. We can only tell you that it works. Many people can say no to one well-researched request; not many say no to two. Because so few people take the time to find out anything about a person or a company and actually pay a compliment, this is an uplifting and positive experience for the person you're talking to. All the "people" experts, from Dale Carnegie to Stephen Covey, tell us, "Make the person feel important—try and understand where he or she is coming from." Take the time to demonstrate your interest before trying to be interesting.

If you say it twice, you are demonstrating that you really mean your compliment—you are not using idle flattery. Try it a couple of times—it's amazing how effective it is.

Why focus on only a few companies at a time?

It might seem as if you are not spreading yourself around enough to find a job quickly. However, our experience shows the opposite. Most job hunters today spend time on many possibilities, trying to get their name and resume in front of as many people as possible, erroneously thinking that things will happen more quickly or that the probability of a "find" is greater. What we hear and see over and over again is that these job hunters are spending most of their time chasing down jobs

♦ In companies that aren't hiring many people at all

- In companies that aren't hiring people like them
- Or in situations where they are competing for a job with hundreds or thousands of applicants

If the job hunter ends up receiving a phone call pertaining to a possible job, he or she has difficulty moving past the first conversation or first interview because he or she cannot effectively articulate a potential contribution. Remember, at least 50 percent of the job candidates we talk with disqualify themselves in the first interview based on their inability to match their skills with our needs. Most of the successful job hunters we have worked with focus their efforts on a very small number of companies at a time and add one new company as one drops out. It works because

1. They aren't wasting time on dead-end, long-drawn-out interview cycles where their chances of success are 500 to 1. Instead, every minute of their time after they have reduced the large group of 200 or more possible companies to three or four is spent talking with companies and hiring managers who typically don't have posted or advertised openings and do not hear from well-researched, well-informed job hunters evaluating opportunities. Hiring managers generally hear from uninformed, desperate job hunters who mail their resumes everywhere hoping to hit a target.

2. The job hunter can maintain a bright, positive attitude because he won't be getting a lot of no's and "Dear John" letters. He is only putting himself in front of hiring managers where he knows the company could be hiring someone like him.

3. The job hunter can articulate her understanding of the company, its competition, and her possible contribution (because of her intense research on the company beforehand).

Job hunters who follow the focus method spend at most four weeks on any given A in their final group before progressing to multiple interviews. If they don't get anywhere, they move the company to the bottom of the A check-back list and add another A company to their active list.

And remember, the successful job hunter focuses on companies where other job hunters aren't looking. Those who focus on a company that is advertising for a position are competing intensely and at length with many other job hunters. It is important to find the smaller, growing companies where the others won't think to look.

Why talk to or network with 500 to 800 people if you are only focusing on three companies at a time?

At first glance, that seems like contradictory information. The pattern of successful job hunters we've worked with generally follows the seven-step focus method in some form. They spend several weeks collecting data on any possible growing, hiring companies in their target or focus industry. They compile a list of companies in their broad industry; competitors, vendors, and suppliers of their current or most recent employees; their friends and acquaintances; contacts at the Chamber of Commerce, newspaper writers; stockbrokers, and others, and they come up with a master list ranging from 100 to 300 companies. If they talk to only two people in each company, they will have from 200 to 600 contacts. Remember, the networking contacts are not necessarily potential employers. They are phone calls or contacts made by the job hunter *for the sole purpose of determining which companies should be on his or her target or focused list.* After the focused list is compiled, the process of determining to which companies the job hunter has the most to offer and which company offers the most to the job hunter continues, and he or she keeps adding more networking calls during this evaluation period. Once the job hunter has decided which companies are most promising, he or she then works on three or four at a time.

You say 50 percent are disqualified on the basis of the phone interview. What do you mean by that? What criteria are you using to screen people?

The day of the phone interview has arrived. You need to be prepared for a call. You should not have sent your resume to someone unless you are prepared to articulate why you sent it and what you can bring to the table; this is focus. Fast-growth companies hire people who have researched them, know them, know something about their products, are enthusiastic, and can't wait to come to work for the company, and can tell them why.

We want to know if you know our company. What value can you add? For example, we advertised for a human resources manager, and we got about a thousand resumes. All the people we called back were from our competitors, such as IBM, Digital, Hewlett-Packard, Sun, and Data General, so theoretically they should have known something about the computer industry and SGI.

I pulled 100 resumes to call for a phone screen, and 90 out of the 100 people, when I asked them why they sent a resume or what they knew about Silicon Graphics, said, "I saw the job posted." At that point, the interview is over. If somebody is not proactive enough to be prepared for a phone call from someone he or she sent a resume to, I'm not really interested in that person. I don't want someone who is just sending out random resumes and hoping to get a phone call.

Some job hunters say, "I'm always prepared if I get to the point of being asked to a face-to-face interview." *What they don't realize is that if they don't pass the phone screen, they don't get the interview.*

How do you handle adversity? Many times we throw out an objection to see how people handle it. "Oh, you don't have enough experience, we're really looking for Big 6 accounting experience." Many just say, "Oh, O.K., bye." We might just want to see how you react to that.

There are never enough resources in a high-growth company to do what needs to be done. Everyone just sort of rolls up their sleeves, gets in there, and works. How do you deal with adversity when someone says, "We can't do that" or "We don't have the resources to deal with that"? Do you just kind of slink away and hope something else comes up? How you handle adversity in the phone interview tells us something about how you handle it in a work environment.

How concisely can you articulate your response? Another thing that a lot of the books teach is to have a two-minute summary of "you." Sell us on you, tell us how great you are; I might say to a job hunter, "Tell me a little about yourself." And five minutes later I'm still listening to this person's outstanding characteristics, and the person has never even asked me what kind of job I'm calling about. You need to step back; you need to be calm enough to say, "Before I tell you about myself, tell me what you are looking for. What is the position you are hiring for? Is this a new position? What do you expect of this person?" If you let me or another hiring manager go on the attack, you are just going to step down, down, down.

When the job listings say a certain skill is required vs. desired, is that a show stopper?

We don't usually split requirements up that way, but some companies do. We had another job, a human resources management position. Our ad said we required an MBA and from six to eight years high-tech experience. The person we hired had only eleven months' experience in our industry. We talked with people from other companies with more experience, but she got the job. Why? Superior communication skills and persistence. She knew how to use persistence with charm. She called the vice president. She was so energetic and enthusiastic, she took it upon herself to visit a couple of our customers to hear from them how great the products and the service were. Then she could give that information back to the hiring manager.

You think you can't compliment people? Don't believe it. If you do your work and it's sincere, they just fall over. Somebody who is less qualified for the job but has that energy and enthusiasm, and has really done his or her homework, will get the job every time.

It sounds more like you're saying that unless you have specific experience in the area of that small company, you can't get hired. In that case, the larger companies seem to be much more flexible about hiring people with different experience because they have the resources to train and to mold people. That might be one reason that they attract more people with less experience than a small company would.

That's a good point. I guess what I go back to is that you have to expand what you think your industry is. Most of you have some kind of work experience. In one position, we wanted eight years of experience, and the candidate had eight months. But, she did other things. She found us. She asked all the right questions—"What do *you* need? How can I help you?" She also kept in touch continuously. She got the job because she didn't give up; she made us like her. She demonstrated great communication skills.

But let me say something about training programs. How many companies are reducing their training programs as part of re-engineering efforts? What is the competition for the training programs in those big companies? You should find out before you waste a lot of time and effort. We've talked to many people who have gotten halfway through a program or just finished their training and been laid off. *There's no substitute for a growing company.*

You also said you hadn't help hire anyone that didn't have experience?

Yes, that is true—but many successful job hunters developed a plan to come to work for their target companies. They found a position that didn't require experience, or they went to work for a fast-growth dealer—and then sought a position after they gained some level of industry experience.

How do you get someone to look at your resume?

Your resume won't get you the job, but it is important. If you talk with the administrator, peers, customers and competitors of your target company so that you know what the manager's challenges are, you can *customize your resume and cover letter.* That gets their attention. It's the follow-up *after* you send your resume that gets your foot in the door. Resumes do not generally get anyone's attention today. Managers in high-growth companies, even if they need someone, are too busy to call anyone. Successful job hunters usually track *them* down.

If you have never heard of one of these companies, how do you recommend finding out what it's doing, especially if it is not publicly traded? Should you call the company and say, "Send me a brochure"?

Yes. Call as a potential investor or as a potential employee. They'll send you information. Again, you are in the driver's seat. Suppose you say, "I'm thinking about interviewing with someone in your company—is there someone there who can send me some information, some press clippings to help me evaluate your company prior to really putting my name in the hat?" All of a sudden, they are interested. You are not just a desperate job hunter. You can also find the title of an executive and call that executive's assistant, and ask his or her advice about how to pursue the company.

The local newspapers also, if the company is really growing, will have quite a few press clippings on that company. A lot of libraries cut news clippings from newspapers and periodicals, and have them filed by company, so you can go seat yourself in front of a file cabinet and look through all the companies in a particular area. Just read the press clippings on them, and if they sound exciting, call them for more information and add them to your list.

In contrast, one of the problems with information from mutual funds is that it typically doesn't have the company location, so you've got to find the headquarters before you can call them. Ask the librarian for the best place to look. Start with the *Directory of Corporate Affiliates*. We won't give you many names of books, because that's what the old guides do, and you can get out of date information. Just ask the librarian, "If I want to find out the headquarters of these companies so I that can call information and get their phone numbers, where do I find it?" They'll take you to the best books.

What's the strategy here? How do you make one phone call lead to another when you are calling these companies?

Successful job hunters are always evaluating the companies, not vice versa. If their business sounds interesting, ask for a time when you can to talk to them. If not, don't ask. Ask yourself, "What do I need to know to approach that hiring manager?" Today, you need to talk to people within an organization to find out what their challenges and concerns are and whether there is a possible job there. If you determine that there is not a position in this company for you at this time, ask what other departments or people might have positions that you could pursue.

Do you counsel people to attack this search differently depending on whether they are currently employed or whether they are in school like I am?

That's a good question. I really don't think so. Obviously your time constraints might be different, and you might have to work harder to convince someone that your background fits their needs if you don't have much experience. But overall, the process is the same. Our most successful job hunters find that the fastest way to great jobs today is to find the hiring manager. Talk to the person where the job is being created! Talk to hiring managers, find out what their needs are and ask them how your background fits in with their needs. You can get hired almost on the spot! In our business, The Focus Group, we have made hiring decisions the same day the individual interviewed. Small companies can move fast. Demonstrating that you can add value to the organization is always important, whether you've got six months or six years of experience.

How do you define the hiring manager?

The person who actually has the job. The person who is going to hire you and have you come to work for him or her.

I'm hearing a couple of things that sound contradictory. You are saying you should talk to these people and ask them how your background fits in with what they are doing or where they are going, but at the same time, you're trying to sell how your background already fits into what they are doing or a particular project. If you have done the research that you're suggesting, you should know that, shouldn't you?

We're suggesting that you ask them for their time so that you'll understand their needs and be able to tell how your background fits in with those needs. You don't want to ask the manager to figure that out for you. There's a difference between asking, "Can you help me understand your challenges so that I can see how my background fits your needs?" and, "Can you tell me how my background fits your needs?" The first is "you"-centered. The second is "I"-centered.

You say to contact the hiring manager. What if you have no clue as to which sector of this company is hiring? How do you find out if a particular manager is, in fact, the person who is looking for someone?

You might not know that right off. You may have to talk to several people within the company to find out. You do know that you have an operations background. You also know what kind of job you want at the company you're going to target. This is where all that preparation and research comes into play. You have to do the research to find which companies are growing, then talk to people within the companies that are growing.

If the company is growing by 50 percent a year, or by more than 30 percent a year, most of its sectors probably need more people. Remember, before you talk to the manager, you should talk to the people who work for him or her. One of the most important questions you'll ask this potential peer is, "Is your manager looking for people?"

Are faxed resumes handled differently from mailed resumes?

That's a great question. Fax is the way to send resumes today. Mail sits in tubs. Faxes get read. Managers like faxes because they are looking for orders or they are looking for information from different parts of the organization. So you'll see them hanging around fax machines, and they'll look at faxes while they're waiting for some great news. But you won't see them hanging around the mail room waiting for mail! When you fax your resume, be sure to use good, laser-printer-style paper. Fancy linen paper with embossed text doesn't fax well, and it won't get you the job.

Is it a problem to do both? Send a fax and follow it with a mailed copy to follow in case something happens?

No, there's nothing wrong with that. Remember, however, always follow up a fax with a phone call to make sure that it has been received.

Is your strategy for approaching a company the same if you are the person who exactly fits the requirements—you've got the eight years of experience, you've got the degrees, you've got whatever the company says it wants?

No, it's the same. It's an easier sell if you've got everything the company is looking for. But the people that were the furthest fit—the ones such as Jan and Mike—were able to come back to us and show us that they had all these other talents that made what was on their resume not as important as who they were as individuals. You still will need to talk to the secretary, peers, and customers to find out what the hiring manager needs, even if you are the perfect fit. Show them that not only do you have the qualifications you also have the desire! For one position, we talked to several candidates who had everything we wanted except enthusiasm. They knew they were a good fit, and they sat back and played hard to get. Well, high-growth companies don't have time for games. We didn't pass them to the next step because we didn't think they were really interested. We aren't suggesting that you appear desperate or sell yourself short—just remember, small companies need to be pursued.

I'm wondering—say the money isn't as good in your target company, but you still feel it's a good company, and you want to get a foot in the door. To what extent do you say you are willing to work for peanuts to get your foot in the door without undermining your value?

We can't stress enough how important it is to analyze the company. In a small company, you may not have the big salary right off the bat. You may, however, have a chance for stock options, equity, or other forms of compensation. What you will have is increased responsibility far beyond your job title, which you might not get in a big company.

On the other hand, there's far less direction and hand-holding in a small company. If you aren't comfortable with a fast-paced environment, a small company might not be for you—but it's still where the best jobs are.

How do you fish out the objections? They are not going to just tell you flat out why they are not interested in you, are they?

It's just part of the process, as you are asking questions. Some of them should be, "Well, what do you think? Does my background fit with what you are looking for? Do I look like I'm the right kind of person?" If the interviewer says no, ask him or her more about it. Get the interviewer talking. You know, when people get objections, their gut reaction is to keep talking and telling the interviewer how wrong he or she is. What you want to do is, acknowledge the objection and then ask a few simple questions. The next thing you know, the person is talking himself out of his own objection.

You mentioned something about Internet earlier. How much goes on Internet as far as recruiting? Are there actually jobs out there? Is that a place to go look as well?

We post quite a few of our technical positions on Internet because those candidates are working on their computers. The number probably will increase over time.

Do job hunters use the computer as a tool for sending cover letters or anything like that?

Well, some do. If a manager is very computer literate, he or she might have access to an e-mail system or something similar. You can ask the secretary if the manager has an e-mail address.

The companies that aren't publicly traded—are they giving equity positions?

It depends on how small they are. The smaller they are, the better the chance of that. What you are hoping for in a small, privately held company is that if you pick the right one—one that is growing and sustainable—you'll have a good shot at getting substantial options when it goes public.

What do you suggest to people in the company when it gets bigger? Do you advise them to get back to something small?

Not necessarily. If the company continues to grow, there's no reason to leave. You want to get in on the ground floor so you can reap the rewards later. You don't want to leave as those rewards start to come in. Also, it looks bad on your resume if you change jobs too often.

What's your opinion of targeting business activity spurts? I've had some success in targeting newly hired managers. There seems to be a correlation between newly hired people and their bringing on additional staff.

That's a very good point. There is a correlation. Most local newspapers will have a section identifying people who've been recently promoted. That might be a good place to look for company and manager names to target. With newly hired managers, almost everybody you talk to will be interested in making changes to suit their ideas. In most high-growth companies, if they don't have a new position now, they will in the next year.

What are some of the biases in small and mid-size companies? As recent grads or a people with a lack of specific industry experience, what is the biggest obstacle we have to overcome?

You don't have enough experience. We want people who can start doing the job the day they walk in. And if you can't do that, you've got to be trained, you have a learning curve. You don't understand the competition. You don't know what the challenges are. It will take you a while to get up to speed, or so we think. If you've done all your homework, however, *before* you come to talk to us, we won't see the lack of experience as that big an objection.

It goes back to trying to understand the business. If you are asking questions about how the business runs and what their goals are, that kind of bias starts to go away. If you are really willing to jump in and understand the business needs and move on, those biases go away.

Say I send an unsolicited letter to a hiring manager at Superstar Company. You've already indicated that he's so busy, he's doing the job of three people. Is he really going to look at that or is he just going to forward it to Human Resources?

You will be blown off. There is no question about it unless you first lay the groundwork and then follow up. This again is where *persistence with charm* pays off. Without it, the hiring manager probably won't take the time to really look at your resume. You can never get someone's attention with just a resume. That's why we advocate this process of making phone calls, talking to an administrator, getting that person inside the company to be your coach and ally. Then suddenly, it's easier to get that hiring manager on the phone when you want to talk to him or her. You can't do that without being persistent and not relying on a single resume to spark the manager's interest.

Say I call and ask for the spelling of the hiring manager's name. What if her name is Jane Smith? If you said, "I don't know how to spell her name," could it backfire on you?

Say, "You know, I always ask for the spelling because you can never be sure with so many different spellings of similar names." But really, nobody calls you on that. And again, what is the worst that could happen to you? You think cold calling is going to be a tough exercise, but you just pick up the phone and do it. It's not as big a deal as you might think. If you just can't find a name, you should look in the annual report for a list of officers and vice presidents. Call one of the higher-level people in the organization and ask to speak to his or her administrator. Say, "Hi, I'm trying to reach the manufacturing manager—I understand you support the vice president of manufacturing. Could you please tell me the name and the fax number for your manufacturing manager?" The administrator will give it to you. If you want, you can even say why you are calling. The administrator will still usually give you the information.

Moving Your Job Search into the "Information Age"

Following are some sources of on-line job postings and career counseling information accessible by modem.

AdNet On-line: Provides job postings, national and international, for many types of companies; usually contains 1,500 to 2,000 listings and is updated twice a week; can be accessed from various subscription services.

Dr. Job: Provides answers to career counseling questions; accessed only through the Genie system's e-mail.[1]

Boston Computer Society: Runs 20 volunteer bulletin boards; members exchange job leads and postings; members also have access to a resource center with equipment, classes, and software packages. Membership cost is less than $50 per year. Contact Pauline Bownes, (617) 252-0600.

Capsule Job Listings: Lists several hundred contract technical positions available nationwide and overseas, updated daily. Also provides a newsletter, which is updated weekly. Call Publicity and Communications, (800) 678-9724.

On-line Career Center: Provides a job database for job hunters and employers. Updated biweekly, this service lists job opportunities across the United States. Available through Internet, which may be accessed via many other subscription services. Call Internet, (800) 444-4345.

Now Jobs Database: Provides job listings; searches available by job title, salary, zip code, etc.; no charge for printouts; primarily lists data processing jobs in the Boston and New Hampshire area. Contact Wayne Davidson, (617) 837-8916.

---

1 U.S. Department of Labor. *Job Search Guide: Strategies for Professionals.* 1993.

Career Placement Registry: Provides information on job hunters to employers across the United States. This service is advertised to employers in general-interest publications such as the *Wall Street Journal* and *Business Week*. Available through Dialog, prices to have qualifications posted vary (approximately $12-$50); postings remain active for six months. Call (800) 368-3093 for a questionnaire.

Federal Career Opportunities: Lists federal jobs across the United States from GS5 to SES levels. The on-line system is updated daily, and job information may also be accessed through a newsletter updated every two weeks. For on-line or newsletter information, call (703) 281-0200.

Many subscription services have a job-posting section included in the basic fee. For example:

America On-Line's Employment Section: Job listings across the United States, updated daily. There is also an on-line resume template that may be used. Call (800) 227-6364.

Compuserve's Classified Section: Similar to a newspaper, this classified section posts listings of job hunters available for work and jobs available nationwide. Call (800) 848-8199.

Prodigy's Employment Advertisement: Hundreds of career opportunities listed on this system, updated biweekly. Also includes a resume posting service to more than two million members. Call (800) 776-3449.

The Best Career Services

By now you've probably realized that we favor a personal, proactive approach, but some people may wonder what career services are available to job hunters. If you're looking for low-cost job search counseling to help you define your mission or assess your skills, we offer the following advice: The best job search counselor to ensure your success is the person you can count on to make the extra call, understand your abilities, and sell your capabilities to your future employer. The best job search counselor...is you!

It's a different job market today, and in approaching the challenge you must be the initiator and be proactive! Career counselors, government agencies, and outplacement firms are not the cavalry who will sweep into your job search and rescue you from the hours of work ahead. In fact, no level of monetary investment in career counseling can make the right job appear, and, amazingly enough, most of the advice and services that career counselors offer can be found in the local library or through other low-cost sources.

Put first things first, and prioritize your objectives. Then develop a plan for using career counseling to focus on areas where you need the most help. You can be your own best career counselor by writing a mission statement for your job search and defining associated goals. Develop a weekly action plan based on those goals. After analyzing your needs, be a wise consumer of all the free services offered to you, selectively utilizing "paid" services when they offer the highest payoff.

What is career counseling and outplacement, and what can it do for you? First of all, career consultants are not search firms. They may have ties to employment agencies, but their job is to equip you to compete in today's job market, not to help you find your next position. These professionals provide guidance on resume writing and interviewing, job leads, networking opportunities, and skills assessment to direct you into high-growth fields. There are many resources available to job seekers—but they provide only some tools, not the solutions.

The least expensive and possibly most effective option is to do it yourself. The library has job-hunting guides, trade magazines, and self-assessment workbooks to help you determine your skills and find compatible careers. In addition, the reference librarians can help you find almost anything you need, such as the names of the fastest-growing and most profitable companies. They often have information on local support groups of other job hunters who meet regularly to provide moral support, exchange job leads, and share job hunting tips. The librarians can direct you to government departments that offer career planning services.

An important first step in your job hunt is to **find a friend or relative who can coach you** on interviewing and phone skills and your resume. You might feel more comfortable using an objective, outside observer, however. The important point is to find someone with whom you can discuss your successes and failures without embarrassment.

If you have a personal computer with a modem at home, you can find on-line job listings through the CompuServ, Prodigy, or Genie network.

In addition, you should seek out a local consumer credit counseling service to help you plan your budget based on reduced income. Sometimes these groups can negotiate alternative payment plans with creditors to protect your assets and your credit rating.

The federal government offers many good sources of help at little or no cost. Several Department of Labor publications, for example, can take you through your job search from beginning to end, and also help with career counseling and industry research. Some of the available books are *Job Search Guide: Strategies for Professionals, Guide to Occupation Exploration,* and *Occupational Outlook Handbook.* You can find the local or national phone number for all federal departments by calling 1-800-347-1994.

State governments also provide excellent counseling and career growth services. In the state government section of the phone book, you'll find the number for your local employment office. This office can show you how to begin receiving unemployment benefits. Although every state differs, most offer similar services such as aptitude testing and evaluation, job retraining, career counseling, and job referrals. Some states offer coaching on resume writing, interviewing, and motivation. Your local office might have a job bank with hundreds of listings of available positions. In fact, some businesses hire their employees exclusively through the state employment offices. Because the counselors at each office have heavy case loads, it will be up to you to keep in touch and follow up with them.

Joining a local networking or support group can be a good way to gain job leads and keep up your morale. Most groups are listed in the newspaper or with the library, or can be located through churches and community centers. Many professional associations also have networking groups for displaced members. If you can't find a good group, start your own by finding people with similar backgrounds at the employment office or through a professional association. In some areas the YMCA also offers job counseling and career planning on a sliding-fee scale.

Another key resource is your former college or technical school and alumni association. Most schools offer counseling and workshops for career planning and job search strategies. Many have special alumni bulletins that list job openings.

There even are some nonprofit outplacement firms, such as the Career Action Center in Palo Alto, California. You can find these agencies by calling the local Chamber of Commerce.

You should try to negotiate **outplacement services** as part of your severance package, but remember if you don't have that option through your company, **many of the same services are available at no cost through other organizations.**

An outplacement firm can provide administrative support and office facilities. The counselors can help you determine your skills and help you focus your search. Most firms have reference materials and can provide workshops on interviewing skills, resume writing, and networking. Some of the larger firms also have job banks with national listings.

In evaluating an outplacement firm, there are several key questions to ask:

- What is the educational/professional background of the consultants and the reputation of the firm?
- What do its former clients/candidates say about it? (Ask for references.)
- How does it quantify its success with people with your background?

Watch out for firms that won't give references, ask for large fees up front, or offer quick promises (i.e., "I can get you a job in three weeks").

The best source of information on an outplacement firm is Kennedy Publications' *Directory of Outplacement Firms*, which might be available in your library. Another resource is the Association of Outplacement Consulting Firms, (201) 887-6667. It can direct you to member firms in your area.

Remember, however, that an outplacement firm is not a search firm. The consultants are trained counselors who can help you explore options, such as starting your own company or transferring your skills to another field. The consultants can also provide emotional support in dealing with your job loss, financial planning for your reduced income, and coaching on your phone and interview skills, as well as psychological support to help you project a positive, high-energy image.

In order to gain the most from any outside resource, you must determine to take charge of the situation:

- ♦ Be proactive—follow up and follow through.
- ♦ Stay focused—be open to new options, but keep your goals in mind.
- ♦ Get more training if necessary—you can teach an old dog.
- ♦ Stay on a schedule and develop a plan.
- ♦ Stay positive!

You have the most to gain from a successful job search, so use all the resources available to give you the tools to find that great job!

Examples of Successful Industry Transfers

The job hunter should always be looking in one group only. Focus! We talked in Chapter 6 about how to go from one industry to another. The secret is to move to a closely related field. Going from a computer hardware manufacturer to a biotechnology firm is usually a difficult stretch. The closer you stay to your industry, the greater the probability of obtaining a comparable salary, because the company will see a shorter ramp-up or "learning the business" period. Following are examples grouped by successful transference capabilities.

Telecommunications
Data communications equipment
Telephone equipment
Printing & publishing
Cellular companies
Communications companies
Radio broadcasting
Cable TV operators

Finance
Insurance companies
Mortgage insurance
Government insurance
Mortgage banker
Commercial banks (national
  or state)
Real estate investment trusts
Savings and loans
Federal sponsored credit
  (Federal Home Loan Mortgage
    Association)
  (Federal National Mortgage
    Association)
  (Student Loan Marketing
    Association)
Personal credit institutions
International banks
Securities industry

Securities and commodities brokers
Investment managers

Transportation
Aerospace and defense
Airlines
Shipping
Trucking and freight
Railroads
Chemical and resin suppliers to the
  automotive or aircraft industry
Radio/stereo manufacturing
Industrial machinery
Air courier services

Automotive
Auto and truck parts
Tires and inner tubes
Truck trailers
Defense electronics
Electrical equipment
Machine tools and metal-cutting
  equipment
Farm machinery and equipment

Health Care
Computer services and software
Biotechnology
Commercial laboratory research
Drugs and pharmaceuticals
Manufacturers of electronic
  instruments for health care
  equipment
Medical insurance carriers
Medical equipment and supplies
Wholesale drug distributors
Medical facilities management
HMOs
Outpatient care companies
Medical labs
Packing and container companies
  supplying the health care
  industry

Chemical
Building materials
Paint and varnish
Rubber and plastics
Agricultural chemicals
Industrial bases
Organic chemicals
Plastic and synthetics
  manufacturers
Drugs and pharmaceuticals
Foods
Household products
Metals and mining
Oil and gas
Packaging and container
  manufacturers for chemicals

Technology
Computer service and software
Computer programming services
Data processing
Packaging of computer products
Computer peripherals
Wholesale computer equipment
Electrical equipment and
  components
Medical equipment manufacturers
Semiconductor manufacturers
CAD/CAE/CAM

Data communications equipment
Telephone equipment
Entertainment
Printing and publishing
Cellular companies
Communications companies
Radio broadcasting
Cable TV operators

APPENDIX D

Summary of the Scripts for Each Specific Contact

Chapter 3

Newspaper Editor Script

Receptionist:	The News and Observer...
Job Hunter:	Hi, is Joe Writer in?
Receptionist:	No, he's not, could I take a message?
Job Hunter:	Yes, that would be great, could you ask him to call me? It's regarding the article he wrote on Company X last month.

Note—A newspaper editor or writer may be under a particular publishing deadline and so have no time to call you back. Try to time your phone call so there are no imminent deadlines pending. You should be able to find this out from the receptionist.

If the reporter or business editor doesn't call you back after two messages (unlikely), the third call should go something like this:

Receptionist	The News and Observer...
Job Hunter:	Hi, I was wondering if you could help me?
Receptionist:	I'll try, what is it?
Job Hunter:	I've been playing telephone tag with Joe Writer. Could you advise me as to the best time to reach him? I'm going to be in and out the next few days.
Receptionist:	Well, I really don't know his schedule.
Job Hunter:	Oh, yes, I'm sorry, you couldn't keep track of all those writers. Is there someone up in the Business department who might?
Receptionist:	Well, his manager Bob Jones might have his schedule.
Job Hunter:	Great, thank you!

Or, you get a call back from Joe Writer:

Joe Writer:	Hi, this Joe Writer, I was returning your call regarding Company X.
Job Hunter:	Thank you so much for returning my call. I want to first say, I really enjoyed the article; you have a nice concise style.
Joe Writer:	Well, thank you.
Job Hunter:	I wanted to ask your advice. I am in the process of leaving Company Z (say this even if you're unemployed) or I am a recent graduate of UNC and I thought you would probably have some insight for me regarding Company X. Do you think they're doing well? Who did you speak with when you wrote your article?
Joe Writer:	Well, I interviewed Sam Johnson, the CEO, and I got the impression that they are doing well.
Job Hunter:	What did you think about the company? Would it be a place you'd like to work if you were me?
Joe Writer:	Well, they are just introducing a new product. There are probably 500 employees, and the CEO seemed like a good guy. What is your background?
Job Hunter:	I'm looking for a position in the advertising or promotions area.
Joe Writer:	I'm not sure if they'd be a good place or not.
Job Hunter:	Do you think I should talk to some more people there? Is there anyone else you met or do you have any other names who work there so I can at least make some contacts? (Newspaper people will appreciate your tenacity and they will empathize. They often have to try to talk to people who don't necessarily want to talk to them.)
Joe Writer:	Let me look in my file...Oh yeah, Susan Water is the V.P. of Sales and Marketing. You could call her.
Job Hunter:	You have been so helpful! Have you seen any other growing, small dynamic companies in the area that maybe I should contact?...Are there any other reporters there who cover business news?
Joe Writer:	Well, there's x, y & z...

Venture Capitalist Script

Job Hunter:	"Hi, this is Donna Lutz. May I speak with one of the partners, please?"
Receptionist:	May I ask what it's in regard to?
Job Hunter:	Well yes, and maybe you could help me, too. I was interested in talking to one of them regarding a new business start-up. Are they currently investing in new start-ups or are they only

accumulating a pool of capital at the current time? (You sound like you are a potential client.)

Receptionist: Well, I'm not really sure, perhaps you should talk to Joe Wells.

Job Hunter: Is he one of the partners? (Most venture capital firms are pretty small—less than 50 people.)

Receptionist: Yes, he is.

Job Hunter: Thank you so much for your help, and what did you say your name was? (You'll probably need her help tracking Joe Wells down in the future.)

When you speak to Joe, this is how the dialogue might go:

Joe: Hi, this is Joe Wells.

Job Hunter: Hi, this is Steve Job Hunter. Thank you for taking my call, Joe. I just wanted to ask for your advice. A friend told me you know just about everything about every start-up business in this area. (Pay a compliment.)

Joe: I know many of them.

Job Hunter: I'm in the process of leaving Company X (or I'm a recent graduate of University X). My background is in Y (give the briefest possible description). If you were me, are there any of these companies that you would make contact with? What kinds of successes have you had recently in identifying successful start-ups? Would giving you my resume help?

Joe: Why don't you fax me a resume and we'll talk after that?

Job Hunter: Terrific, you have been so helpful. I'll drop it off with your secretary tomorrow. (You might get the opportunity to at least introduce yourself in person, but if you say I'll bring it to *you*, the person will see this as a possible infringement of their time and they will tell you to just put it in the mail.)

Remember, most people are helpful if they are approached benevolently, and

1. Are asked for their help directly.
2. See a demonstrated interest in understanding their business on the part of the person asking.
3. Are made to feel important, as they are helping those less fortunate, especially if the less fortunate person is sincere in expressing gratitude and appreciation.
4. Are complimented and asked again for their advice.

Script for Council on Economic Growth

Here's a sample role-play with Jan Smart, who works for the Council on Economic Growth:

Secretary:	Council on Economic Growth, may I help you?
Job Hunter:	Is Jan in? This is Steve Job Hunter.
Secretary:	Yes, may I ask what it is in regard to?
Job Hunter:	Yes, I'm with Company X and I wanted to ask her advice on some personal issues (or) Yes, I'm at the University of North Carolina and I wanted to ask her advice on a personal issue.
Secretary:	I'll put you through.
Jan Smart:	Jan Smart.
Job Hunter:	Hi, Jan, this is Steve Job Hunter. I'm in the process of leaving NTI and I wanted to ask for some advice from you. Is that okay?
Jan Smart:	I'm pretty tied up today. (Expect a rebuff.)
Job Hunter:	I've heard you are the expert on new companies in the area—I'd appreciate just a few minutes of your time.
Jan Smart:	Sure, go ahead.
Job Hunter:	First of all, tell me, how are things going in attracting new businesses? It sure seems like you're doing a great job! I remember seeing an article in the newspaper a while ago about Company Z purchasing land on Weston Parkway. That was a real coup. (Other possible questions: How long have you been here? How many new business have you worked on?)
Jan Smart:	Thank you very much. Well let's see, we brought in four new businesses in the last year, and we have good prospects for at least three new ones right now.
Job Hunter:	That's terrific, it must be really challenging competing against all the other areas wanting new companies. How have you guys done so well? (Remember, sincere compliments and questions work miracles at opening people up.)
Jan Smart:	*Continues talking about the reasons for their success.*
Job Hunter:	Jan (people love the sound of their own name, use it a couple times in conversations), you obviously have a lot of contacts. I was wondering, if you were me—recently graduated from UNC in business (or in the process of leaving an accounting position at Company NTI), which of those companies would you call about a possible position?
Jan Smart:	Well, I would call Company J, since they are also in the technology field.
Job Hunter:	That's a good idea. (Always acknowledge their ideas as being good.) What else could you tell me about Company J?
Jan Smart:	*Continues dialogue.*

Job Hunter:	Do you know the names of any people who work there as a starting point for me?
Jan Smart:	Well, Stan Jacobs is the President, and Julie Target is in charge of the logistics of the move.
Job Hunter:	That's terrific, is there anyone else you can think of?
Jan Smart:	No, not really, that's it.
Job Hunter:	Jan, you've been such a help to me in my job search. Are there any other places you think I should call or people you know who might be interested in my background? I'm a real "can do anything" type of person.

Chapter 5

Librarian Script

Vince:	Hi. I was wondering if you could help me.
Librarian:	Yes, what do you need?
Vince:	I would like to find the fastest-growing companies in the health-care field. I was told to look in the last two years of business magazines such as *Forbes, Fortune, Business Week, Inc.* and *Financial World*, which all have periodic listings of the top, growing companies. I would like to look particularly for those issues. Then once I find some company names, I need to find out where their headquarters are located if it's not mentioned in the magazine.
Librarian:	Okay. Over here are the periodicals themselves from the last two years. Just look at the covers for your specific issue. They are arranged in alphabetical order, so begin with *Business Week*, or you can find the location by looking them up by title on the card catalogue or computer, just like any other book. The last couple of months are in the magazine section, which is over in that room, arranged alphabetically. The index of *Directory of Corporate Affiliates* will give you the location of the headquarters, and a page reference for a brief summary.
	Something else that might interest you—we have a book called *Hoover's Handbook of Emerging Companies*, which consolidates those lists and also lists the companies that are increasing their new hires the most rapidly in the United States. But, you have to remember that its information is about a year old; you still should review the magazines to find the most recent lists.
Vince:	You know, it's been years since I've done research in a library; and I've got a lot of research to do. Could you

	possibly show me how to find the company headquarters in that book? By the way, could I ask your name?
Librarian:	(smiling) Certainly. It's Sue. And I'll be glad to help you. (She shows him where the magazines, and the *Directory of Corporate Affiliates*, are and looks up a sample company name.)

Economic Development, Industrial Recruiter Script

Vince:	I hope you can help me. Do you know who could tell me about any local businesses in the health care industry that are rapidly growing? Do you have a recruiter or an industrial recruiter?
Karen:	Well, that would be John Sampson.
Vince:	I think you have a listing of major employers in the area. It would be great if you could fax a copy of the health care listings in addition to any company names you get from your colleagues.
Karen:	Yes, let me find out who you need to talk to.
Vince:	Thank you for your help, I really appreciate your time. My fax number is 350-4539. My phone number is 350-5862. Thanks again.
Karen:	No problem. I will send you some information.

Chapter 6

Receptionist Scripts

1. O & M Inc.: secretary/receptionist.

Job Seeker:	Hi. I would like to ask some questions about your company if you have time.
Receptionist:	I don't have time now. I'll transfer you to someone else. Got voice mail.

2. Applied Pharmaceutical: secretary/receptionist.

Job seeker:	Hi, I have heard great things about your company—how fast it is growing and that it is a great place to work.
Receptionist:	Yes.
Job Seeker:	I am currently job hunting and was wondering if you were hiring?
Receptionist:	There are always positions available for the right people.

Job Seeker:	I would really like an opportunity to apply. What is your advice to get my resume some attention?
Receptionist:	Send an excellent cover letter and try to place yourself in the context of the company.
Job Seeker:	What do you mean?
Receptionist:	Well, make yourself sound like you would fit here. What is your forte?
Job Seeker:	General pharmaceuticals. (Vague.)
Receptionist:	You need to be specific...if you can talk with Bob..."
Job Seeker:	Bob who?
Receptionist:	Bob Nelson in personnel. He is the best, and he's very funny.
Job Seeker:	In your opinion, what does your company generally look for in a new employee?
Receptionist:	The most important thing is commitment. It isn't always an easy place. Your job has to be a priority. Competence is also impressive.
Job Seeker:	Do you have any final advice?
Receptionist:	Um, don't describe yourself as a people person. Bob hates that phrase.
Job Seeker:	Thank you so much. You have been extremely helpful.
Receptionist:	Oh, you're welcome. No problem.

3. Biotec Pharmaceuticals: secretary/receptionist.

Job Seeker:	Hello, I am job hunting, and your company came up in my search, and it looked great. I wonder if you have time to answer some questions about it?
Receptionist:	I don't know very much. I am a temporary. Let me transfer you to someone else.
Job Seeker:	Thank you.

4. Star Pharmaceuticals: personnel

Job Seeker:	Hi, I am currently job hunting, and I've heard what a great company Star is, and I wanted to find out more about it.
Personnel:	Well it is a good company, but right now we are under a hiring freeze.
Job Seeker:	Oh. When do you expect it to be lifted?
Personnel:	No time soon.
Job Seeker:	I've heard about how fast you were growing. What aspect of business is booming?

Personnel: As I said, we are a good company, but we are downsizing right now. If you are still looking in a year, you could get back to us.

Job seeker: May I keep in touch with you as long as I am not a pest?

Personnel: (Laughs.) Sure, and I'll let you know when the freeze lifts.

Job seeker: Thank you very much.

Personnel: You are welcome.

5. Innovative Health Group (president answers the telephone after 6 p.m.):

Job seeker: I've heard a lot about your company...about how you've been growing. I wanted to learn more about Innovative Health Group. I'm evaluating the fast-growth health care companies in the area. What exactly are you involved in?

President: Actually, we are part of the health care initiative to control costs, and we help organizations streamline.

Job Seeker: What is your customer base?

President: We work for hospitals, HMO's, service producers, and insurance companies.

Job Seeker: What do you look for in the people you hire?

President: We are industry focused and look for individuals with strong backgrounds in health care administration. It's a growing company, but we are small and quite specialized. Why don't you send your resume so I can better predict if we can use you?

Job Seeker: Great. The way your company is growing...by leaps and bounds...

President: Yes, we probably will have places for the right people. What was your name again?

Job Seeker: Laurie Day. Could you send me some information about your company?

President: Sure, what is your address?

How to Find a Hiring Manager's Name

Receptionist: Hello, this is XYZ Company. May I direct your call?

Job Hunter: I'm sending a fax to your manufacturing manager. May I get the correct spelling of their name? OR —

I think I spoke to your manufacturing manager in the past and I can't recall the name. OR —

May I speak to your manufacturing manager, and could you give me the correct pronunciation of their name (or their direct number[1])? (At this point, if you get the manager on the phone and aren't prepared to talk to him, hang up).

---

1 The best way to reach the hiring manager is on his or her direct line before 8:30 a.m. or after 5:00 p.m.

Here is another sample script to follow:

Job Hunter: May I speak to the secretary for the manufacturing department?

Secretary: Manufacturing Department, this is Sally Jones.

Job Hunter: Hello Sally, this is Joe Smith from ABC Company. I'd like to send a fax to the manufacturing manager and I need the correct spelling of their name.

Secretary: Could you tell me what this is in regard to?

Job hunter: Yes—I'm sending some information I thought would be of interest.

How to Use Voice Mail to Your Advantage

Secretary: Hello. This is Sally Hill. I am away from my desk right now. Please leave a message.

Job Hunter: (At this point you can hit "0" for an operator.) —OR— This is Joe Smith of ABC company. I'd like to send a fax to the Manufacturing Manager. Could you please return my call and leave me the correct spelling of their name and the fax number? I can be reached at 555-555-5555. Thank you.

President's Secretary Script

If you call a company and find the receptionist unable or unwilling to give you the name of either the manufacturing manager or the manager's secretary, call the president's office and enlist the help of the president's secretary.

Again, you have information, ideas, and insight. Call the president's administrator, saying:

Job Hunter: Hello, may I speak to the president's administrator and could you please tell me his or her name?

Receptionist: Yes, his name is Bob Gordon.

Bob: President's office.

Job Hunter: Hello, is this Bob? This is John Jay of NTI.

Bob: Yes, this is Bob Gordon.

Job Hunter: Hi, Bob. I would appreciate your assistance. I've been trying to send a fax to your manufacturing manager. Could you please give me the fax number and the correct spelling of the name?

Assistant to the Hiring Manager Script

Job Hunter: Jane, you must have a lot of knowledge and insight on your department. What do you think makes XYZ such a great company? or How did you get started here?

Sample Script: The Key to the Kingdom Is the Administrator

Secretary: XYZ Company, this is Susan Mitchell. How may I help you?

Job Hunter: Hello, Susan. I understand you're the assistant for the manufacturing department. Is that right?

Secretary: Yes.

Job Hunter: Hi. My name is Joe Smith of ABC Company. As the support for the manufacturing department for your company, you must have a good idea about what makes your company and your department such a success. I could really use your advice. Could you spend a few minutes of your time with me?

Secretary: I have a couple of minutes, I guess.

Job Hunter: I've spent a good deal of time trying to understand your company and its industry. It seems to be a team with winning strategies and great people. I need help trying to figure out how my skills might fit into your organization. Susan, what do you like at XYZ Company?

Secretary: It is changing all the time. Nothing stays the same way long, and I love the hectic pace.

Job Hunter: I've heard some positive comments about your boss, Barbara Jones. What do you believe are some of the most significant accomplishments of her department?

Secretary: Barbara has developed a cohesive team which works together to solve problems and make the whole process work more effectively.

Job Hunter: What factors do you think have made her successful?

Secretary: She values the contribution of each team member. She expects a lot and she receives it.

Job Hunter: What kinds of things does she look for in people she hires?

Secretary: She hires committed team players who aren't afraid to look at a new way to do things, even if it means changing the way we work.

Job Hunter: I would be interested in understanding how your quality assurance is handled. Could you tell me who handles quality assurance? Does that person report to the manufacturing manager?

Secretary: Yes, quality assurance is handled by John Davis, our production control manager.

Job Hunter: Can you think of any other people I should talk with in the manufacturing area so I don't bother your boss prematurely?

Secretary: You may want to speak to the Operations Supervisor, Mary Decker, or to Pete Johnson, Materials Manager.

Job hunter: All right. That's great. Thank you so much for your help, Susan. I really appreciate it!

Secretary: Sure. No trouble.

Peer Script

Peer:	This is John Davis.
Job Hunter:	Hi John, this is Joe Smith of ABC Company. Susan Mitchell, your associate, suggested I give you a call. She indicated that, as the Production Control Manager, you understand a great deal about XYZ and the strategic importance of manufacturing. Do you have a minute? I would greatly appreciate your advise.
Peer:	Sure, what do you want to know?
Job Hunter:	I've been researching your company and am very impressed with your philosophy of TQC in manufacturing. I'm evaluating becoming part of the team. John, how did you join the company? Do you like working here?
Peer:	This is a great company. Sales have increased 1,200% in four years. Our ability to ship low-cost, quality products keeps us competitive.
Job Hunter:	The company has been growing, and I understand there has been considerable hiring taking place. Is that true in the manufacturing department?
Peer:	To grow as fast as we have, we are always on the lookout for good people who can contribute to our growth rate. We run lean and mean, and that is a significant reason for our success.
Job Hunter:	You've been very helpful. I'm planning to speak to your boss, Ms. Jackson. Is there any insight you can give me on what she's looking for in the people she hires?
Peer:	She looks for flexibility, a strong work ethic, a can-do-anything attitude. You won't get as much training as you might elsewhere, but we look for people who can make their own way, who are proactive and take initiative.
Job Hunter:	John, do you have any further advice?
Peer:	Be persistent, but be patient in some ways too. Susan Jackson is handling a lot of balls at once. She desperately needs to hire another quality engineer, but she just has not been able to take the adequate time to find the right candidate.
Job Hunter:	What would you recommend I do?
Peer:	Learn about what we're trying to do here and then leave her a voice mail on what you could be able to do help us right now. But you might need to make multiple attempts. If you don't catch her when she has a moment to think about this issue, you won't get her attention.
Job Hunter:	Would you recommend I speak to anyone else in your department?
Peer:	You might want to talk to Pete Johnson, the materials manager, or Mary Decker, the operations supervisor. And our di-

	vision across town might be hiring too. Talk to Sam Light, the manufacturing manager.
Job Hunter:	I really appreciate your time and all of your suggestions. Maybe we could get together and I could buy you lunch. You could share with me your ideas on TQC and the manufacturing process issues.
Peer:	That sounds great. And if you have any more questions, feel free to call.

Most companies divide the sales organization by product and geography. Because companies know many people call into their organization trying to find the name of the sales rep for their location, salespeoples' names are the easiest to obtain. And because most job hunters don't take the time to ask their opinions, sales representatives aren't being inundated with similar calls and will be glad to help most of the time.

Sample Scripts to Obtain Sales Representatives' Names

Receptionist:	Hello, Growth Co., Inc.
Job Hunter:	Hi, I'm trying to reach the sales representative who represents North Carolina—could you please tell me who that is?
Receptionist:	Yes, we have two reps. Bill Barlett handles Raleigh and Eastern North Carolina, and Sue Wilson handles Greensboro and Western North Carolina. To which person would you like to speak?

(Write down both names—you might want to speak to both.)

Or you might be told that there are multiple sales reps. In that case, be as specific as possible. For example:

Script to Find a Sales Rep:

Job Hunter:	Hello, I'd like to speak with the sales rep who handles North Carolina.
Receptionist:	What location and product are you interested in?
Job Hunter:	Well, I'm in Chapel Hill and I'm looking to speak to someone who handles your industrial product line.
Receptionist:	OK, that's John Dunn.
Job Hunter:	Is there a sales rep for this area who handles consumer products?
Receptionist:	Yes, that is Linda Griffin.
Job Hunter:	Thank you. Could I speak to John, please?

Once You've Been Transferred to the Rep—Sample Script with a Sales Rep:

Job Hunter:	John, this is Sue Long with Health 2. I understand you've done a great job representing ABI in North Carolina.

John:	Well thank you. How can I help you?
Job Hunter:	You must know an awful lot about ABI. I've been following their great progress, and I'm trying to understand more about the company. I'm in the process of evaluating the company for a possible career change.
John:	I'd be happy to help you, but I'm going to a meeting in just a few minutes.
Job Hunter:	I can understand how busy you are. As a successful rep, I'm sure your knowledge about ABI is one of the most insightful in the company. Could you just spend a couple of minutes before your meeting?
John:	OK. What do you want to know?
Job Hunter:	What do you like best about ABI?
John:	Oh, it's the fast pace. The benefits are great, and our customers love our products.
Job Hunter:	What makes your customers so receptive?
John:	Innovation has set us apart. We put together programs to match our customer's exact requirements. Our competitors do not do that. We try to make it easy to do business with us. A great company remembers who the customer is! We try to say yes—even if it means working on a request for 15 hours straight.
Job Hunter:	What are some of your biggest challenges?
John:	Making sure no one takes our market after we've done all the R&D, which keeps our products and services the most unique in the industry. We need to create enough barriers to make it difficult for others to grab market share. Sometimes it is not the company who does something *first*, but the one who can get the message out and market it—I'm sure you know what I mean. I'll tell you, I've got more information I'd be happy to share. Why don't I get in my car, and you can call me while I'm driving. The number is 967-1286.

Sample Script with a Sales Rep

Actual Conversation of a Successful Job Hunter Who Tried First to Understand What the Company Was About

(Called the company and asked the receptionist for the name and phone number of the sales rep who handled the territory where the job hunter lived.)

Sales Rep:	Hi, this is Suzanne Bay, can I help you?
Job Hunter:	Hi Suzanne, this is John Harrison, and I am calling to ask for some advice. I have been following ABI's success over the years and I am trying to decide if I should contact them re-

garding possible positions. I wanted to get your opinion of how you like working for them first.

Sales Rep: Sure. What company do you work for now?

Job Hunter: I'd rather not say because I'm just in the preliminary stage, but it is in the same industry. Could you tell me how long you've been at ABI?

Sales Rep: I've been with them only six months.

Job Hunter: Great. You must have a fresh, fairly unbiased opinion then. How did you get your position?

Sales Rep: Well, I replied to a want ad for another position I didn't end up getting. I was so impressed with the company that I kept following them in the news and through our industry meetings, and I just kept in touch, and they ended up opening a new territory for me and basing it out of this area. You see, the company is just booming, and when you keep in touch and seek out opportunities, a job will eventually be created if they're continuing to grow and hire as this company is. In fact, they really don't advertise positions much at all.

Job Hunter: You know, I notice from the news they sort of struggled along the first few years and then have been doing well the last three years. What has happened? Is Fred Johnston still the CEO?

Sales Rep: Yes, he is. He came from the NAC Company and started this eight years ago, just focusing on one product, really. Then he brought in two other partners—James Cornell, who was a great sales person and had a lot of contacts, and Susan Kemp, who had a lot of ideas for several new products, and things just took off.

Job Hunter: That's fantastic, Suzanne. What do you like best about the company?

Sales Rep: I like the energy and enthusiasm and the concrete vision of the company.

Job Hunter: What is the vision?

Sales Rep: To be the best in our business. With services and products such as we have now, we are the best, and the company is working hard, filling the line in with a full set of products and services for our whole industry niche.

Job Hunter: What do you see as their competitive advantage? Why are they the best?

Sales Rep: Our research and development laboratories do a better job than anyone in the industry, and the quality of our services ranks second to none. You know, I wish you could tell me a little more about your background. How did you get my name?

Job Hunter: I just called corporate and asked for the sales rep's name in this area. Well, I work in the quality assurance area of com-

	pany ZBA—one of your customers, actually. Based on what I've told you, who should I contact at corporate? Do you think they need people with my background?
Sales Rep:	You need to contact Dr. Peter Lyson.
Job Hunter:	What is his title?
Sales Rep:	Director of Quality and Standards.
Job Hunter:	Great. Do you know anyone who works for him that I might talk with more about the department before I contact him directly?
Sales Rep:	You could talk to Davy Tate or Ann Dixon; they could give you some good insight into this area.
Job Hunter:	You know, I'd love to meet you. Could we meet for lunch one day? Maybe I could share some information that might be helpful to next time.
Sales Rep:	Yeah, let's do that.

(Go on and set a date)

Sample Script for a Competitor

Med-X Company is a key competitor of Superstar, one of your three focus companies. Here is a sample role play to follow when finding the name of the sales representative.

How to obtain sales rep's name

Receptionist:	This is Susan.
Job Hunter:	Hello. My name is Jane Bell of CTL. May I speak to your sales representative who handles the hospital accounts for the state of North Carolina? (It is important to be as specific as you can be when asking for sales representatives.)

[It is important to be as specific as you can be when asking for sales representatives. This level of detail lets the receptionist know to which sales rep she or he would transfer you.]

Script for a competitor's sales rep

In this role play you are calling the sales rep from Med-X to see what she thinks of Superstar's new product, the 1248B. Med-X has a product, the H2L, which competes directly with the Superstar Product.

Sales Rep:	Hi, this is Sally Smith.
Job Hunter:	Hi Sally, this is Jane Bell of CTL. Sally, I've heard a great deal about your product offering, especially your new H2L product.
Sales Rep:	Market acceptance has been great. What can I help you with?

Job Hunter:	I wanted to know specifically how you thought it compared with the 1248D from Superstar?
Sales Rep:	The 1248B is a good product, but it has been known to have quality problems and is not nearly as well known as the H2L.
Job Hunter:	Oh really, what do you mean?
Sales Rep:	Well, the brand recognition of the H2L means we have more sales volume and a larger revenue base for future R&D. Additionally, we believe our ability to stay ahead is based on our shorter R&D cycle time to bring products to market.
Job Hunter:	I see. And what product do you think will ultimately dominate the market?
Sales Rep:	That's hard to say. What else can I help you with?
Job Hunter:	You seem very enthusiastic about your company—what do you like about it? How did you come to work for Med-X?

(It is fine not to reveal why you are calling if the rep doesn't ask and is willing to give you the information, but most good sales reps will want to know why you're calling and who you are. Never be untruthful; just use persistence with charm!)

What to say when the SR Asks, "Why are You Interested in Our Product?"

Job Hunter:	Sally, I've admired your company's products and ability to compete in this market. I wanted your advice on which company's future looks the best. I'm evaluating companies in this market and I am in the process of making a career change.
Sales Rep:	Well, I'm not sure I'm the best person to talk to about this.
Job Hunter:	Sally, you have been an outstanding representative for your company, and I hear you know more about the HZL than just about anyone. I'd just appreciate your advice.
Sales Rep:	OK, where do you want to start?
Job Hunter:	What are the future strategies for your company?

Chapter 7

Examples of Using Charm

If you obtain some relevant information or news about the specific person you're calling, say: *"I have admired your work and some of the things you've accomplished as I heard from Joe Smith (or read about in an article in the local newspaper), and I was interested in learning how you've become so successful. Perhaps you can offer me some advice on my job search or input on my resume."* or

"I understand you are one of the best people to talk to regarding the 'ins and outs' of this industry. Can you give me some advice regarding my career search? I am a recent graduate of the University of Georgia."

or

"I understand you know a lot of people in this area. Could I ask for your advice regarding my possibly changing companies?"

or

"You have been so successful in your area. My background is in advertising. If you were me, how would you pursue career opportunities in this company? Could you recommend anyone else I should contact?"

Continue:

"How did you get started in this business?"

"What are the aspects of this company that make it especially successful?"

"Could I take you to lunch to learn more about your company/industry?"

"Can you recommend any of your associates whom you think I should talk with?"

Sample Voice Mail

Job Hunter: Hi Susan, this is Amy Hurring. Congratulations on the great press coverage HiGrowth, Inc. has had recently. The feature article in July's *Fortune* was particularly impressive. Susan, I've heard some good things about your department, could you spend a few minutes talking with me sharing what makes your team so successful. I'll call you again tomorrow morning at 9:30 to arrange a convenient time. Again, congratulations, and I look forward to talking with you.

Practice your voice mail messages and your introduction.

Use Administrators to Help You Reach the Hiring Manager

Job Hunter: Hi Jane, this is Susan White with ABC Co., and I've been playing telephone tag with John. Jane, you've always been so helpful. Could you please see what you could do to schedule a call with John?

Jane: I don't usually make appointments for John. Why don't you call at 7:45 a.m.? He's usually here.

Or, try this:

Job Hunter: Jane, this is Susan White, with ABC Co. Your organization is such a fast-paced group, and I realize you are incredibly busy. Could you help me to speak with John. Do you schedule his calendar? When would you recommend I call?

Jane: You can call him at 10:30 on April 16.

Script: A Conversation with the Administrator to the Customer Service Vice President

The administrator opens new doors and provides a wealth of information. Here is another role play. Does the job hunter, Sharon, gain from the conversation? Does she move her job search closer to her goal?

James: Superstar Company. This is James.

Sharon: Hi James. The reason I'm calling is that I've heard so many great achievements about your customer service department. And I am evaluating Superstar as a possible future employer. James, I know you have a lot of insight about the department. Could you spare a few moments? I'd really appreciate your advice on Superstar.

James: I'd really like to but I'm tied up right now. And that's really not my forte—perhaps you should speak with Linda in Human Resources.

Sharon: I appreciate that you're busy right now, but I understand you have the real inside knowledge on the customer service department and you seem to make things happen. Could you spare a few minutes?

James: Oh, OK. (Expect a rebuff, but make an informed compliment and ask again. It works!)

Sharon: What do you like about Superstar?

James: Superstar is a fast-growth company and there is always a lot going on at once. The people are very supportive, too.

Sharon: How did you get to Superstar?

James: Funny that you should ask. I had a friend who had heard that Superstar was a good small company. When I called to see if there were any openings, I spoke with Jackie and she set up an interview later that day. I started right after that! Superstar's not so small anymore.

Sharon: That's great! How do you see Superstar in the future?

James: We are growing so fast that this is the time that will make or break us. We are ahead of our competitors in technology, but if we don't keep our customers happy, we will be in trouble. Things have been pretty hectic (ring, ring)—can you hold one moment?

Sharon: No problem.

James: Thanks for holding. Now what were you saying?

Sharon: I really appreciate your time—I only have a couple more questions. Have you heard of any hiring taking place?

James: There is nothing formal, but I know that Jackie needs some help. You should really talk to Anne Williams who is the customer service manager and she should be able to give you more information.

> Sharon: Thanks a lot James. Is there anyone else in the department you would recommend I speak to?
>
> James: Try Susan Steele, the XYZ customer service manager.
>
> Sharon: Thank you again so much for your time. Is there any other advice you can give me?
>
> James: Sure. Why don't you send me your resume and I'll try to get it to Jackie.

Still, there may be some situations where you need to get right through to the manager and feel more comfortable asking directly for him or her. These sample scripts suggest ways to get in touch with the manager quickly. If they don't work, you need to ask for help.

"Hello, Jane, this is Sarah Shey. Joe Smith suggested I contact Ed regarding some competitive information."

"Hello, Jane, this is Luis Munoz of G.D. Goodsell. I wanted to congratulate Ed on the XYZ product introduction."

"Hello, Jane, I'm calling with regard to my letter of June 14."

"Hello, Jane, may I speak to Ed? We've been playing telephone tag."

Role Plays with the Hiring Manager

> Job Hunter: I have talked to some people in your organization, and I understand your team is in the process of designing a new customer service system. I have had some experience at XYZ Co. designing and implementing quality systems, and I would like to understand a little more of your goals in that area.

Or, for someone with whom you have had some contact in the past:

> Job Hunter: I would like to ask for your help because I cannot think of anyone else who is a) better connected, b) more informed about the industry, or c) who could point me in the right direction. (etc.)

Manager Role Play

> Sharon: Hi Jackie. This is Sharon Long of Mertec. From my conversations with Bob Samms at Customer, Inc., and with your associate, James, I've learned that your customer service department has developed some of the most innovative and effective programs in the industry. I was wondering if you could give me a few minutes of your time so I can understand more about your business and see whether my background might fit in with your organization in the future.
>
> Jackie: I'd like to, Sharon, but Human Resources handles these kinds of calls. You should probably contact them, and ask to speak with Jan Start.

Sharon: Certainly, I'd do that, Jackie, it's just that I've heard from customers and your associates that you know more customer service than anyone and I'd just appreciate a couple of minutes.

Jackie: OK, but not any more than that —I've got a conference call.

Sharon: Jackie, what are your most important goals for the customer service department?

Jackie: Our number-one goal is to keep our customers satisfied, but with our growth and shipping problems this has been almost impossible. You know, everyone waits until the last minute to order, and then they want it yesterday. We're just having trouble keeping up.

Sharon: How has that affected customer satisfaction?

Jackie: I've got the vice president of sales and the CEO checking with me daily to get products out on time. It's gotten so bad, we're allocating deliveries. The most frustrating part is that I like to run a proactive operation, but it's impossible with this kind of growth. I don't like being in the position of always re-acting to everything.

Sharon: Have you had any way to get the customer's insight on the problem?

Jackie: We've tried, but there has not been equal access for every-one. If someone yells loud enough, then we spend extra time trying to mollify them—it's basically the squeaky wheel get-ting the grease.

Sharon: At Mertec, we ran into similar customer problems. We ran several very successful programs. I once put together a SWAT team of all our executives and then assigned each ex-ecutive to a key customer.

Jackie: Well sure, that sounds great, but everybody is so busy around here. I don't know if I could get their attention. It's one thing for the VP of Sales to call me and complain about delivery time, it's another to ask her to spend an hour and a half at the customer site listening to them complain about it.

Sharon: What role has the Marketing VP played during this situation?

Jackie: He's interested, but he's working on new product launches for the new markets we're trying to penetrate. He doesn't have the time to work out customer satisfaction problems until they become marketing problems.

Sharon: That is a tough situation—maybe a plan for a proactive SWAT team, with all the logistics nailed down before you took it to the executives, could make the difference.

Jackie: That sounds good—it's much easier to get their buy-in if they don't have to tie up their staff in doing much of the up-front work. But then I'd have to pull someone from my staff to do it, and we're all stacked up with six weeks worth of work marked "Urgent."

Sharon: I see your point. Perhaps this is where my experience could help you. I was the person they always turned to for all the new ideas and plans in my department. I could do the groundwork to make the plan work. What do you think?

Jackie: You know, I'd like to talk about this further, but I've got to make this conference call.

Sharon: Sounds great, thanks for your time. I'll look forward to meeting with you.

Jackie: Sounds good.

Sharon: How about getting together this morning?

Jackie: No, I've got a meeting.

Sharon: How about lunch?

Jackie: Okay, meet me at my office at noon.

Recovering from a Rebuff

Executive: We aren't hiring anyone now; send your resume to personnel.

Job Hunter: Susan, thank you for your help; do you think you'll be hiring in the next year?

Executive: Yes, we will.

Job Hunter: Well, I'd just like to come by and meet you, shake your hand, so you can match my face to the name, and personally give you my resume.

Executive: Oh, that's not necessary.

Job Hunter: You're right, but I've heard and read so much about Company X (or you) that I want to make this extra effort! It will take only a minute of your time.

Executive: Fine, arrange a time with my secretary.

Job Hunter: Great, I look forward to it.

How to make them interested in talking to you

Job Hunter: John, hello, this is Bob Smith of XYZ. I'm calling in regards to my letter of July 3, and wanted to congratulate you on the recent huge increase in Asian business. After talking to your associates, Bill Wheeler, Jane Snow, and some others, I understand your group was the major factor in winning this business.

John: Thank you, but what can I help you with?

Job Hunter: I've heard so many positive things about your company, and I'd like to learn if I might add any value with your team in the future. I'd be interested in learning more about your challenges. Could you take 15 minutes with me in the next week?

John:	I don't think that's possible. Can I give you five minutes now?
Job Hunter:	Thank you! You've got an impressive product and marketing strategy. What do you see as the main goals for your department? What do you think must go right to meet these goals? What are the biggest obstacles?
John:	Truthfully, as demand has increased, our yields haven't kept with the quality expectations of our customers. We need to turn this around, and we're working at it feverishly.
Job Hunter:	You've made a big impact already. From what I understand, though, if your demand remains at the same rate, you might actually be in danger of losing customers from a customer service prospective. Won't that have an impact on growth?
John:	Absolutely. I've got the CEO calling me twice a day asking about what our largest customers are saying and doing. The last thing we can afford is customers canceling orders!
Job Hunter:	As you might recall from my letter, my background is as customer service manager from XYZ Competitor Co. Our organization faced those same challenges. How about letting me take you out to lunch next week and we can discuss the solutions we came up with?
John:	That's a good idea. I'll tell you what; call my assistant and let her know I suggested an hour meeting. I've got to run, but it sounds like you might have some great insight for us.

Chapter 8

Finding Out the Hiring Manager's Challenges or Problems

Job hunter:	Which areas are not meeting profitability expectations?
Manager:	Truthfully, we've not generated the profitability we anticipated in our customer-service repair program.
Job hunter:	Bob, do you see this as a result of productivity or inventory control challenges?
Manager:	Actually, it's a situation where both need improvement, but we're not sure which one to concentrate on first.
Job Hunter:	We had some similar challenges at XYZ where I worked for the "No Growth" division. Inventories were not being tracked accurately. We implemented a simple incentive program with our field engineers. It improved inventory turnover and increased productivity by 25 percent. Is this a concern for you?
Manager:	It sure is. Tell me more about it.

Chapter 9

How to Turn a No into a Yes

Job Hunter: How many more people are you planning on talking with? How do I stack up in comparison?

or

Job Hunter: I know it's hard to remember one of the first (last/middle) people you talk to, but I am committed to doing everything I can to work for you (your company). Is there anything you can recommend for me to do in order to move to the next step?

or

Job Hunter: "Do you have any concerns about me and my ability to do this job?"

Responses after receiving an objection

"That's a good point. You must have thought about that. Could you share your reasoning with me?" or

"How did you come to your decision?" or

"Could you share with me what factors determined your decision? or

"Could you elaborate on that?"

Example 1

Job Hunter: Susan, thank you for taking time to share with me your ideas for new research methods. How do you feel my experience matches your requirements?

Interviewer: You have some good experience, but we might need someone with more specific experience related to statistical analysis in an industry setting.

Job Hunter: Could you share with me what specifically concerns you?

Interviewer: Sure. You have never worked in this industry environment.

Job Hunter: Yes, you're right. My experience has been focused in an educational setting—I can see how an industry focus has differences. What do you feel are the most important attributes of industry experience?

Interviewer: In industry, our situation changes constantly. We're directed by our customer.

Job Hunter: Yes, flexibility is very important. How do you see flexibility impacting the daily priorities? Do you see not only flexibility but also the ability to do what it takes to make the difference?

Interviewer: Exactly. You see why it is so important.

Job Hunter: Your customers expect the best and they want it now. My career has been built on my ability to be flexible, as we discussed in my handling of the XYZ situation. My managers always have pointed out my capability to get the job done with no questions and a willingness to do anything without thinking something was beneath me. Is that the type of flexibility and roll-up-your-sleeves initiative characteristics you're looking for?

Interviewer: Maybe it does make sense for John to talk to you also. I might have been hasty in my earlier assessment.

Example 2

Interviewer: I'm concerned that you haven't been employed for more than a year now.

Wrong: The economy has been terrible, my industry is in a negative spiral; no one wants someone with my experience or lack of experience (a new graduate).

Correct: You're right: I would wonder too if I were you. I made some mistakes, such as relying on search firms to do the work I needed to be doing myself. I have finally figured out that people find their own jobs and have to work hard to find them.

Script with a Coach

Example 1

Job Hunter: Susan, your insight has been most helpful. Your ability to articulate the needs of the department provided excellent background for me.

Coach: Thank you. I'm glad it helped you out.

Job Hunter: Susan, I'm meeting with John Jay, the hiring manager. Could we get together for lunch so you could share your ideas on the philosophy of finance for ABC?

Coach: I only have 30 minutes.

Job Hunter: How about Friday? We could meet at the company cafeteria.

Coach: O.K.

Example 2

Job Hunter: Susan, you've clarified for me why ABC is such a great company with the zeal for excellence in design, manufacturing, and customer service. No wonder they are leading the industry.

Susan: Yes, ABC is an amazing company.

Job Hunter: That is exactly why I am considering this team. Could you share with me what the decision criteria will be for selecting the candidate?

Susan: We're looking for the best fit and for the person who can grow into this job and contribute to our 50-percent growth.

Job Hunter:	Susan, we've had some more time to spend together. How do you see my ability to fit this job?
Susan:	You seem to have a good grasp of our company, but it's tough competition these days.
Job Hunter:	How many candidates are you down to? Where do I fit in?
Susan:	It's down to three candidates. I'm not sure where you are, but I don't think you're the leading candidate.
Job Hunter:	Could you give me some clues as to why I'm not considered the best person for the position?
Susan:	Well, you don't have as much experience as one of the other candidates.
Job Hunter:	How important do you think this additional experience is? Is Mr. Jay the only one who feels this way? Is there any advice you could give me on what I need to do to demonstrate to Mr. Jay that I'm the right person for this job?
Susan:	You might want to get someone to give you a reference from your last position. Customer references carry the most weight with him.

Follow-up Questions after a Rejection

Ask follow-up questions such as those below.

"I would like to ask for your help."

"Are there any other small companies doing well that I should contact, based on my experience?"

"Where would you call if you were me?"

"Do you know any other people I should talk to?"

"Is there a trade association representing this industry? Is there someone at the trade association I should talk to?"

"Who would you recommend I talk with concerning other job opportunities in this company or others?"

APPENDIX E

Index to Telephone Scripts

Index

About the Authors

Jackie Larson and Cheri Comstock have been helping match quality candidates with growing companies since they left executive sales positions in Hewlett Packard to form their own company, *The Focus Group*.

Since 1990 they have been a recruiting arm for Silicon Graphics, Incorporated, one of the nation's fastest growing companies with sales growth in this period from $289 million in 1989 to $1.5 billion in 1994. Larson and Comstock have reviewed over 16,000 candidates and have helped hire top-producing sales representatives, technical engineers, and managers for this innovative computer manufacturer.

Relying on their perspective from the hiring side of the desk, Larson and Comstock developed The Focus Method®, a seven-step approach to landing a great job within a growing, hiring company. Along with *New Rules of the Job Search Game*, Larson and Comstock have written numerous articles for regional and national periodicals, and have spoken and appeared on radio and television.

In addition to writing and corporate recruiting, Larson and Comstock offer career counseling and job search strategy seminars. They have spoken at universities, corporations, and associations to spread the word about the "New Rules" of today's job market.

Comstock is on the Board of Directors for two companies (one on the *Inc.* 500 list), and Larson has completed her MBA and was a Fuqua Scholar at Duke University. Jackie Larson lives in Cary, North Carolina, with her husband Bill and her two children. Cheri Comstock and her husband Dave live in Chapel Hill, North Carolina, with their two children.

New Rules of the Job Search Game, The Workbook

This workbook is a hands-on tool to assist you in all aspects of the job search, designed to be used independently or in conjunction with *The New Rules of the Job Search Game*. It allows you to have one place where you can chart the course of your job search, keeping track of contacts, appointments, and finances. It employs dozens of tried and true voice-mail and telephone scripts, in addition to those listed in the book, containing:

- best ways for obtaining the "right" person's name
- how to obtain return phone calls
- best openers for getting hiring managers to talk
- best questions to ask interviewers
- a plan for turning around objections and rejections

This workbook provides an **easy way for you to get motivated** and tackle the difficult task of conducting a successful job search. Using it, you will ensure you are working on the right activity at the right time, ultimately **shortening the time to land the job of your choice.**

To Order

CALL: 800-RULES95

FAX: 919-967-1615

E-MAIL: FocusMthd@aol.com

MAIL: The Focus Group
P.O. Box 9243
Chapel Hill, NC 27515-9243

Name _____

Address _____

Telephone _____

PRODUCT	PRICE	QUANTITY	TOTAL
New Rules of the Job Search Game Workbook	$29.95	_____	$ _____
Shipping and Handling	$3.95	_____	$ _____
Sales Tax (NC residents only)	6%		$ _____
Total			$ _____

Payment Method: ❑ Check or money order payable to The Focus Group enclosed
❑ Credit Card Payment

❑ Mastercard ❑ Visa ❑ Discover

Card # _____

Expiration Date _____

Name on Card _____

Signature _____

How did you first learn of *The New Rules of the Job Search Game*?

❑ Bookstore
❑ Friend/Relative
❑ My company _____

❑ TV or Radio Program _____
❑ Magazine or Newspaper _____
❑ Other _____

Would you be interested in receiving information about companion audio tapes?
❑ Yes ❑ No